IMAGES
of America

SCHROEPPEL

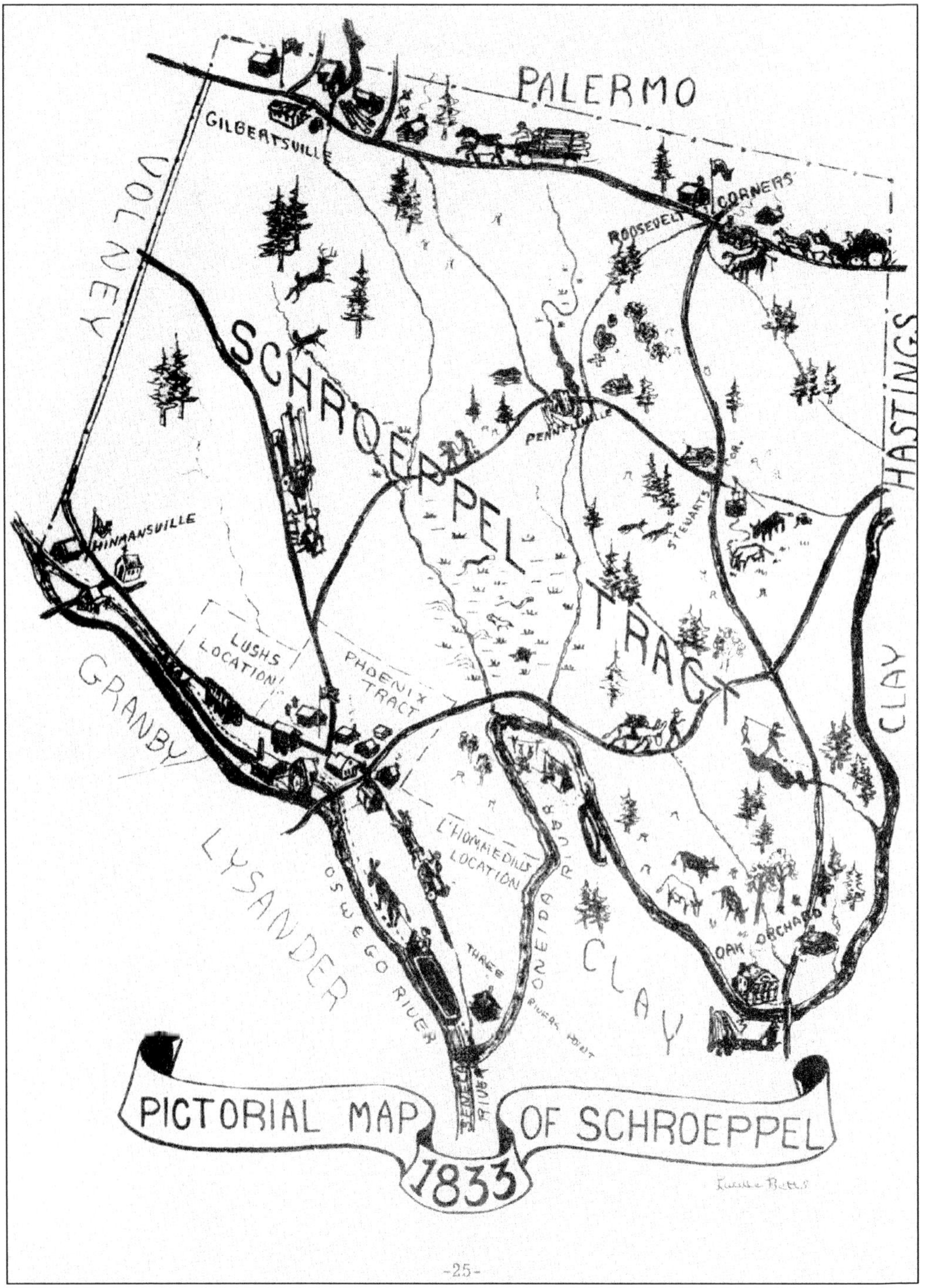

This is a map of Schroeppel from *The Story of Schroeppel*, by Evelyn L. Sauers. (Lucille Betts.)

IMAGES
of America

SCHROEPPEL

Peter W. Huntley

ARCADIA
PUBLISHING

ISBN 978-0-7385-1308-9

Published by Arcadia Publishing
Charleston, South Carolina

Printed in the United States of America

Library of Congress Catalog Card Number: 2003107575

For all general information, contact Arcadia Publishing:
Telephone 843-853-2070
Fax 843-853-0044
E-mail sales@arcadiapublishing.com
For customer service and orders:
Toll-free 1-888-313-2665

Visit us on the Internet at www.arcadiapublishing.com

This book is dedicated to the memory of my mother and father, Wayne E. and Florence S. Huntley, who worked for many years, even while in poor health, to preserve local history. A large part of the information contained here would have been lost in time if not for their efforts.

Contents

ACKNOWLEDGMENTS

I would like to thank Nancy Bowman and Linda Sanders for their assistance in the final editing of this book. I would especially like to express my gratitude to Richard Huntley for allowing unlimited access to his large collection of local photographs and artifacts. Thank you also to Lora and Doc Jones, Frances Chesbro, the *Oswego Valley News* in Fulton, the Oswego County Weeklies, Don Dauer, Roy Huntley, Linda Sanders, the Mexico Historical Society, William F. Brown Jr., Sandy Powers, Joan (Wood) and Robert Coulter, the Utah Historical Society, and the many other individuals who allowed their photographs to be a part of this book.

Along with each photograph is the name of the individual from whom the picture was obtained. This serves not only to show my appreciation for the donor's generosity but also to provide future researchers with a way to track sources. Some photographs have double credits. The first name is the original source (usually an estate) followed by the source who loaned the photograph for this project. Occasionally, the original photographer is credited as well. Photographs with no source information are from either the files of the town of Schroeppel historian's office or my own collection.

Schroeppel's files include work by past historians George W. Chesbro, Evelyn L. Sauers, and Barbara Dix. Additional historical information was taken from town historical files containing the work of Dean Biancavilla and John Byard.

Aside from the publication of this book as a whole, the rights to all photographs remain the property of the sources indicated.

INTRODUCTION

There is no photograph that can completely display the look and feel of an old worn staircase. There is nothing that can replace the inner feeling one gets when standing where generation after generation have stood before. There is no way a picture can present the smell of wood that has become inundated with the odors of years of life. There is much more to preserving the past than the viewing of a photograph, which may have been taken from the wrong angle, under the wrong light, or at the wrong time.

Yet, in many cases, for the town of Schroeppel, the only thing that is left to pass on to future generations is the photograph. The forces of nature combined with neglect have successfully erased the majority of the physical remembrance of this town's past. As recently as the fall of 2002, two structures with local historical significance, one of which was built by one of the town's founding fathers, were burned. Historically, time has not been kind to preservation.

Within these pages, you will find the people and places that were a part of the town of Schroeppel. Here, bits and pieces of history are interwoven with the images that others thought worth saving. If you are from the town of Schroeppel, this is your heritage.

The town of Schroeppel is located in the southern portion of Oswego County, in the heart of central New York State. It is roughly 20 miles north of the city of Syracuse. Human inhabitance in the area that would eventually be known as Schroeppel can be traced back between 9,000 to 11,000 years ago. The town of Schroeppel has a rich prehistoric past, most of which has yet to be discovered.

Following the Revolutionary War, an agricultural area was gradually carved from the dense forest. Throughout Schroeppel's history, up until the 1950s or 1960s, agriculture continued to be the main focus of the town's economic life. Farming was the town's major industry. During this period, two major railroads served the town, as well as a trolley line and the Oswego Canal system. Business, usually in some way tied to agriculture, prospered.

The family farms within Schroeppel began to die out slowly c. 1950. One by one they faded from existence, and thus the industries that they had supported began to fail. Schroeppel's economic foundation was crumbling, and with it, a way of life was dying.

In the 1980s, vast numbers of people moved away from the city of Syracuse and formed an ever-increasing ring of suburban housing. This ring eventually reached the town of Schroeppel. Empty farmland was viewed as prime real estate. The game of buying land cheap, rezoning, developing, and reselling the land at enormous prices began. The value of land took on a completely different meaning.

Today, the town of Schroeppel finds itself in constant turmoil, with numerous conflicting views on the direction the town should be heading. Schroeppel is a township that is trying to grow without destroying itself in the process. What the final outcome will be is a story for a future historian to tell. A glimpse of what the town of Schroeppel has been in the past can be found here.

One

Archaeological Sites

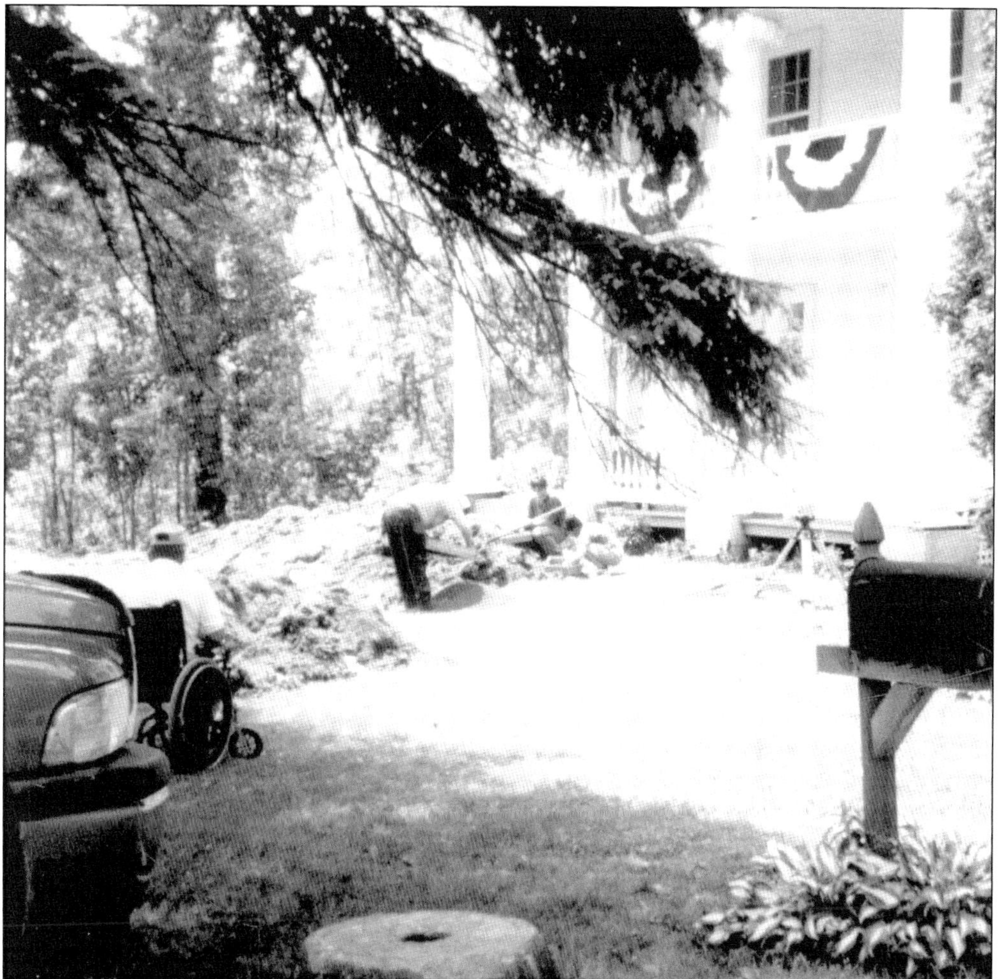

Chief Paul Waterman (left) watches as Doug Pippin, David Babson, and Kimberly Dennin conduct a salvage search in front of the Schroeppel Mansion, at Oak Orchard, in 1997. The round stone (foreground) is the grinding stone from the Schroeppel gristmill that was never finished.

Individuals trained in the field of archaeology refer to the town of Schroeppel as one large archaeological site. As this area was used fundamentally for farming until the 1950s, in many ways it has remained unchanged from the way it was left at the end of the ice age. Farming follows the landscape. Although modern farming is a little more invasive, hills remain hills and lowlands remain without being filled with soil from another area. Plow blades only turn the first layer of soil, and even then, year after year they rotate that soil in basically the same spot. One of the biggest threats from development is that bulldozers and other large machinery can destroy archaeological sites in minutes.

Throughout much of Schroeppel's early history, local farmers spent hours walking or riding behind horse-drawn equipment. Much of that time was spent looking at the ground, and most farmers occupied themselves by looking for arrowheads and other artifacts that were turned up by the plow. Needless to say, many impressive collections were found in the area. One farmer with such a collection was Caleb Potts. In 1953, Herbert Brown, an amateur collector from nearby Fulton, heard of the Potts collection and stopped by the Potts farm to view it. During that visit, Brown purchased some 60 items. Although he was no expert, Brown had enough knowledge in the field to realize that the Potts collection contained some very early pieces. He got in touch with Dr. William A. Ritchie at the New York State Museum in July 1961. Ritchie, who had previously received similar information about artifacts in the area, came to the Potts farm in 1962. There, he, Brown, and Robert E. Funk excavated part of the site. Ritchie returned in August 1963 with a field crew. Later, he detailed the Caleb Potts Collection, along with the other items found in the area, in the book *Archaeology of New York State*. The c. 11,000-year-old Paleo Indian site in Pennellville subsequently became known as the Potts Site.

The Potts Site was also studied by Richard Michael Gramly and Jonathan Lothrop of the anthropology division of the Buffalo Museum of Science in Buffalo in 1982 and 1983. This study was conducted under a fieldwork grant from the National Geographic Society, and a report of it can be found in "Archaeology of Eastern North America," volume 12, 1984.

Sometime during the 1800s, Calvin Corey found a large bone, believed to be from either a mastodon or a whale, on his farm in the swamp area across the road from the Potts Site. Gramly and Lothrop took pieces of the bone for testing and dating.

There are 14 locations within the town of Schroeppel marked on the New York State Archaeological Sensitivity Map. There are many other locally known sites that are not marked, including the Chesbro Site, the Clark Site, and three sites around Peter Scott Swamp. W.W. Meredith of Euclid wrote in the *Grip's Historical Souvenir of Phoenix* (1902) of his personal knowledge of several American Indian villages or camps along the Oneida River from Brewerton to Three River Point. "The largest of these is at Candee Hill," he wrote. It is also known that prehistoric circle mounds were found between Phoenix and Three River Point.

Another area in the town of Schroeppel that may be even more important than the Potts Site is that of Oak Orchard. Oak Orchard is the name of an area that is divided by the Oneida River. Part of the Oak Orchard area is in the town of Schroeppel, and part is in the town of Clay. Little formal archaeological work has been done on the town of Schroeppel side of the river. A report printed in May 1966 compiled by R.M. Coble, with the help of Clay historian Frances Sotherden, stated that members of the Archaeological Society of Central New York working on the Clay side of the river reported finding artifacts dating to 2500 B.C. These inhabitants were thought to be ancestors of the Greenland Eskimo. Coble wrote, "Weapons for hunting caribou and also pottery made by the Stone Bowl Makers who lived at the great bend of the Oneida from 2500 B.C. to 500 A.D., were also found." Relics from the French and Indian War, as well as clay pots of the Iroquois Indians, were discovered as well.

At one time there was a massacre of Native Americans in the Oak Orchard area by either the French or the English. The main burial ground of those killed (Onondaga or Oneida) was located on the Clay side of the river. Prof. W.W. Clayton wrote in *The History of Onondaga County*, "Oak Orchard Reefs, near the bank of the Oneida River, are evidences of an extensive

Indian burying ground. These reefs were a common fording place for the Indians and formerly were much resorted by them for fishing. During the Revolution or the French War, there was a massacre of the Indians at this place. We are informed by a resident of the town, that in 1843 he had a conversation with an aged Indian who used to visit this burial place of his ancestors and sit long there in musing silence, and that this Indian related to him the tradition of the massacre of a large number of his tribe. The same gentleman has seen scores of Indian skulls exhumed, many of which were pierced with bullet-holes and marked with sabercuts." (Clayton, W.W. *The History of Onondaga County, New York*. Syracuse: D. Mason & Company, 1878.)

Evidence shows that the Paleo Indians were also in that area at one time. In the 1990s, developers began pushing to develop the Oak Orchard area on the Schroeppel side of the river. A struggle ensued to try to save the information on prehistoric life that had been locked in the soil since the ice age. Joining in this struggle was Chief Paul Waterman of the Onondaga Nation, who came to the town many times to try to preserve the dignity of his ancestors burials and any information on early native life at Oak Orchard and other areas throughout Schroeppel. Today, most of the area on both sides of the river has been developed or its archaeological information has been destroyed.

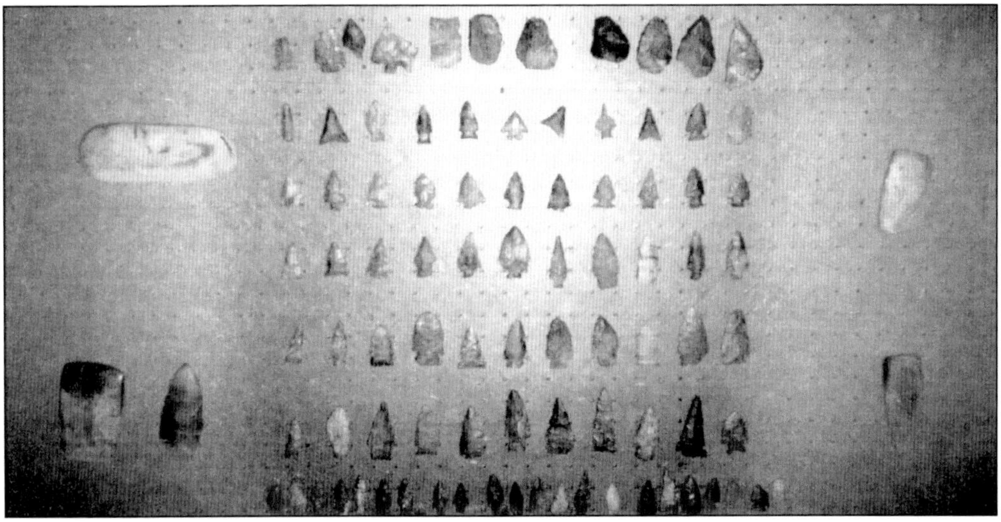

This photograph shows a third of one of the many local farm collections from the town of Schroeppel. Through the natural flow of life from one generation to the next, most of these local collections have become divided among descendants. Many of these people no longer live in the area, and others who were not interested in such items have either sold their inheritance or have given it away. In almost all cases, related information, such as the exact location where each item was found, has been lost over time.

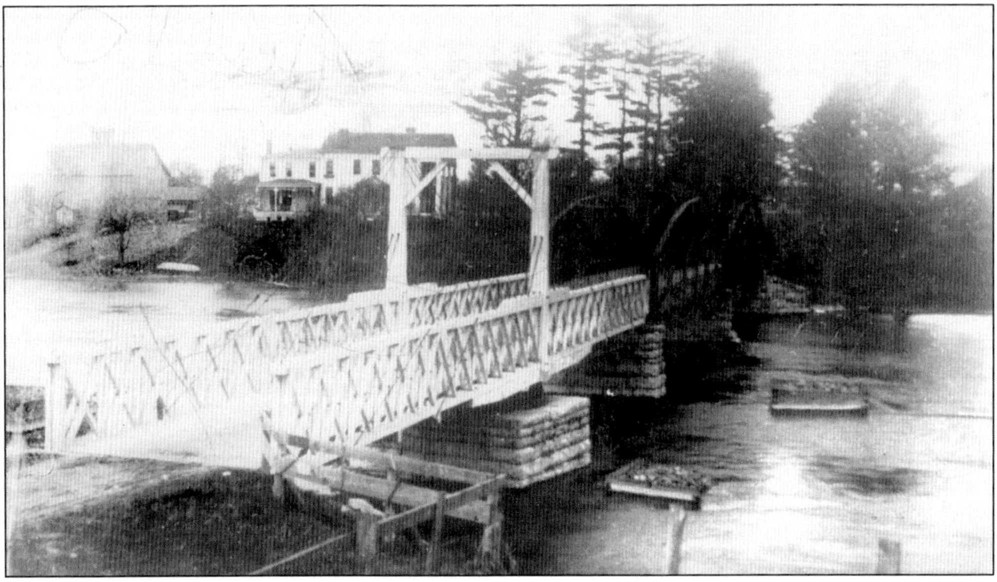

This view of the Swing Gate Bridge (also known as Schroeppel's Bridge) at Oak Orchard is from the Clay side of Oneida River. The Schroeppel Mansion is in the background, with barns that no longer exist. The front lawn of the mansion to the road and river was the site of archaeological salvage work in 1997. (Courtesy of Richard Huntley.)

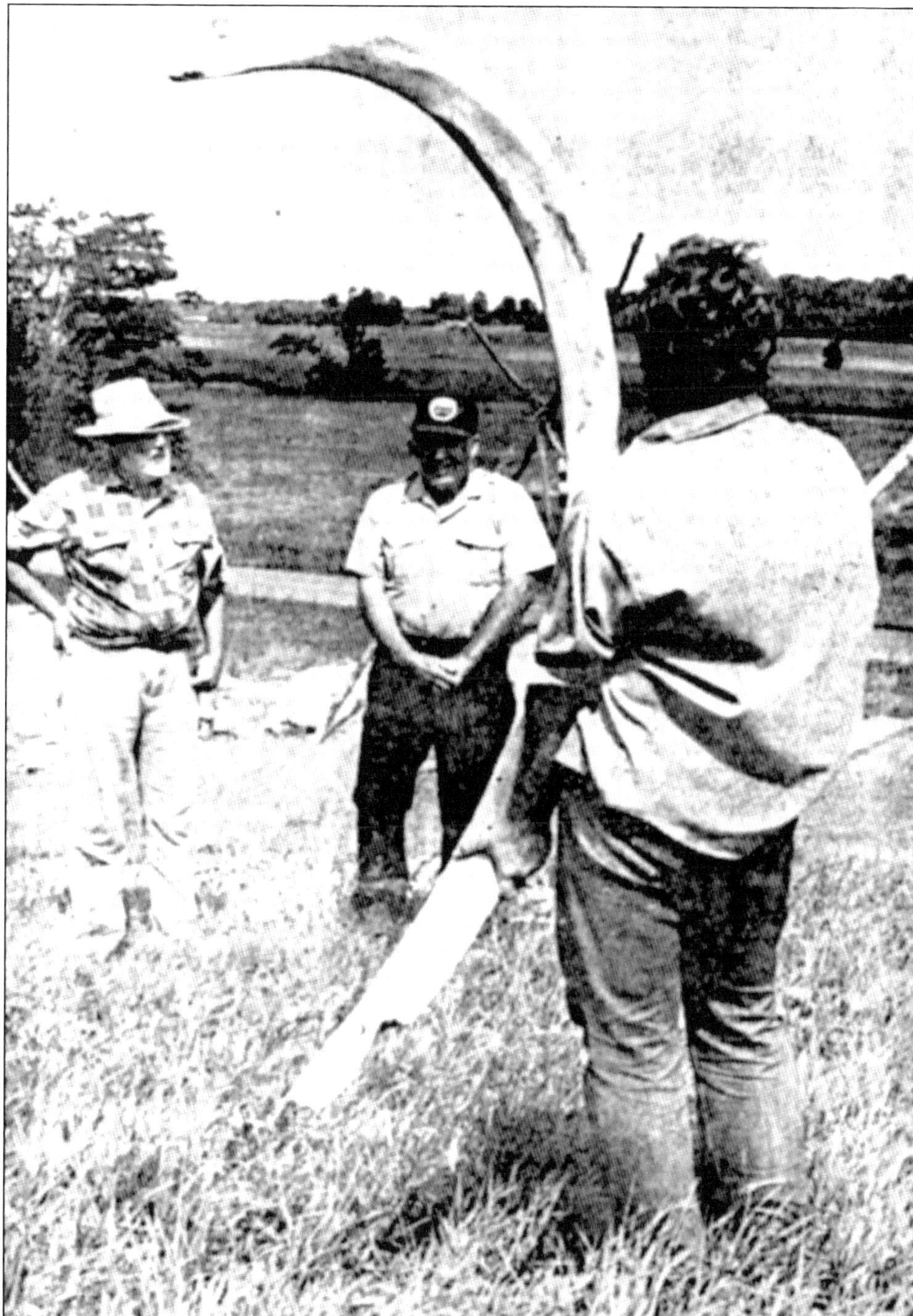

Buffalo Museum of Science curator Richard Michael Gramly examines a bone that was found in Pennellville by Calvin Corey. The bone, dated as being some 11,000 years old, is believed to be the rib of a mastodon. With Gramly is Martin Chesbro, whose wife Frances's grandfather was Calvin Corey. (Courtesy of Carolyn Hendrickson, the *Phoenix Register*, September 1, 1982.)

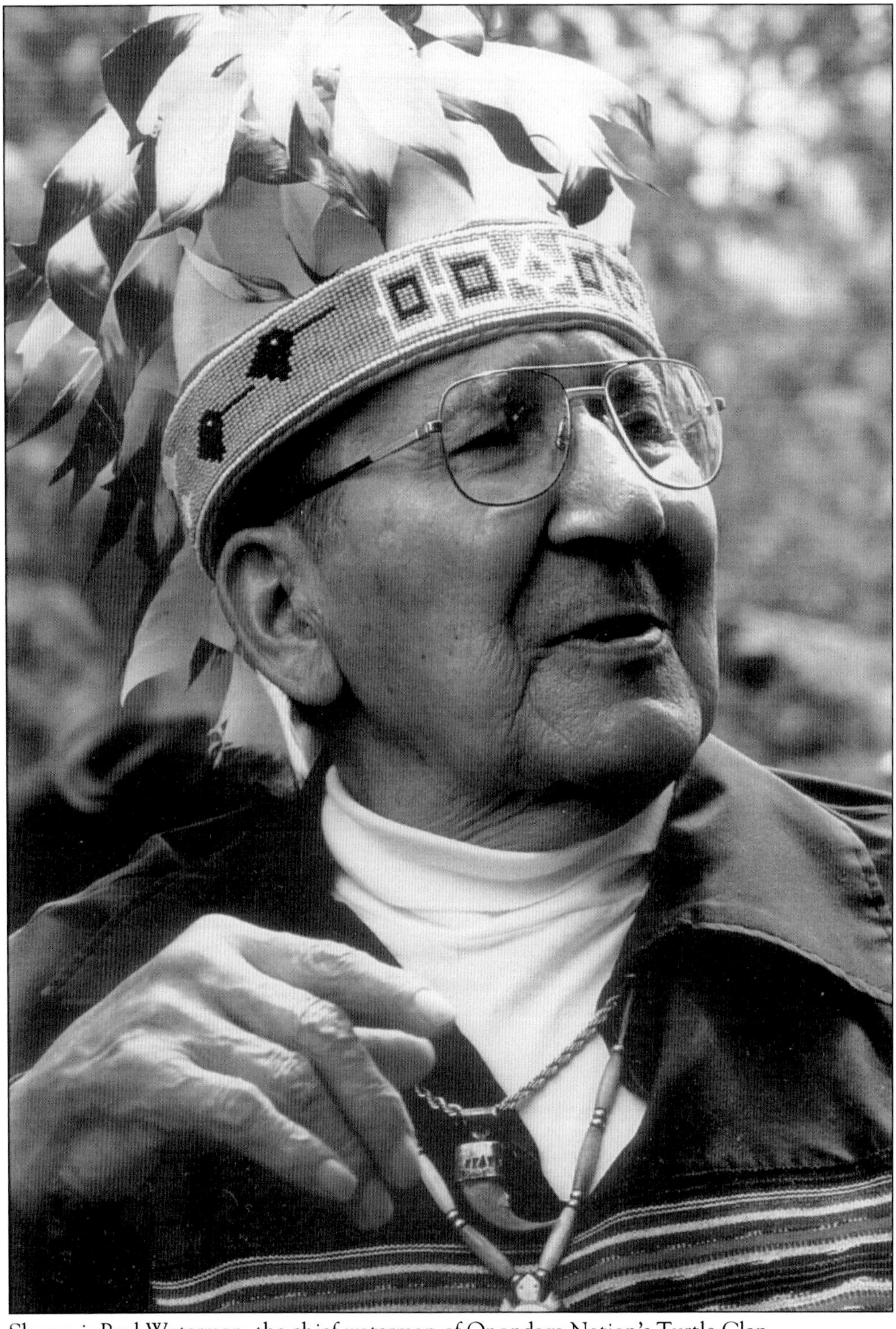

Shown is Paul Waterman, the chief waterman of Onondaga Nation's Turtle Clan.

"I SPEAK FOR THE ANCIENT ONES"

I 'm from a place called "ga-.nak ta gwe yo yeh", meaning the place that is called freedom. The closest word in English would be utopia, also known as the capital of the Iroquois Confederacy. In our language is called "On oo da ge", meaning the people of the hills. Other people call us Onondagas.

When I look out, I visit a sacred site called "ga na da heh", meaning the village way on top, and I visited that place and I wondered why my ancestors chose that place. From there I can see the smoke stacks at the nuclear plant in Oswego. I can see all the lakes, creeks, and the Oneida River, which flows into Oswego and Lake Ontario. And from the top of the hill I can see the ancient ones with the little villages along the river. And today I call these little villages and sacred sites of the Onondaga's , the ancient ones "ho de guy yohn sonh". When I refer to the ancient ones, they are the people who had a really tough time with the dinosaurs. The reason why they can't find remains is because, our people say that our people have returned to Mother Earth. The other reason, "ta de o dah dant", the dinosaurs, were known as meet eaters and leaf eaters. This is why we can't find the remains of the ancient ones. But we can find the tools and the projectiles known as fluted points among the dead dinosaur remains. We can find the tools but not the remains because they returned to Mother Earth. In our words, "sa hu te da way ye", meaning that they returned to Mother Earth. In our beliefs, this where we came from.

So now this is why I'm so dedicated in preserving these sacred sites. This for the people we call "da ha de goo su doon ye", meaning the coming seven generations. And this is why I say, preserve the river and the sacred sites along the river.

Destroying sacred sites of my ancestors would be like going to your cemeteries and digging up you grandmothers and displaying them in the town square. We are civilized people; we have sacred sites and places. This is why we call ourselves, "on way on weh"; true or real humans.

My main duty as chief of the Onondaga , Turtle Clan, is to see that the seven coming generations have clean water to drink and fresh air to breath. I give thanks to the Creator, and I also give thanks to the Four Protectors—"ga ye nyew way da ge"- for watching over my people. I also give thanks to the "we saw say hey noo", the Thunder People who cleanse the land for the seven generations and they continue to do so today. And we give thanks to them.

I was told to speak for the ancient ones, and tell this to the coming generations. Da Ne Too.

Chief Paul Waterman
Onondaga Nation

This statement was given by Chief Paul Waterman during one of his many visits to the Schroeppel town board meetings.

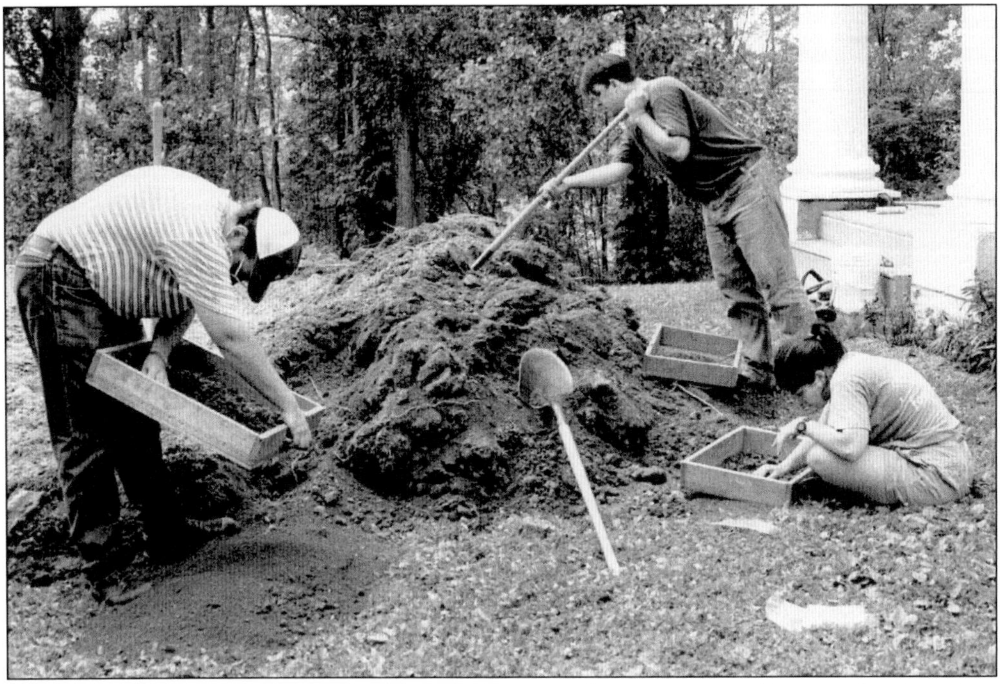

On June 21 and 22, 1997, Doug Pippin, a graduate teaching associate of historical archaeology at Syracuse University, along with graduate student David Babson and Kimberly Dennin, a student at Hobart and William Smith Colleges, worked on a two-day salvage search after the front lawn of the Schroeppel Mansion had been bulldozed. The work was done at the request of Chief Waterman, who was also at the site. Among the items found were 42 different types of flint, bone fragments, and a prehistoric knife. (Courtesy of the *Oswego Valley News*.)

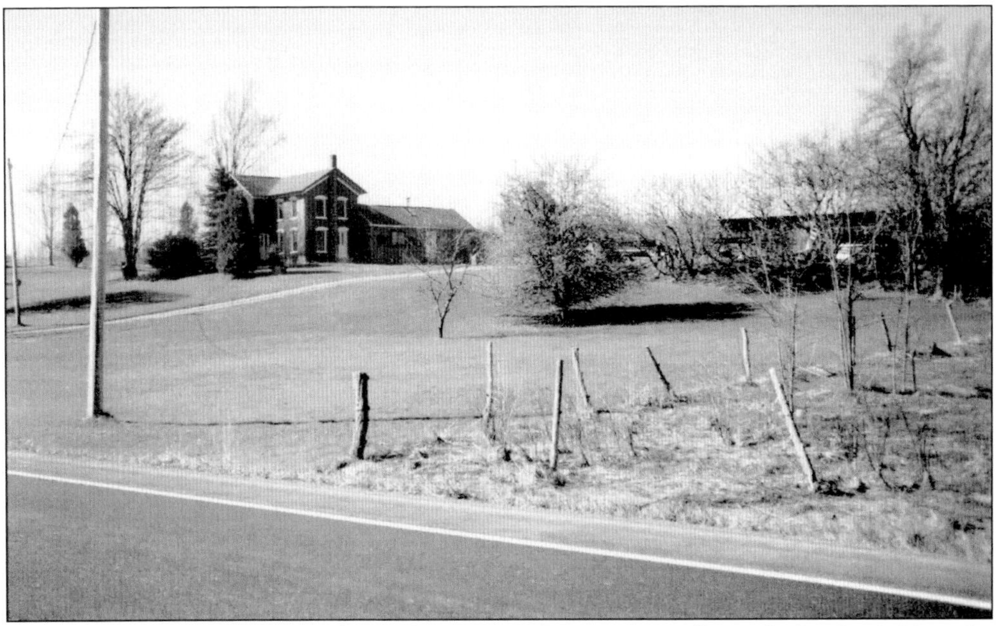

The farmhouse of Caleb Potts, located on county Route 264, still stands. In the field to the south is a new home and barns on the site of the 1982–1983 dig.

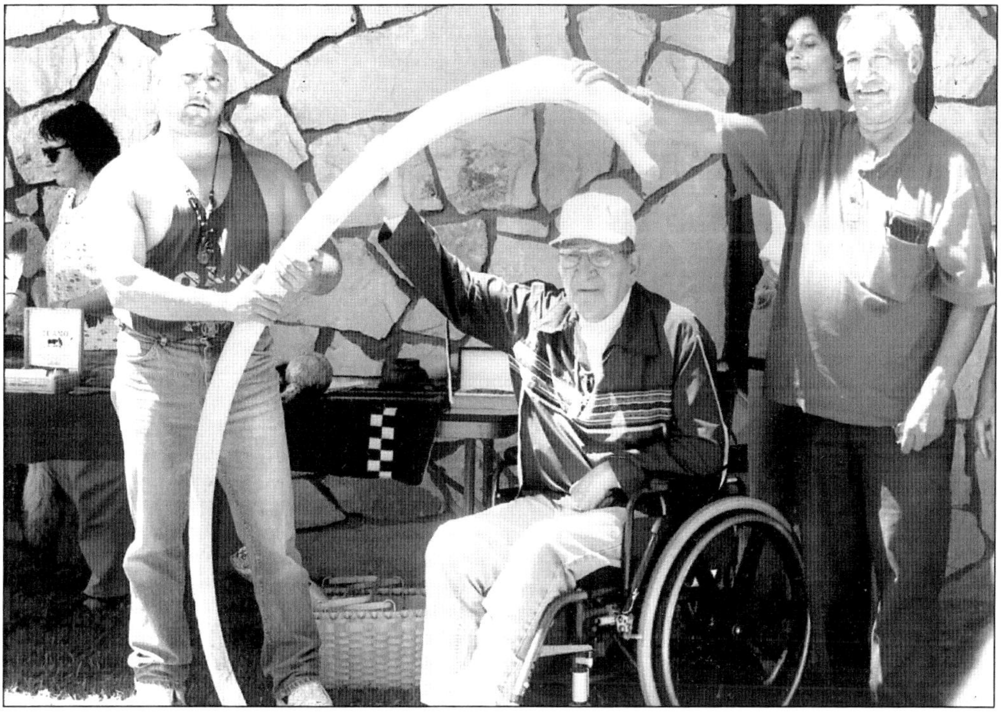

Following his address to the small crowd gathered for the July 25, 2000, tobacco ceremony, Chief Paul Waterman of the Onondaga Nation holds up the bone found in Pennellville by Calvin Corey. The bone, possibly that of a mastodon, symbolizes the town's rich heritage of historical artifacts. With Waterman are Athre Sawatis (Andrew David) Tawit (left) of the Mohawk Nation and Finlay Anton Sekowe of the Oneida Nation. (Courtesy of the *Phoenix Register*, August 2, 2000.)

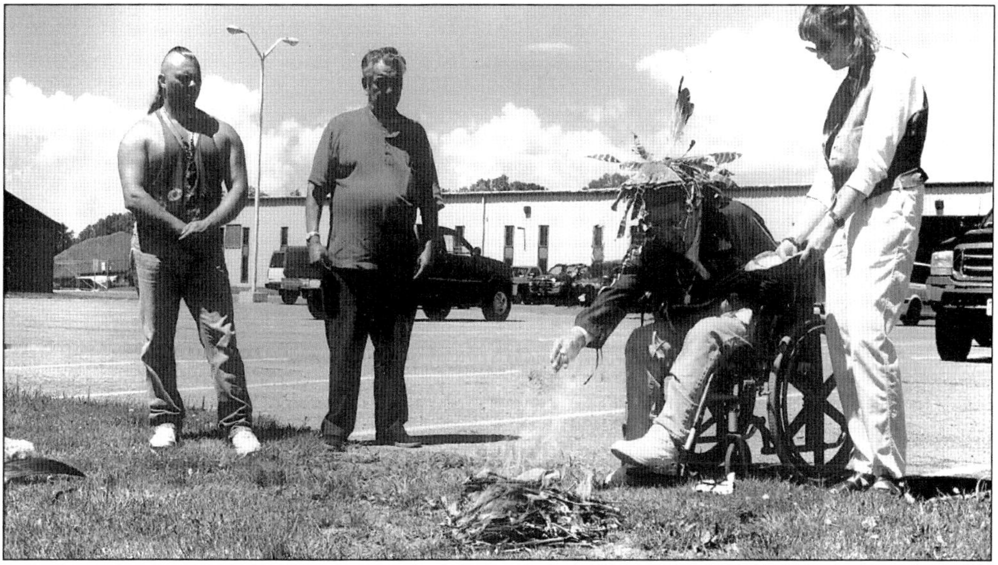

Chief Paul Waterman places sacred tobacco on a small fire. With him at the edge of the parking lot at the town of Schroeppel offices, from left to right, are Athre Sawatis Tawit, Finlay Anton Sekowe, and Sandy Powers. (Courtesy of the *Phoenix Register*, August 2, 2000.)

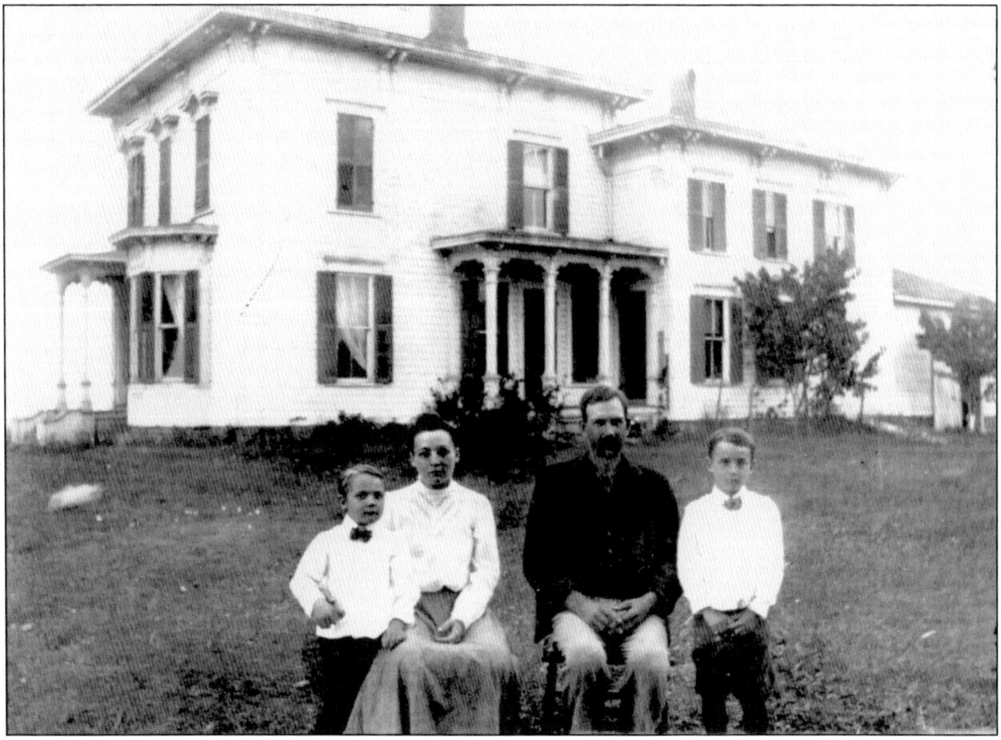

George F. Chesbro (June 18, 1874–January 9, 1949) is pictured with his wife, Clara, and sons Hugh and Addison. He is considered to be the first historian of the town of Schroeppel, although a formal town position did not exist during his lifetime. He had a close relationship with the Onondaga Nation. He worked with the Onondagas and others in a constant search for local Native American history. He, along with several members of the Onondaga Nation, rediscovered the location of the Oak Orchard burial grounds. (Martin Chesbro, courtesy of Frances Chesbro.)

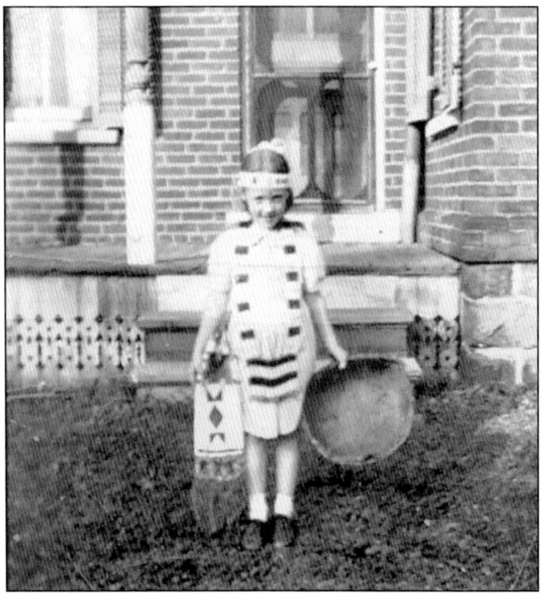

Nancy Chesbro displays some of the beadwork and a basket given to her grandfather George F. Chesbro by the Onondaga Nation. (Martin Chesbro, courtesy of Frances Chesbro.)

Two

THE TOWN OF SCHROEPPEL

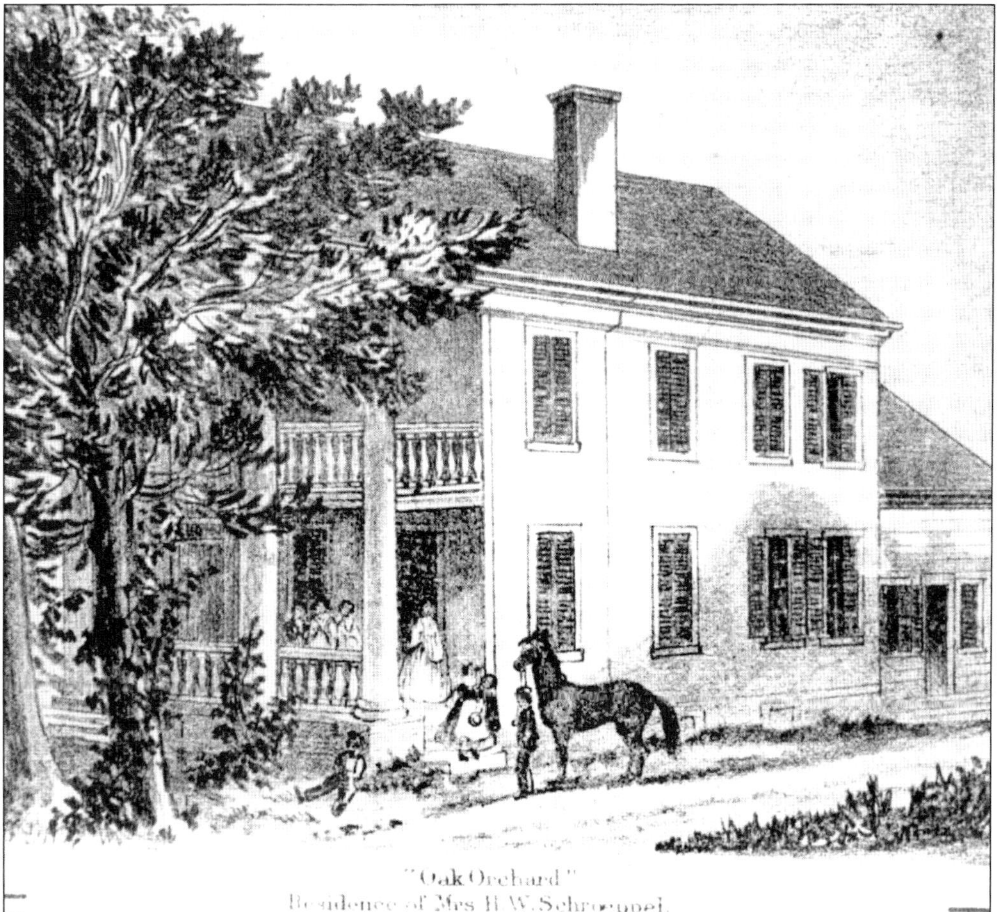

This is a photograph of an early steel engraving of the Schroeppel Mansion, which was built in 1818 by George Casper Schroeppel. At the time, it was the residence of Mrs. H.W. Schroeppel.

The town of Schroeppel was set off from Volney by an act of the legislature passed on April 4, 1832. It contains an area of 26,778 acres. The town was named after George Casper Schroeppel, who at one time owned most of the area that now makes up the town. (Some historical materials state that the town was named after George's son Henry.) Three small tracts were added to complete the town. A total of 350 acres of land were granted to Steven Lush. Known as Lush's Location, this area was along the river just below the village of Phoenix. Also, 1,200 acres of land were granted to Ezra L'Hommedieu and sold to Daniel Phoenix, and later became known as the Phoenix Patent. This area includes the village of Phoenix. Ezra L'Hommedieu was granted 1,000 acres, known as the L'Hommedieu's Location, that occupied the angle at Three Rivers formed by the junction of the Oneida and Oswego Rivers and completed what today is known as the town of Schroeppel. L'Hommedieu had a total of 2,200 acres to begin with. All of these early landowners were speculating on future land development following the Revolution. They were men who knew the inner workings of the New York State government and, thus, were able to bid on land ahead of the general public. The first town meeting was held at the home of James B. Richardson in the village of Phoenix on March 5, 1833.

Throughout this area's history, different locations have served as the center of business and commerce. Before Schroeppel was formed, Gilberts Mills was the main center for commerce in the area. After the completion of the Oswego Canal system in 1828, business and commerce began to shift gradually to areas along the river, and Phoenix eventually became known as the main center for business in the town. Nearby Hinmansville was also a very active canal settlement at this time. In 1869, the Midland Railroad (later known as the Ontario &Western) was built through Pennellville and commerce moved to the Pennellville area. In 1885, a railroad was built through Phoenix and commerce started shifting back to Phoenix. With the bankruptcy of the Ontario & Western in the 1950s, the majority of Schroeppel's commerce shifted to the Phoenix area. Although a wide variety of businesses existed, the foundation of Schroeppel's economy was based on agriculture or industries associated with agriculture until the 1950s.

A limited amount of historical information is available on Gilberts Mills and Hinmansville. These two areas were already in decline before photography was prevalent. Aside from short paragraphs in a few books, very little has been preserved.

During the Civil War, 436 men and boys from the town of Schroeppel joined the Union army and navy. The town has a long list of men and women who have represented Schroeppel in our nation's many wars and conflicts. Three Revolutionary War veterans are buried in the town of Schroeppel: Ebenezer Allen of Gilberts Mills (October 27, 1761–April 18, 1845), Cornelius Wallis of Pennellville (1765–1858), and Timothy Olmstead of Phoenix (1759–1848), a music composer who played the fife in a Connecticut regimental corps and later served in the War of 1812.

Schroeppel has three known Revolutionary War veterans: Cornelius Wallis (right), buried in the Pennellville Cemetery; Timothy Olmstead, buried in the Phoenix Pioneer Cemetery; and Ebenezer Allen, buried in the Gilberts Mills Cemetery. Wallis (the name also appears as Wallace) was born on April 20, 1765, in Manakatling, New York. He lived with his family at Fort Gumaer. His father was a guard and a scout. Wallis, a private, enlisted in April 1779 and served at various times until the end of the war for a total of 15 months. Although his father fought for the Revolution, his uncle was a Tory with the English. At 14 or 15 years old, Wallis was taken prisoner and brought before his uncle, a Tory officer. The judgment was, "I don't want to harm the boy, but I would like to get my hands on his blankety, blank Father."

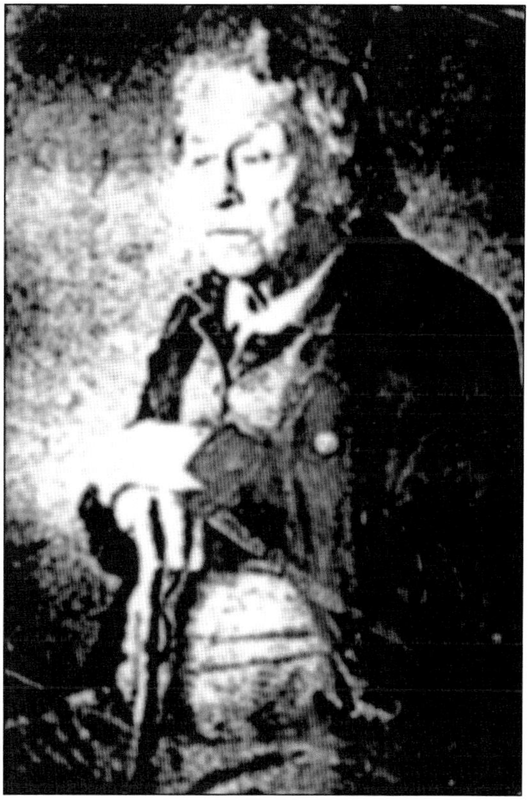

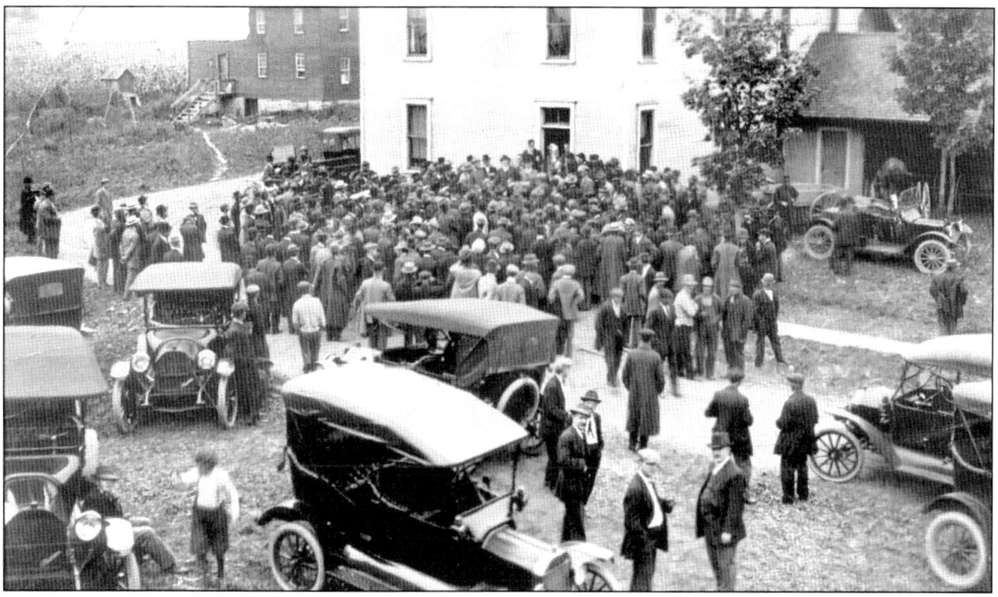

The Schroeppel town caucus takes place at the Pennellville Grange Hall in 1915. (Photograph by R.S. Kellar, courtesy of Lora and Doc Jones.)

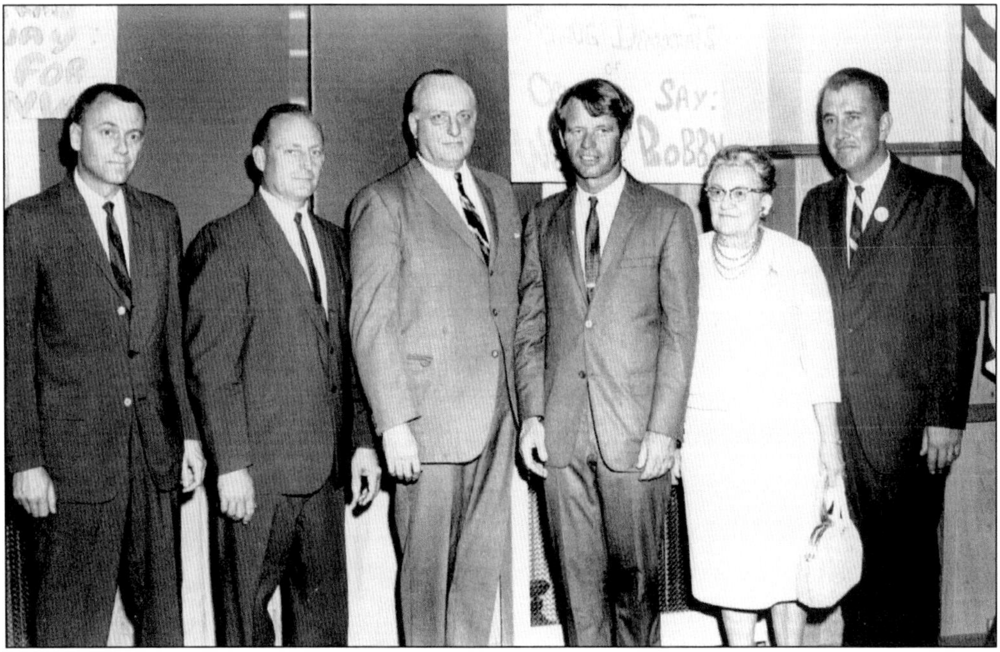

Sen. Robert Kennedy (fourth from the left) and Oswego Mayor John Conway meet with Schroeppel Democrats in 1965.

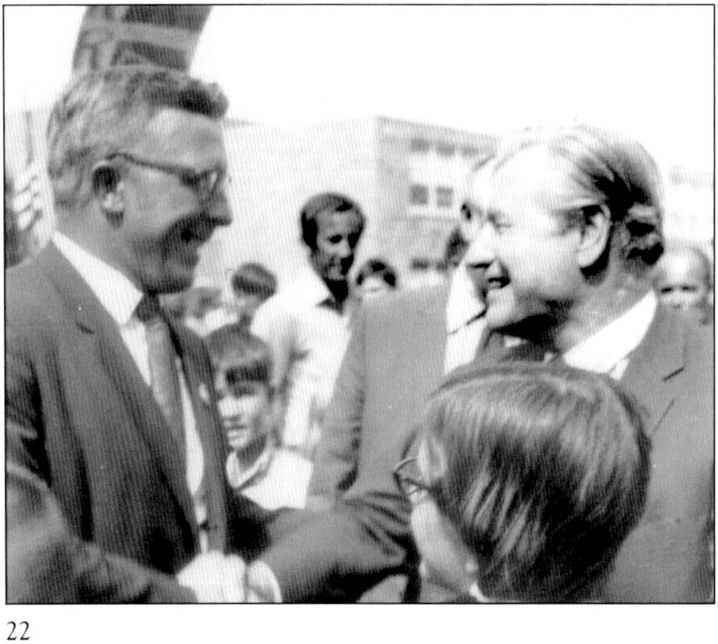

Art Ospelt (left), supervisor of the town of Schroeppel, greets New York Gov. Nelson Rockefeller.

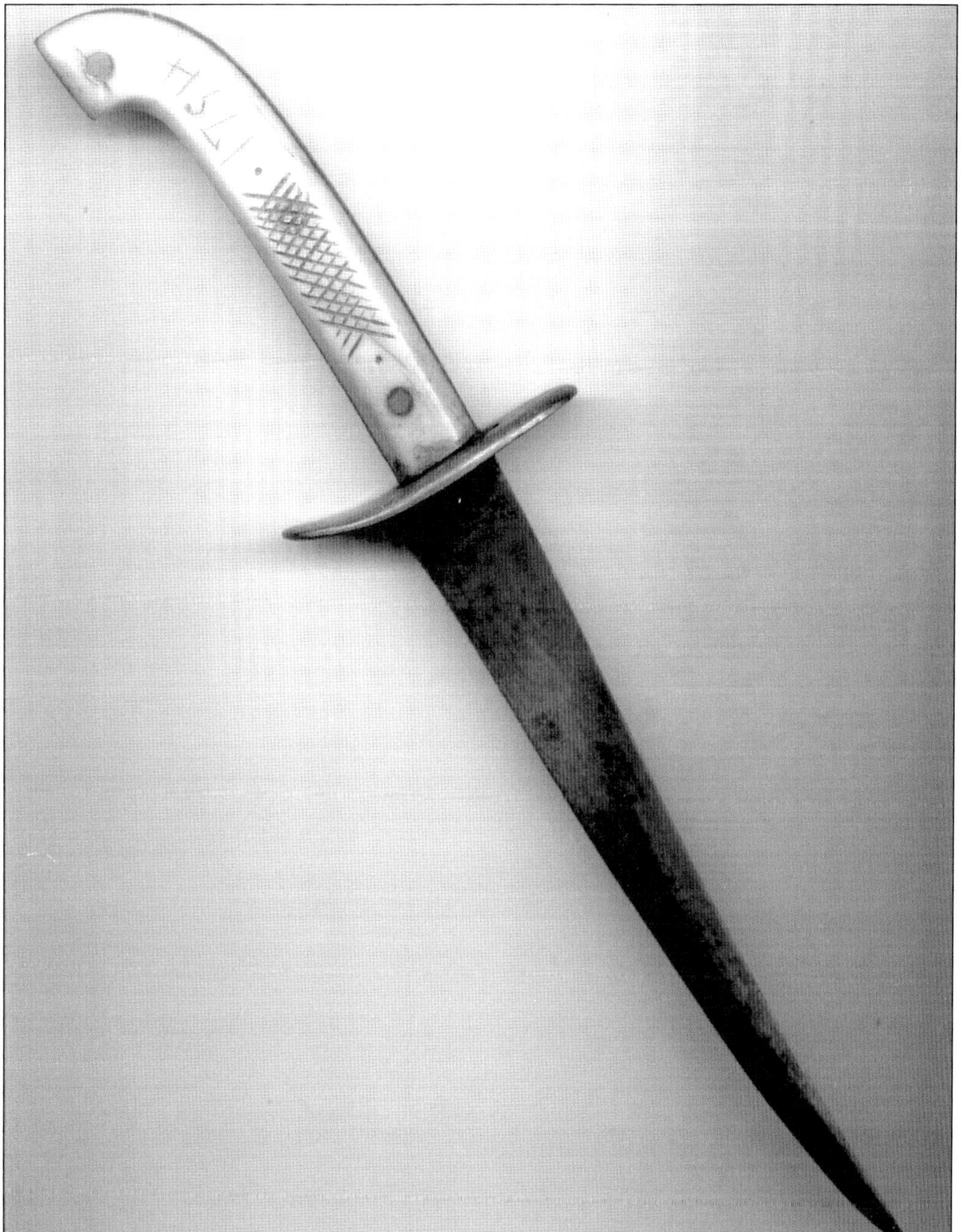

The story of the pirate of Peter Scott Swamp is a part of the lost history of this area. At one time, a pirate was said to have lived in the swamp area just east of the village of Phoenix. This knife, from the estate of a Phoenix collector, belonged to the pirate. Carved into the handle of the knife is the date 1794. Unfortunately, information about the pirate was never written down and was lost with the death of the local collector. Peter Scott Swamp was named years after the pirate's time for Col. Peter Scott, whose troops spent the winter c. 1815 near this area after the War of 1812. The troops were returning to Albany from Oswego when the river near Phoenix became frozen and blocked their passage.

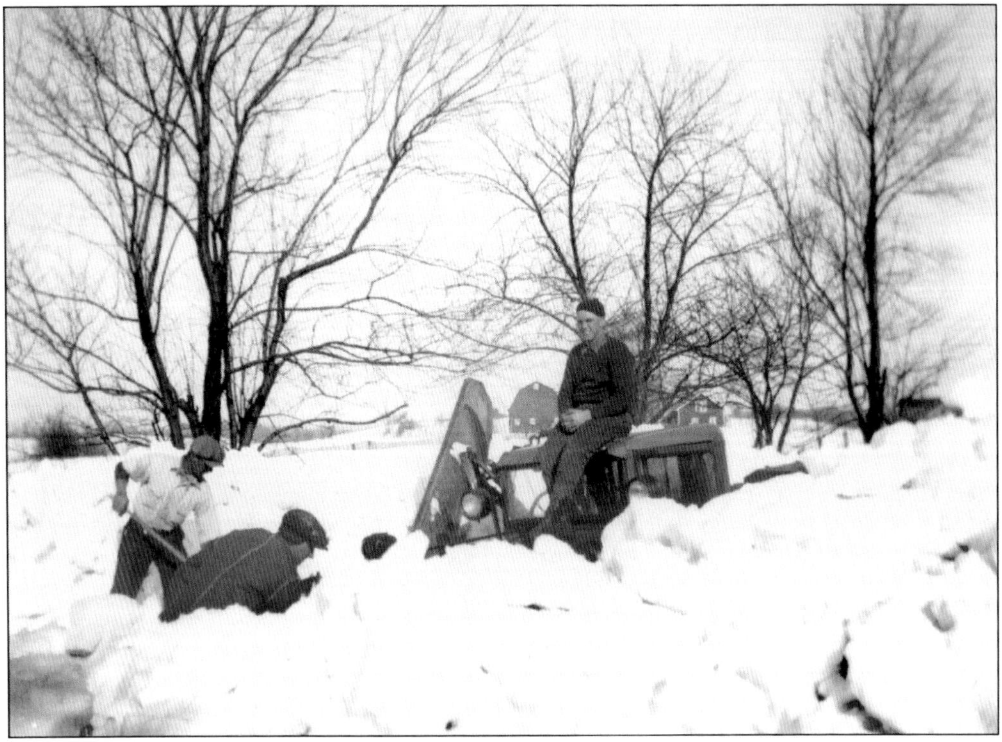

Schroeppel highway crews work to clear the roads of snow.

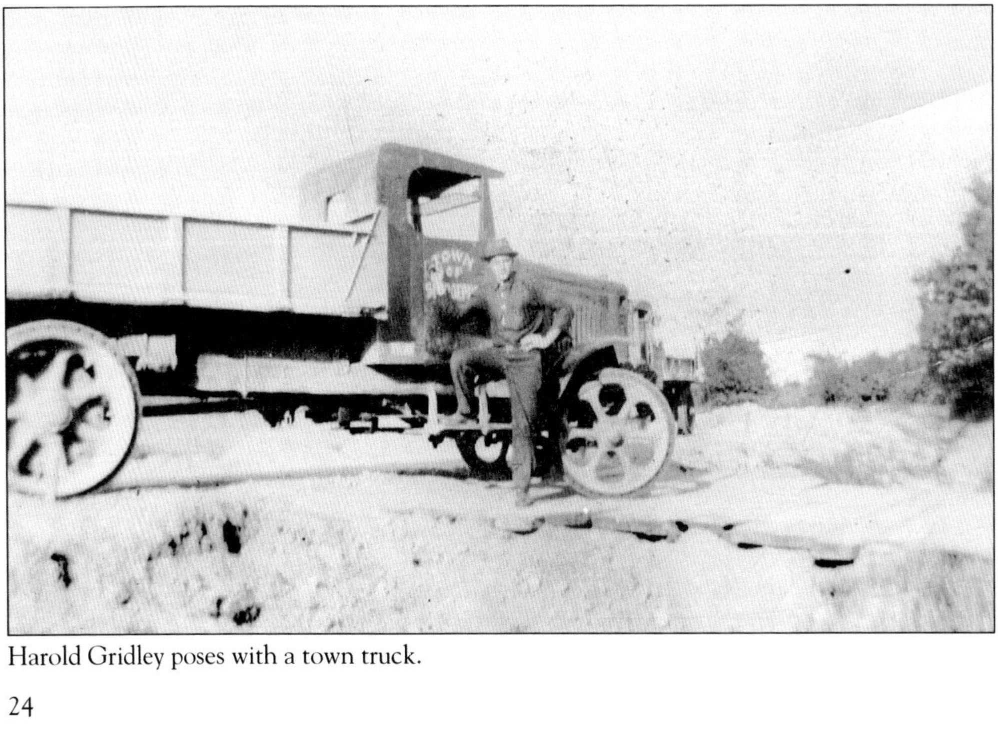

Harold Gridley poses with a town truck.

Three

Oak Orchard

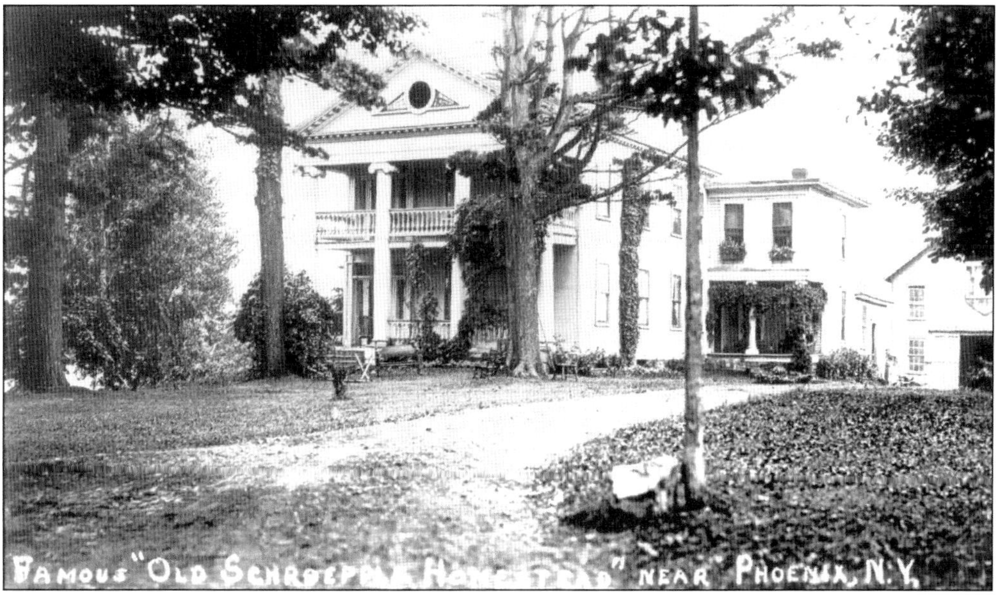

The Schroeppel Mansion was built by George Casper Schroeppel in 1818. This Greek Revival home was the first frame house built in the area that became the town of Schroeppel. Schroeppel owned most of the land in this town that later carried his name. His son Henry added the back section of the mansion after his father's death in 1829. The upstairs of this mansion was the location of the early school in this area. A secret tunnel ran from the basement of the mansion to the shore of the nearby Oneida River.

Located in the southeastern section of the town of Schroeppel is an area known as Oak Orchard. This area was first settled in 1807 by David Winters, who was followed in 1811 by George Foster. Foster was more often referred to as "Tory" Foster than George because of his allegiance to the English during the Revolutionary War.

Amidst the sprinkling of log cabins, George Casper Schroeppel directed the building of the first frame house in the town. The home was finished in 1818, the year Schroeppel's son Henry settled at Oak Orchard. While the home was being built, George Schroeppel lived in a flat-roofed shanty. He also built the first sawmill in the town in 1819 and started a gristmill that was never finished. The grinding stone for the gristmill is still in the front yard of the Schroeppel Mansion today. Oak Orchard never developed into a settlement with stores or other businesses. Schroeppel died in New York City in 1829. His body was later brought to Pennellville by his daughter Mary Pennell for burial in the family plot at the Pennellville Cemetery.

There are many conflicting versions of the life story of George Schroeppel and his marriage to a French princess. The wife, Louisa Marie Adelaide Eugenie, was the daughter of Louis Phillipe Joseph, the Duke of Orlean, who was killed in the French Revolution. She eventually left her family in America and returned to France and is said to have entered a convent in Switzerland where she ultimately died. Yet, her life story is as much a mystery as is that of her husband.

This area known as Oak Orchard is divided by the Oneida River. Part of the Oak Orchard area is in the town of Schroeppel, and part is in the town of Clay.

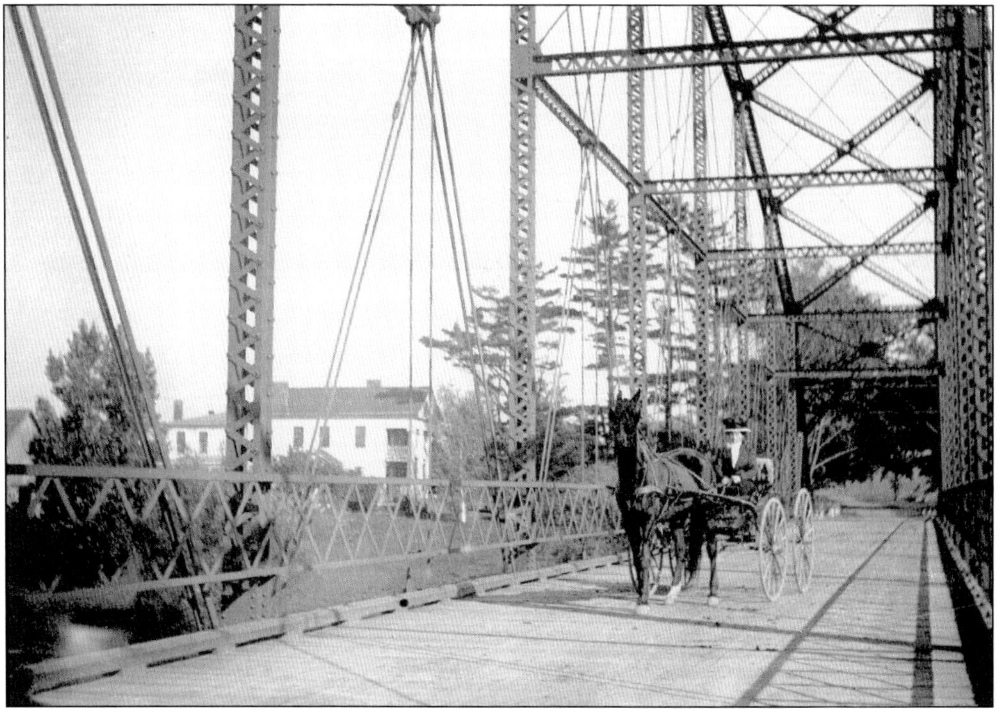

Schroeppel's Bridge is the name of the bridge that crosses the Oneida River, linking the town of Schroeppel with the town of Clay. There have been many bridges at this location over the years that were referred to as Schroeppel's Bridge. The site was originally a fording place in the river and a fishing area for early Native Americans.

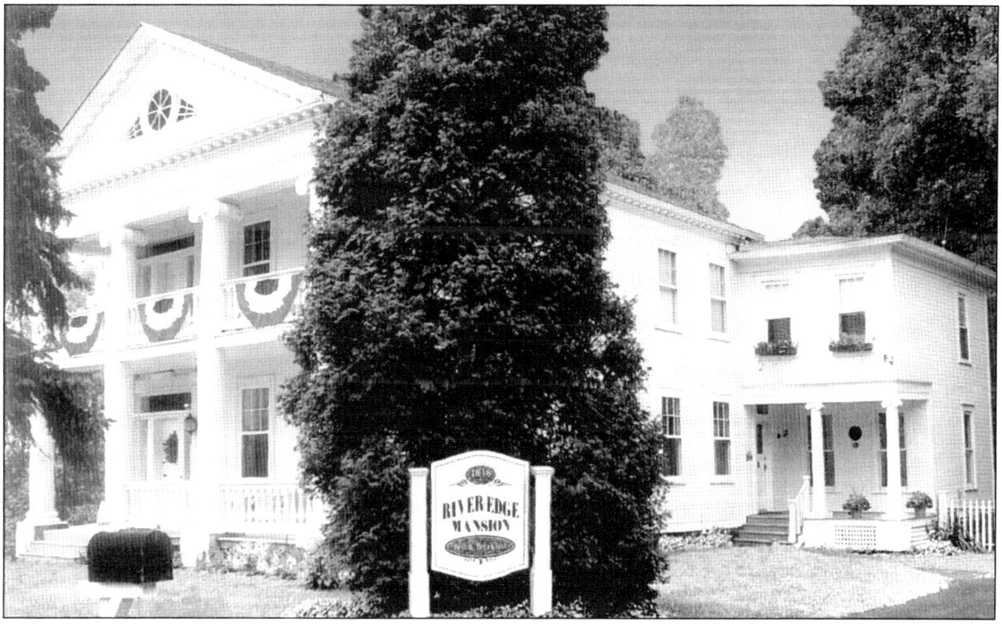

Today, the Schroeppel Mansion is the River-Edge Mansion, a bed and breakfast owned by Dean Wright and Kelly Ciulla. The home was restored by Greg and Dolores Storie, its previous owners. In 1948, Raymond and Regina O'Hare purchased the mansion, which was in shambles, and completely restored it. By the time the Stories bought it, this grand building, once visited by General Lafayette, was again in need of restoration.

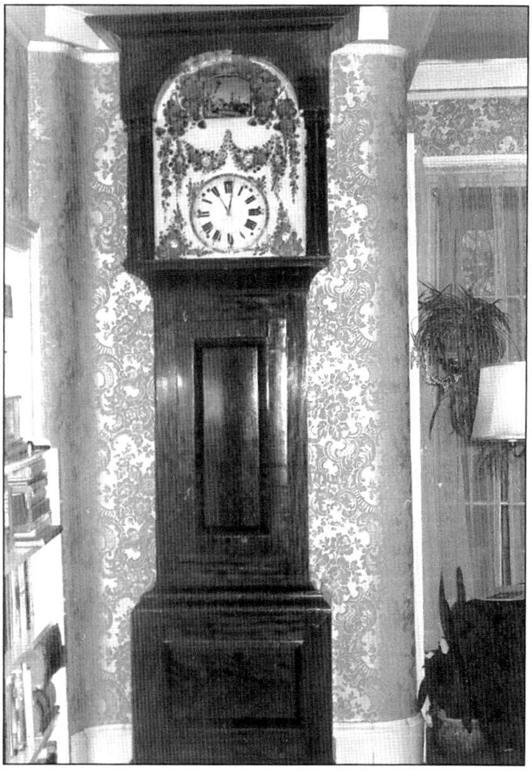

The Schroeppel clock was made in the Black Forest of Germany for Henry Schroeppel in 1833. It was owned for years by J.C. Birdlebough, a local clock collector and principal of Phoenix High School. It can be found today in the Bates House in Oswego, the home of the Oswego County Historical Society. Before the clock strikes, one of eight tunes is played on a pipe organ inside. At the same time, a butcher strikes down a steer in the little stage at the top. The clock's works were made by Felix Fuller, and the organ was made by Ferdinand Meyer.

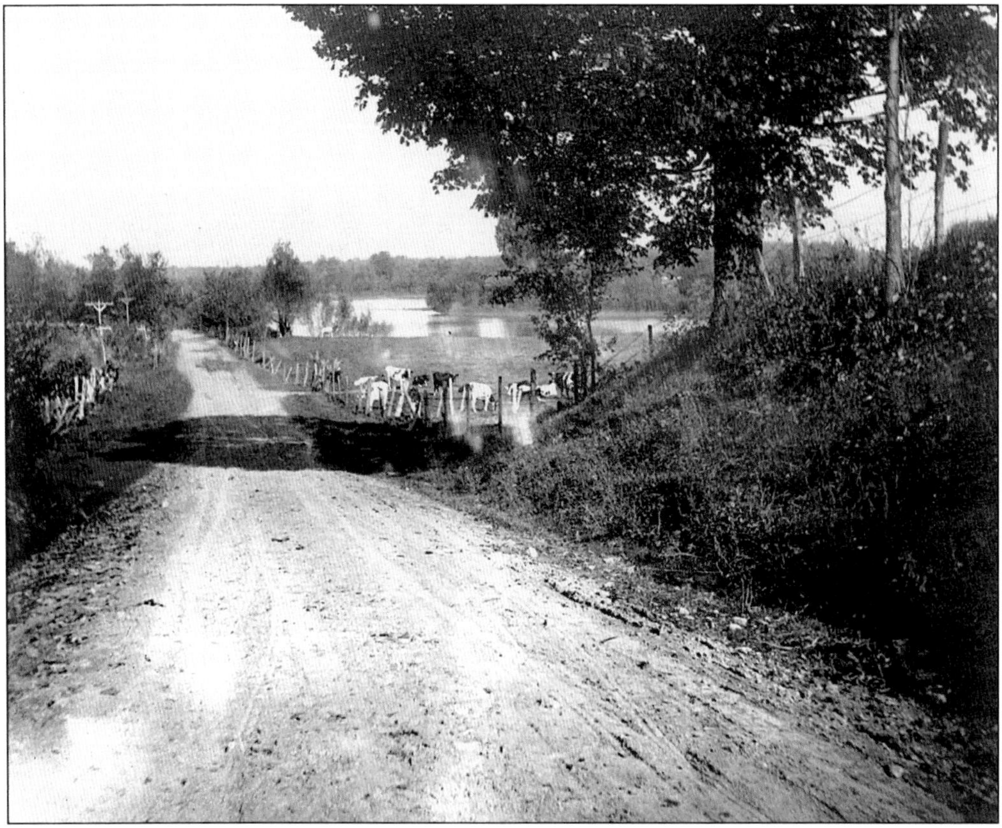

Oneida River Road is pictured *c.* 1917.

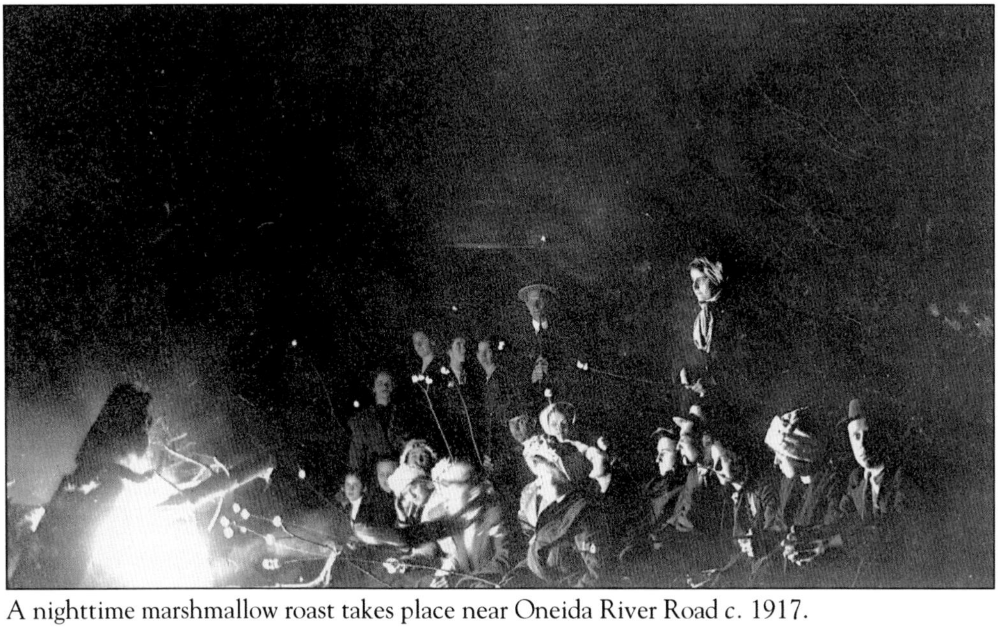

A nighttime marshmallow roast takes place near Oneida River Road *c.* 1917.

Four

GILBERTS MILLS

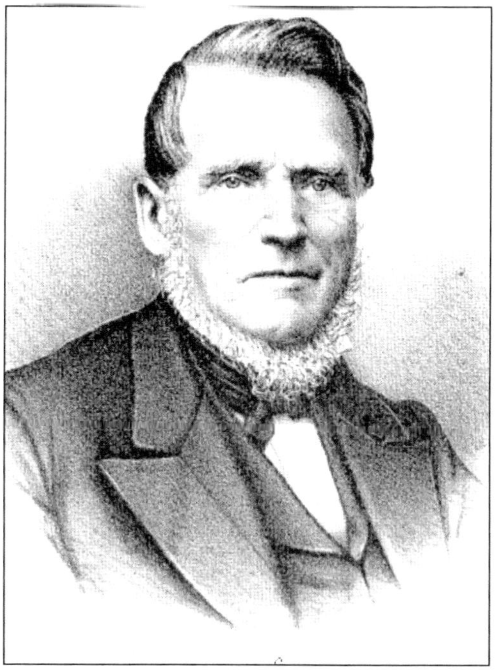

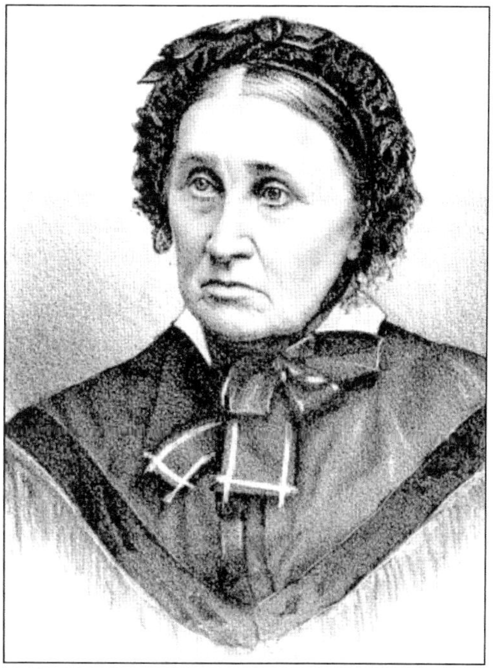

Portraits of Mr. and Mrs. Andrus Gilbert are shown here. (*1789 History of Oswego County, New York*. L.H. Everts & Company, Philadelphia, 1877.)

Gilberts Mills was first settled by Archibald Cook in 1818. In 1819, Andrus and Hiram Gilbert came to the area and built a gristmill along the side of Six Mile Creek. In 1821, Andrus Gilbert built the first store in the township. In 1822, Samuel Merry became a partner of Gilbert in the store, which burned in 1848. A few years later, the Gilberts also erected a sawmill. Salt was discovered in 1864, and a well was drilled. The salt business was operated by Capt. E.S. Cook. At one time, Gilberts Mills had two stores, two blacksmith shops, two shoe shops, a gristmill, a sawmill, and a post office. The area had not sold liquor since 1831.

The recorded history of Gilberts Mills is mostly like the above paragraph—a series of highlights. It offers only a vague view of the way life was in this area, as there are few details. Today, Gilberts Mills is a country crossroads. The new housing in the area consists of single units on existing roads rather than the track developments found in other parts of the town. There is nothing in Gilberts Mills today that gives any indication that this was the area where real growth in the town of Schroeppel began; that this area was, in fact, the economic and cultural center of the township for many years and, at one time, larger than nearby Fulton. The Gilberts Mills post office opened in 1847 and was discontinued in 1904.

Construction began *c.* 1868 for the Midland Railroad, which bypassed Gilberts Mills and ran through nearby Pennellville. The economic life in Gilberts Mills soon after went into a steep decline and never recovered. Business followed the railroad and moved to Pennellville.

Local history today does make note that Gilberts Mills was a heavy abolitionist area in the early 1800s, and that it was the final stop in the town of Schroeppel along the Underground Railroad. Escaped slaves who made it to Gilberts Mills were placed in false-bottom hay wagons and taken to Oswego where they were placed on ships bound for Canada and freedom. A few stories have survived that tell of the Underground Railroad and the southern plantation owners and bounty hunters who would periodically search the Gilberts Mills area for their lost property.

Local history also holds a number of fragments from Gilberts Mills's past that are slowly becoming clearer. It was not until 2001, as a result of the research of Volney historian George Wise, that the existence of a Revolutionary War soldier's grave in the Gilberts Mills Cemetery was known. Although it has always been known that Gilberts Mills was the home of a locally famous artist named Frank Mason, it was only a few years ago that the extent of the Mason family fame in the art world was truly understood. According to local oral history, the daughter of Archibald Cook, the first settler of Gilberts Mills, was one of the many wives of religious leader Brigham Young. Although indications are that this is true, it has yet to be historically proven. Gilberts Mills was the home of many prominent individuals of the period. It may have had its own newspaper and supposedly had a gunsmith who made Gilberts Mills firearms. Again, however, there are few known details and little historical proof.

One thing that is known is that Gilberts Mills was named after the Gilberts. Developing areas were often referred to by what was located near them. In the case of Gilberts Mills, it was the mills that the Gilberts had built, although the area was known as Gilbertsville for a while.

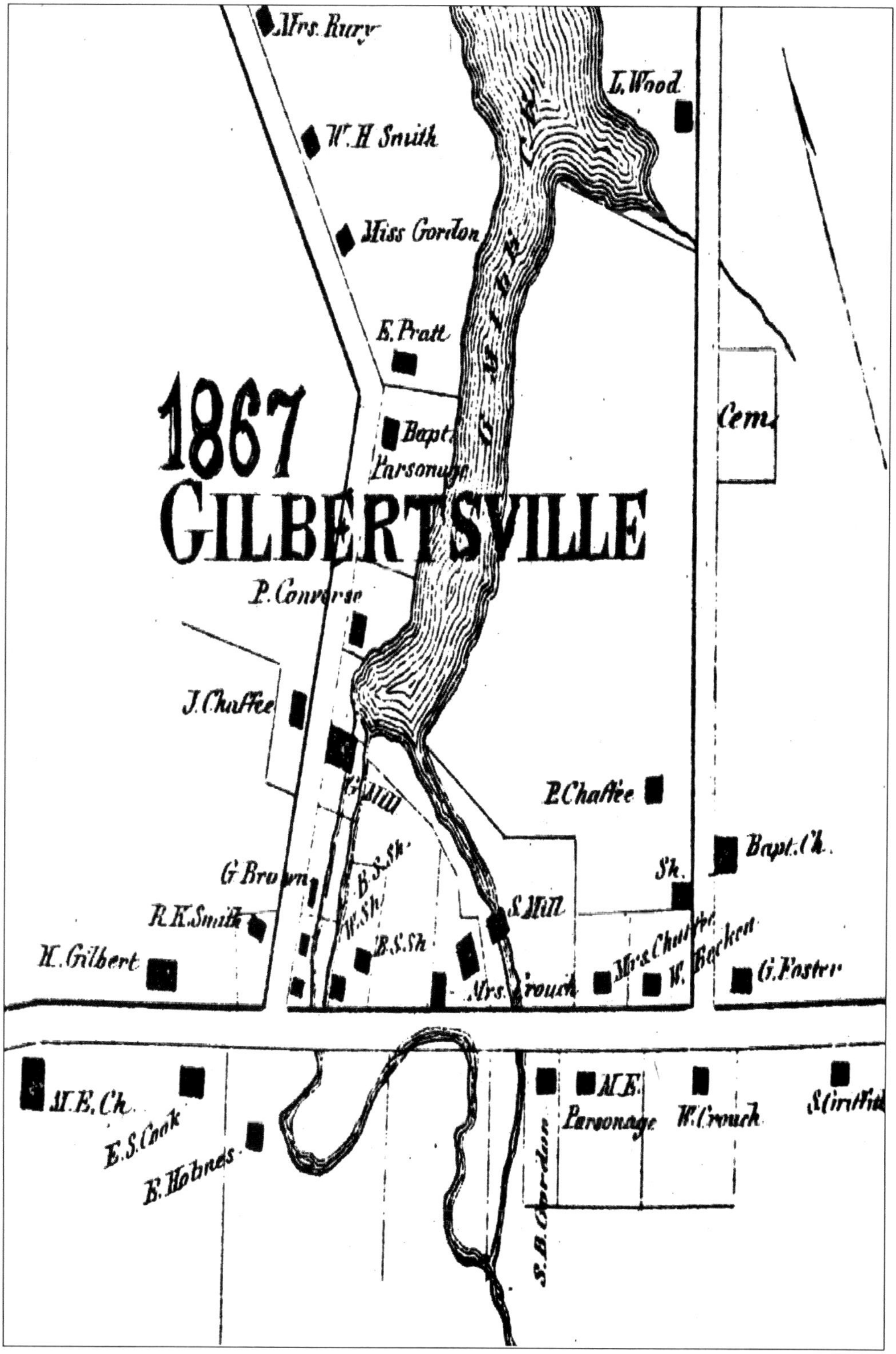

This is an 1867 map of Gilbertsville.

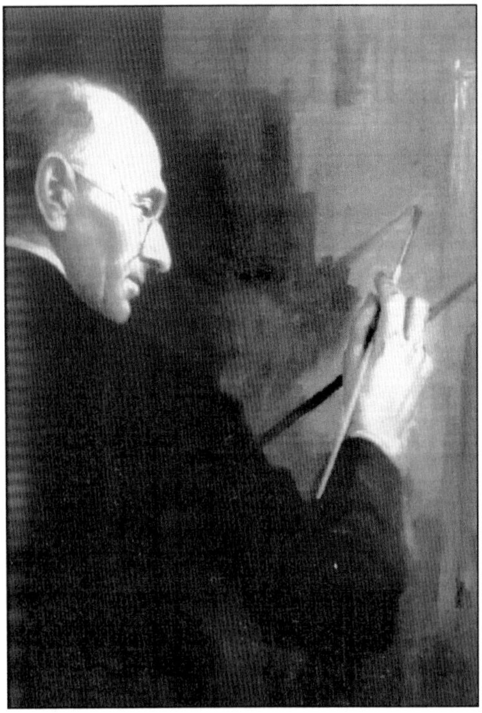

Frank Elliott Mason was born in Gilberts Mills in 1859. When he was 12 years old, artists from England boarded at the Mason home in Gilberts Mills. Young Frank carried the men's equipment and learned to paint. He married Sarah Wilson from Gilberts Mills in 1881 and had three children: Nina, Roy, and Max, all of whom went on to become famous artists. Max was born in Pennellville, where the Masons moved. Frank worked for Hunter Arms in nearby Fulton as an engraver before the Masons moved to Batavia. While living in the Gilberts Mills-Pennellville area, Frank taught art to many local residents. This is a painting of Frank Mason done by Nina Mason Booth. The image was taken from *The Masons of Batavia*, by William F. Brown Jr. (Hodgins Printing Company, 56 Harvester Avenue, Batavia.)

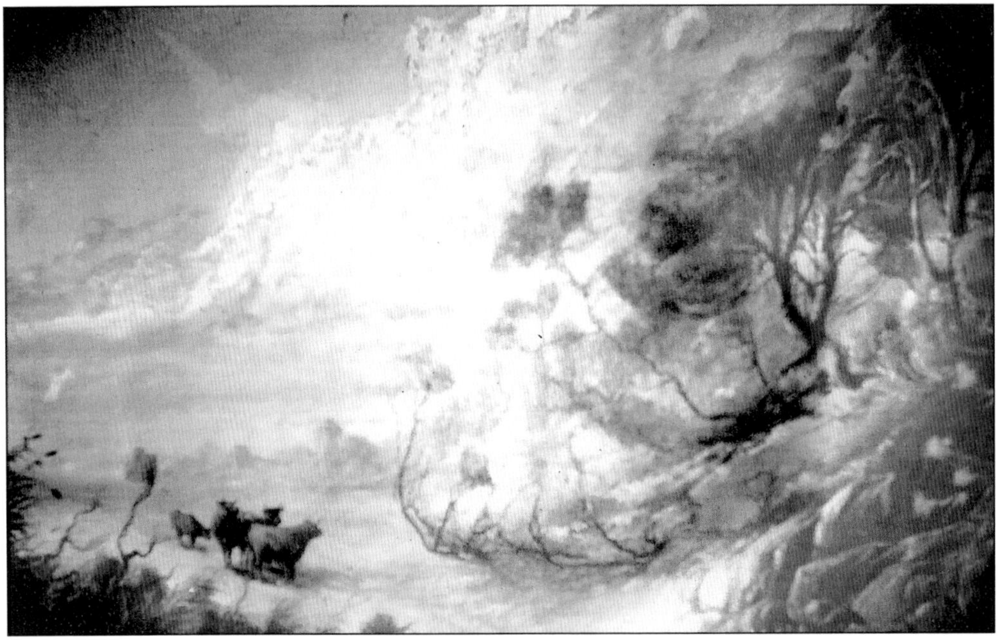

This is a photograph of a local painting entitled *Ole Virginia*. It was done in 1888 by Frank E. Mason. Ole Virginia is a local name given to an area that was on the Gregg Farm, across Fish Creek and along Sutton Road. This was the first time this type of cattle (either Jersey or Guernsey) had been brought to the Pennellville area, and Mason recorded the moment with this painting. The painting was given to one of his Pennellville students, Frances (Fanny) Parker. Several of the paintings done by the Masons are of the Gilberts Mills–Pennellville area.

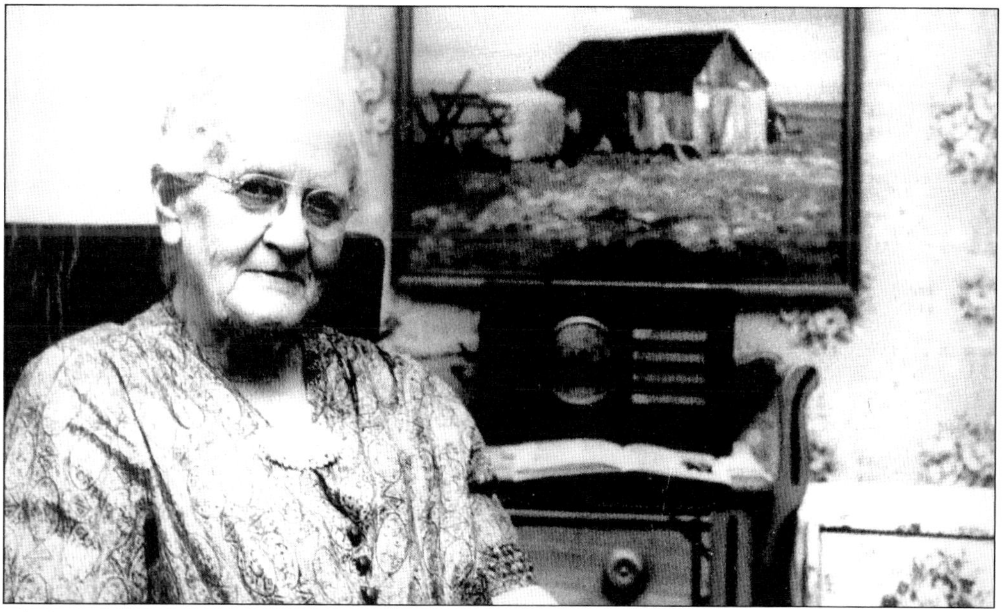

Edith Gregg, who taught at the brick schoolhouse on Biddlecum Road, is shown here in retirement in her room at the Pennellville Hotel. Behind her is a painting that is believed to have been done for her by one of her favorite students, Max Mason. The painting is believed to be of the barn that was on the Mason property at Gilberts Mills, which was across from the school. (Photograph by John Hyvonen, courtesy of Marian Creamer.)

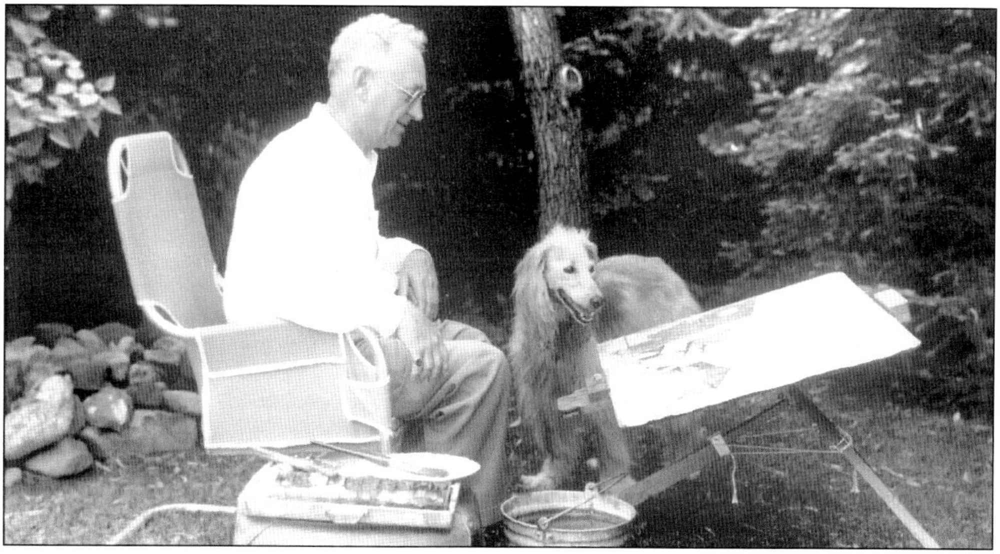

Wildlife artist Roy M. Mason is considered one of the top landscape painters of his time. His main interest was in sporting and wildlife. Born on March 15, 1886, in Gilberts Mills, the award-winning artist is listed in *Who's Who in America, 1969–1973*. His work received numerous awards, including 17 major prizes. Museums and galleries from coast to coast own his paintings, including the Metropolitan Museum of Art in New York City, the Toledo Museum in Ohio, and the Art Institute of Chicago Museum. His work can be found in a large number of prints, calendars, and on the cover of magazines such as *True*, *Readers Digest*, and *Colliers*. (William F. Brown, *The Masons of Batavia*.)

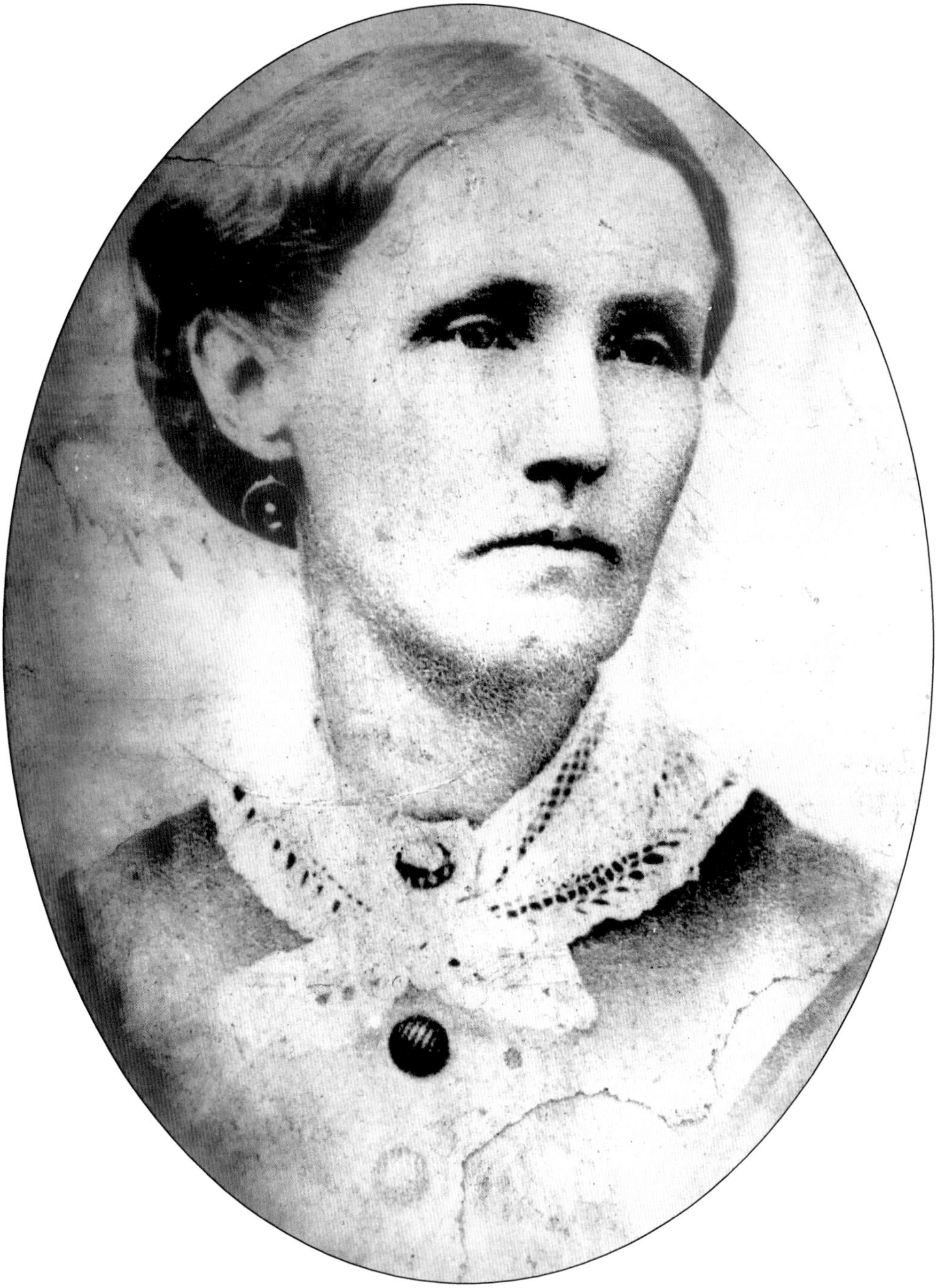

Harriet Elizabeth Cook was the daughter of shipbuilder Archibald Cook and Elizabeth M. Campbell. She was the fourth wife of Brigham Young and the second of his 70-odd plural wives. It is said that she was tall, blue-eyed, slender, and the granddaughter of Ralph Waldo Emerson. After she was converted by Mormon missionaries, she was promptly disowned by her parents. She married Brigham Young on November 2, 1843, at age 19. (Courtesy of the Utah State Historical Society, all rights reserved.)

Five

Hinmansville

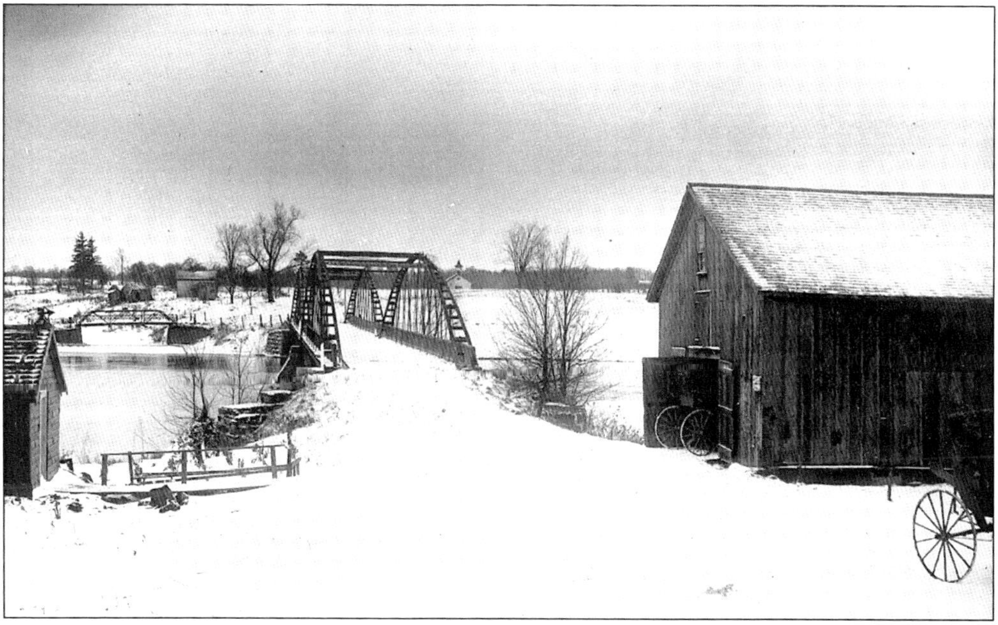

This photograph shows the Hinmansville Bridge.

Hinmansville was formerly known as Six Mile Creek and was first settled by John F. Withey in 1821. The Oswego Canal, which was completed in 1828, runs alongside the area. In 1827, Benjamin F. Sweet erected the first frame house here. This area was inherited by George Casper Schroeppel's daughter Marie and her husband, John E. Hinman of Utica. Hinmansville received its name from the Hinmans and refers to an area that includes both sides of the river.

The Hinmans were instrumental in the construction of many buildings in the area, which laid the foundation for a village. John E. Hinman oversaw the building of 25 small houses for canal workers. The Hinmans were also influential in having the Oswego Canal channeled closer to the settlement. Once a busy canal settlement, Hinmansville had a schoolhouse, church, general store, grocery, blacksmith shop, shoe shop, and tavern.

Today, Hinmansville is a rural area in which only the remnant of a cemetery remains—one grave marker lying on the ground. The stone is that of B. Hinman, Esq., who died in 1845 and was a brother of John E. Hinman. There were at least 25 burials in Hinmansville, but all the markers have been stolen or destroyed. No cemetery records are known to be in existence. The ownership of the cemetery and the responsibility for its care are cause for periodic debates. Historically, Hinmansville, also referred to as Hinmanville, is often an area in the town of Schroeppel that is overlooked or forgotten.

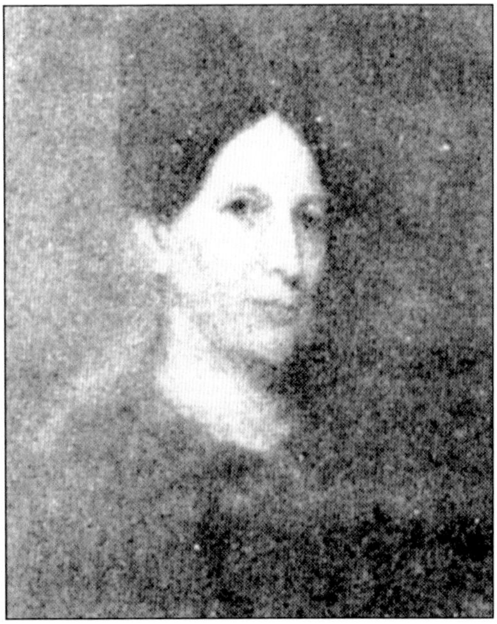

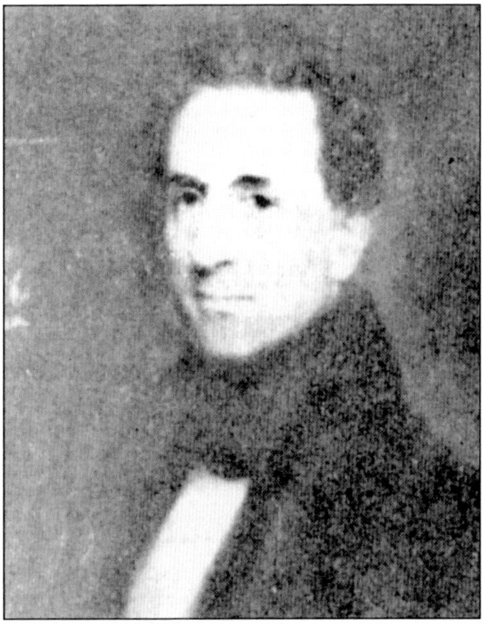

Marie Schroeppel was the daughter of George Casper Schroeppel and the wife of John Hinman (right), the mayor of Utica. She inherited the Hinmansville area after her father's death.

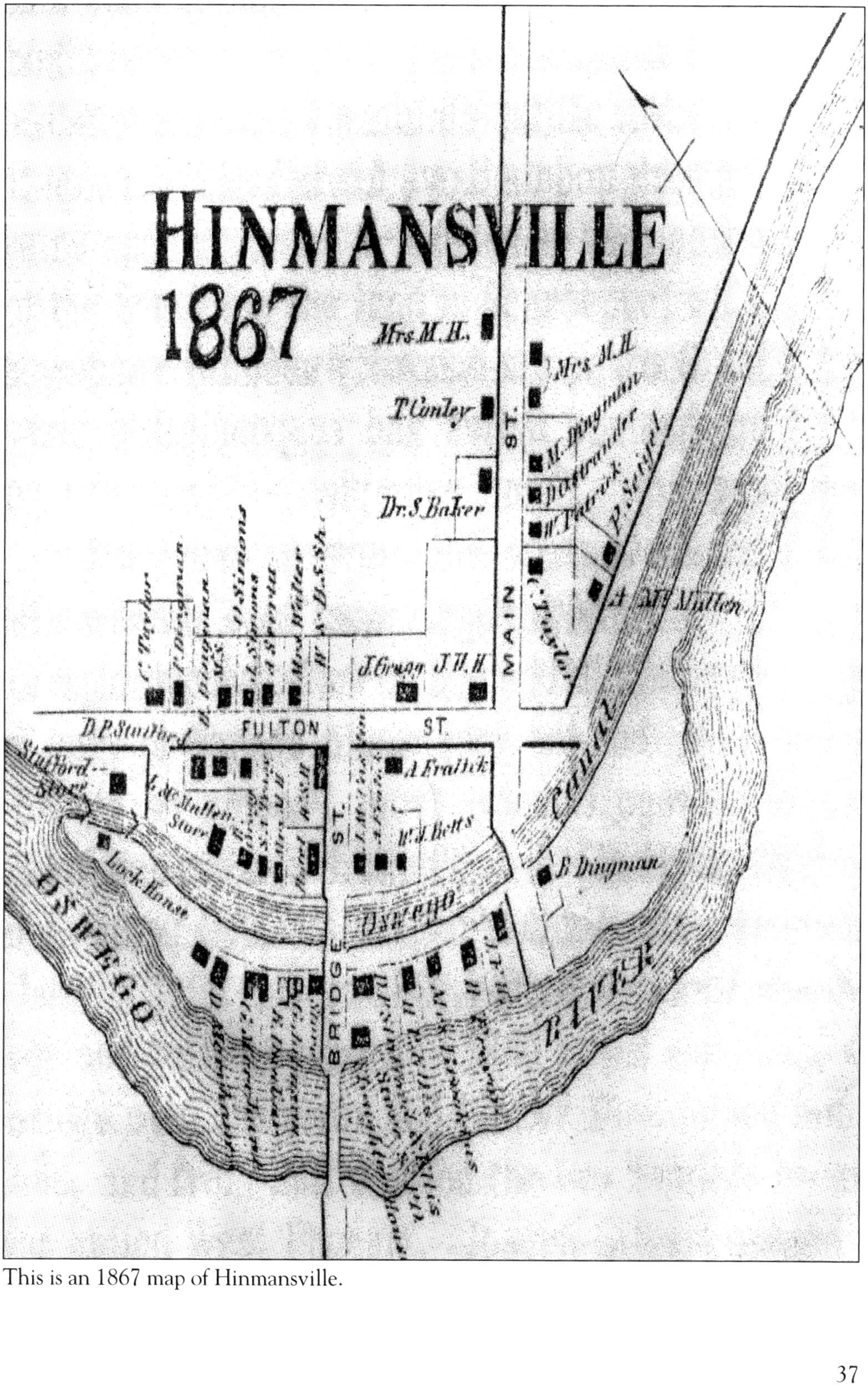

This is an 1867 map of Hinmansville.

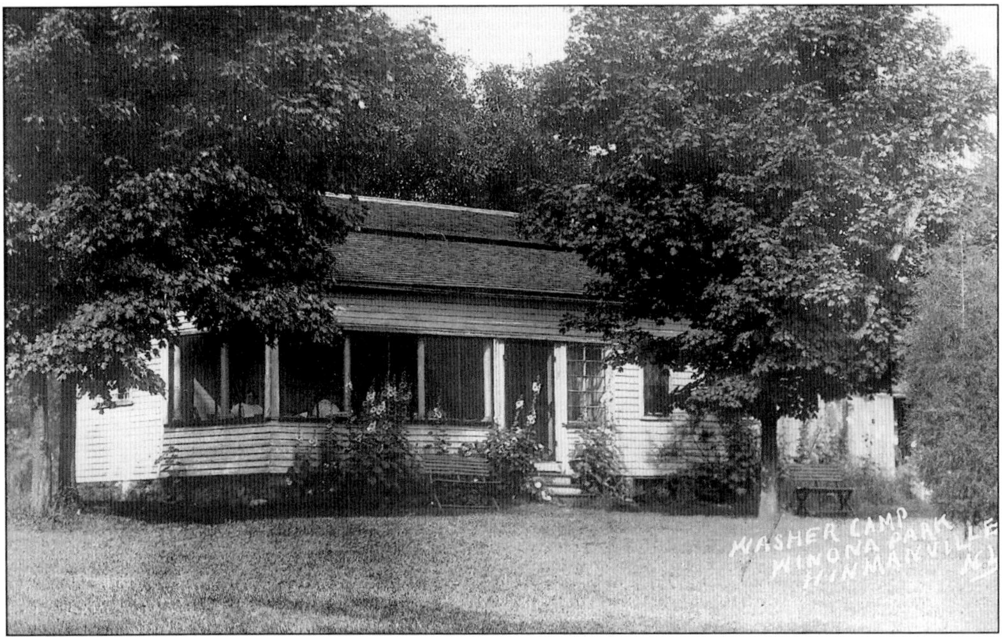

This is Washer Camp in Winona Park in Hinmansville. (Mrs. Washer and Donald P. Kelly, Friends of History, Fulton.)

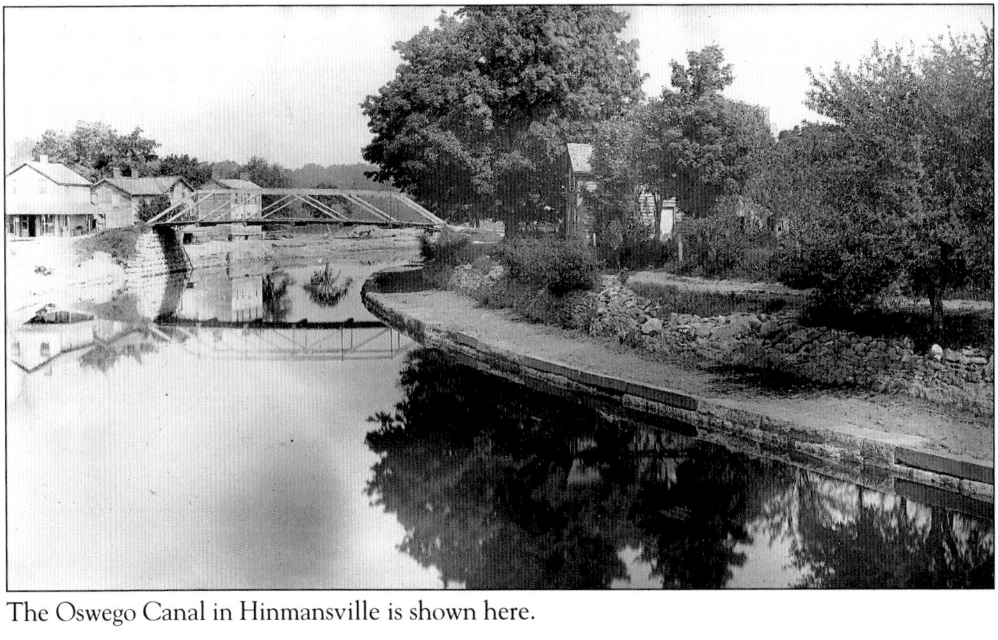

The Oswego Canal in Hinmansville is shown here.

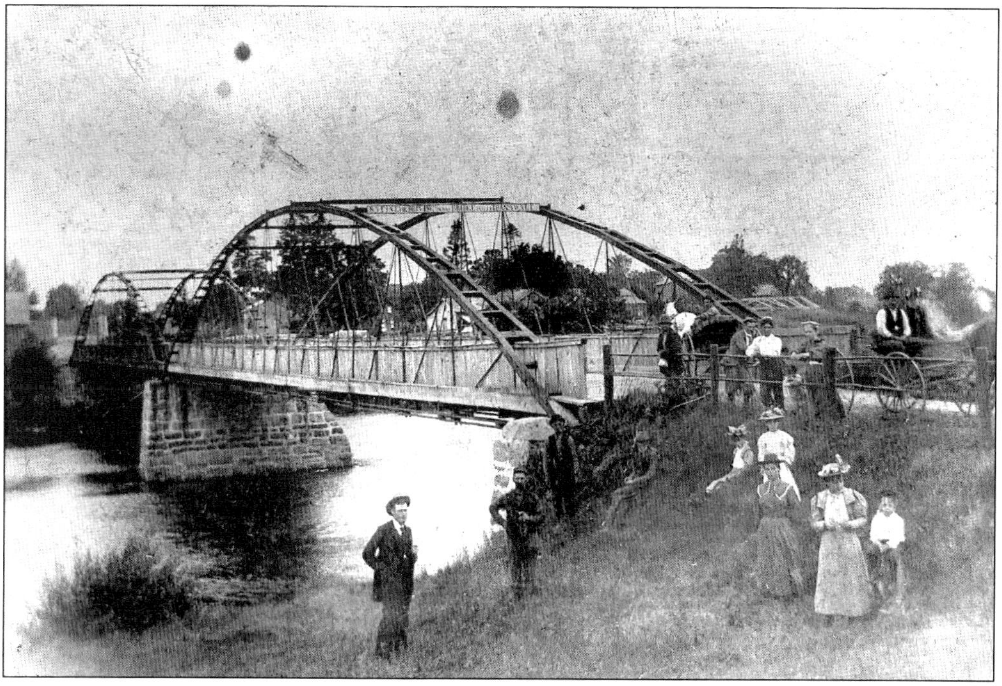

A family enjoys an outing near the Hinmansville Bridge

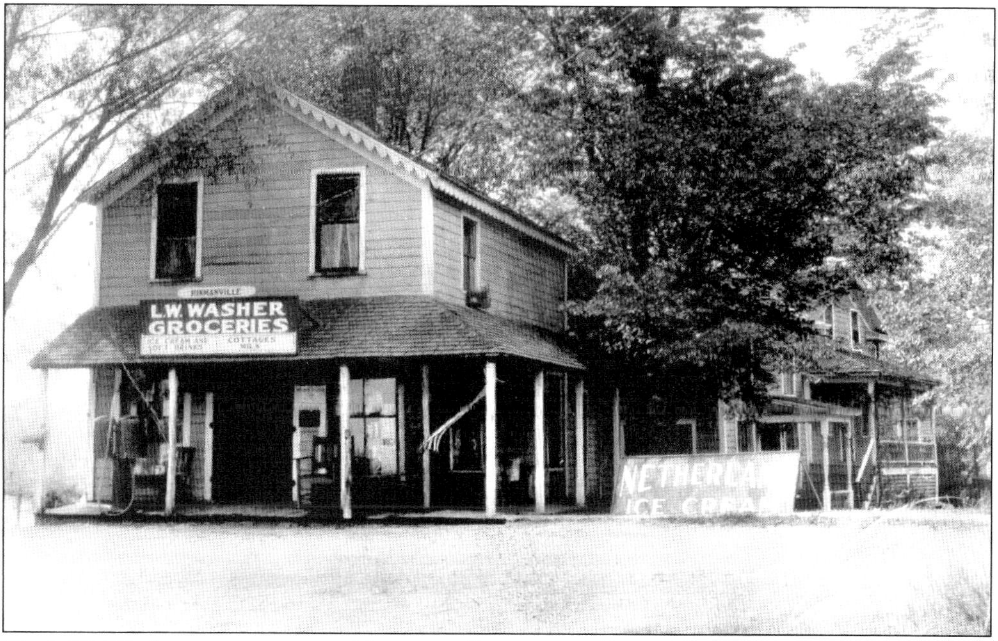

The L.W. Washer grocery store in Hinmansville is pictured here. The large sign (right) advertises Netherland ice cream. (Courtesy of Richard Huntley.)

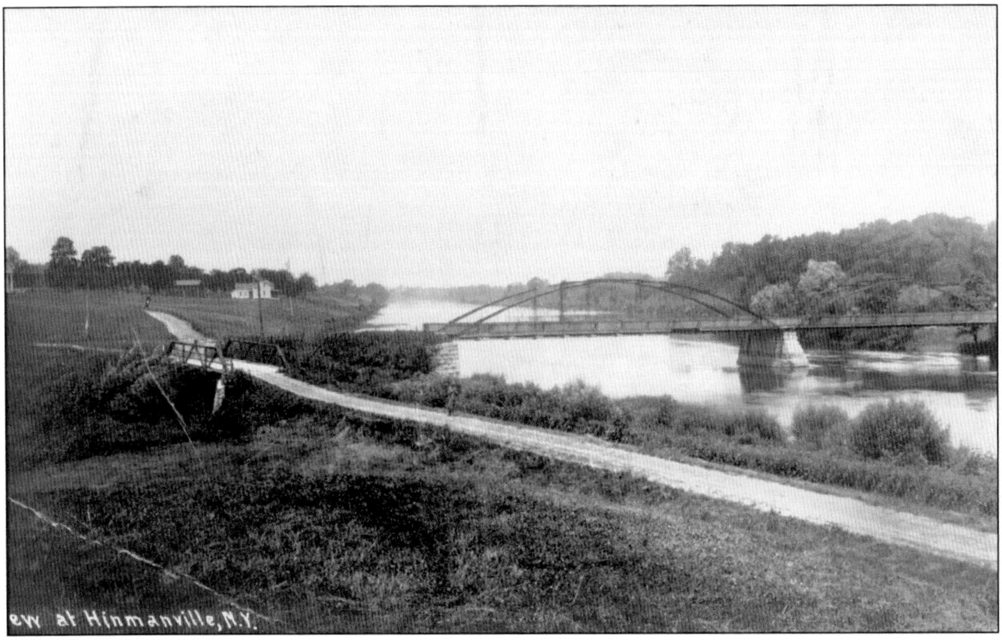

This is a view of Hinmansville. (Photograph by R.S. Kellar, courtesy of Richard Huntley.)

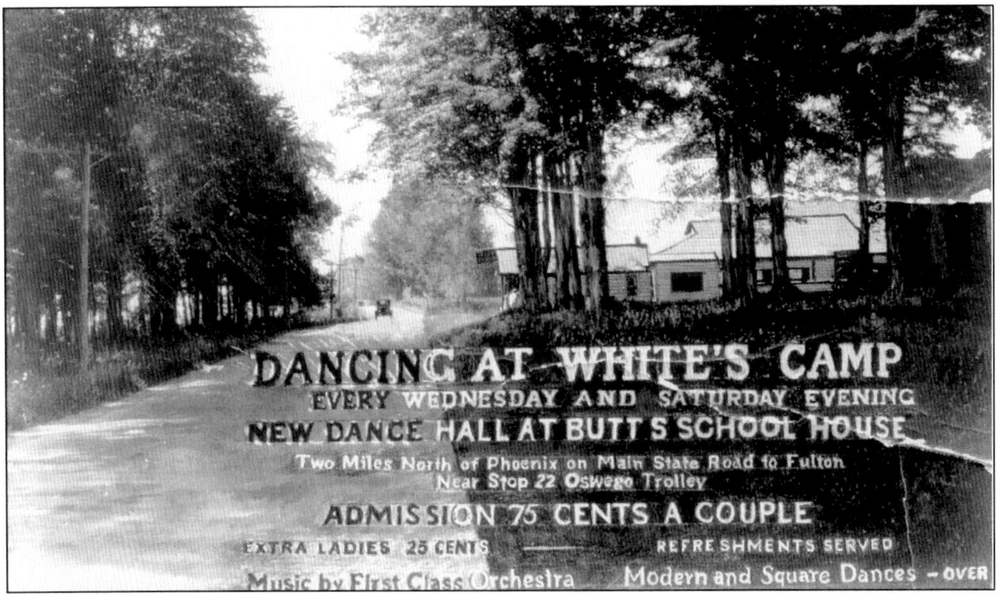

Dancing was held at White's Camp in Hinmansville every Wednesday and Saturday evening. (Courtesy of Richard Huntley.)

Six

Pennellville

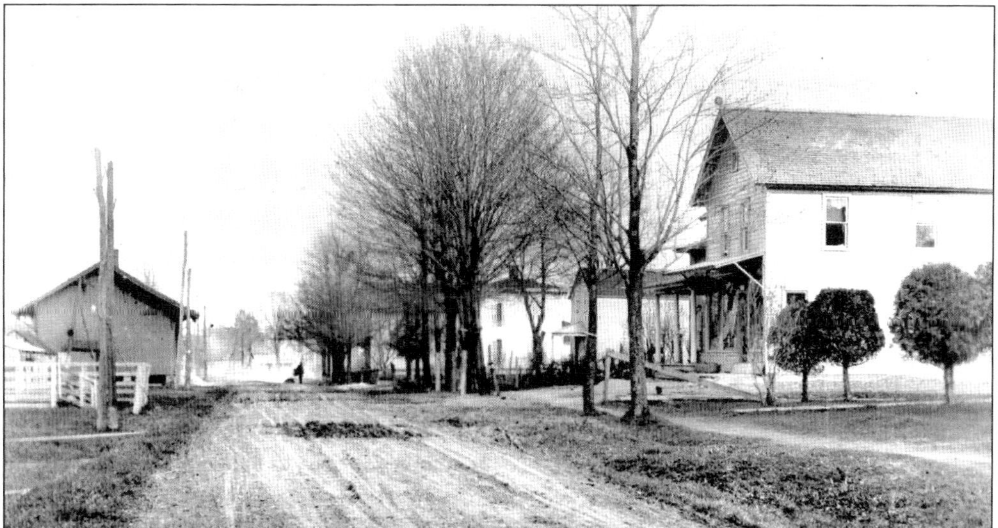

This view looks east toward the Pennellville Hotel. Conrad's store is on the right, and the Ontario & Western cattle yard and train station are on the left.

The area that is today known as Pennellville was the area inherited by Mary Hannah and her husband, Dr. Richard Pennell, from the estate of Mary's father, George Casper Schroeppel. At one time, the area was known as Pennell's Mill after the sawmill Pennell had Lauren Seymour build in 1833. The mill was built along a stream that historical accounts say was called *Ah-in-ah-ta-na-ga-nus* by the Native Americans, signifying "big fish water." This is one of the mysteries of local history, as the word is not from the language of either the Onondaga or the Oneida, the two main tribes known to have frequented the Pennellville area.

Although Pennellville was named after the Pennells, this was their summer home, not their permanent home, as they lived in New York City, where Richard was a prominent doctor. Their main house here was at the end of Grange Street, next to where the new Methodist church and school are located. However, they may, from time to time, have lived temporarily at other locations around the area aside from their main residence. Like George Casper Schroeppel, they were interested in developing the area and making money by selling the land off in small parcels. More than 90 land transactions are attributed to the Pennells. The Pennell name (Mrs. P.) on various locations on early maps indicates ownership of that property and not necessarily residence there. Sometime in the 1800s (a firm date is unknown), half of the Pennells' main residence was moved a short distance to a field, where it was converted into an apartment house known as the Bee Hive, which later burned. The remaining part was used as the caretaker's quarters.

In 1888, a family secret became public in a trial held in Pulaski more than 20 years after the death of Dr. Richard Pennell and his wife. In 1852, a baby boy was born from the short marriage of Pennell's son, George, to his first cousin Mollie Schroeppel. Dr. Pennell had told the couple the child had died, but in reality, he gave the child away and provided for its care. As a result of a sealed letter Mollie had left that was opened upon her death and her mother's search for her grandson, the boy was found. The child sued to regain the name Pennell and his share of the inheritance, and he won, as told in the Thursday, June 7, 1888, issue of the *Palladium*.

The boom years came to Pennellville when the New York and Oswego Midland Railroad laid its tracks through the village. The railroad was built through areas that bonded for its construction and bypassed areas that did not. Although this policy brought growth to the areas where the railroad went in, it eventually was the reason for the bankruptcy of the railroad, as it bypassed some important markets like Syracuse. Still, in its heyday it brought many businesses to Pennellville and made Pennellville the economic hub of the town of Schroeppel until a railroad was eventually built through Phoenix. The Midland tracks through the village were laid using the main road as the railroad bed to reduce the cost of construction.

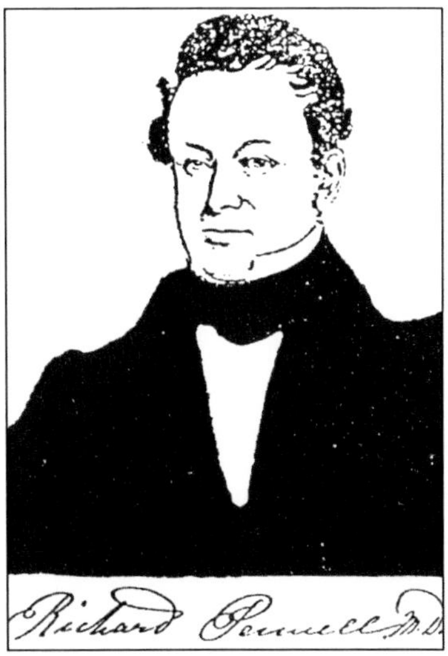

Richard Pennell, M.D., and his wife, Mary Hannah Schroeppel, inherited the area that is now known as Pennellville from Mary's father, George Casper Schroeppel. (Courtesy of Mexico Historial Society.)

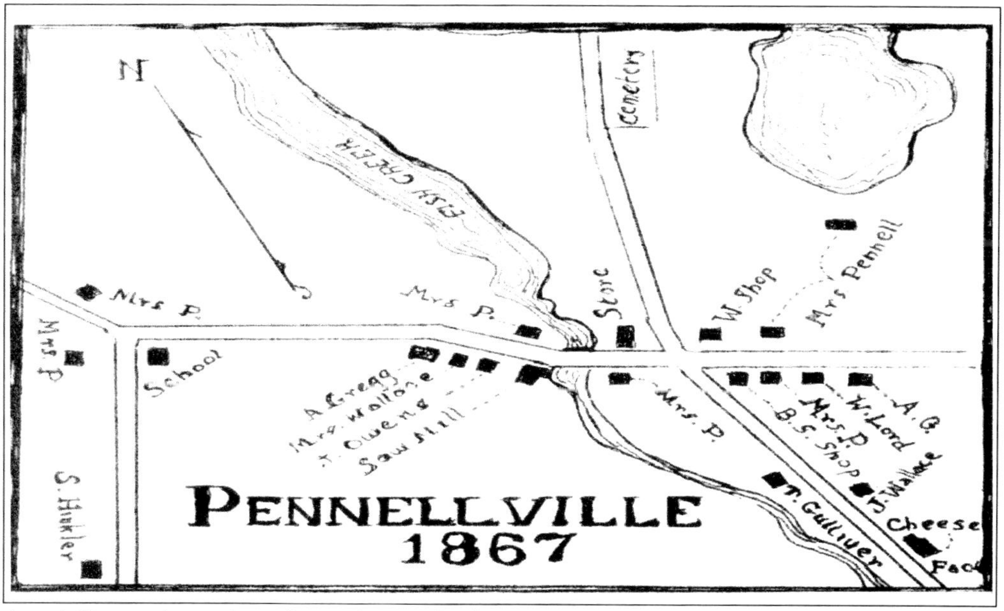

An 1867 map shows the village of Pennellville.

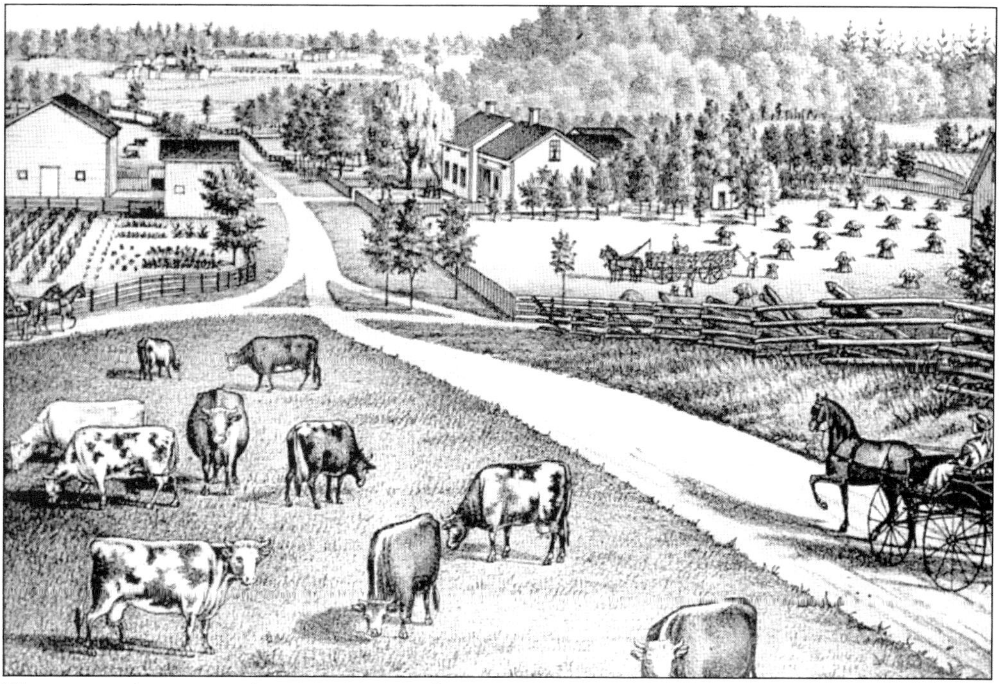

This print, from a steel engraving in *The History of Oswego County 1789–1877*, shows the original four corners (today, it is only three). Pictured is the location of the residence of Reuben Sutton, one of Schroeppel's early founding fathers, near the corner of Sutton and Evans Roads. Nearby, another home was built by Sutton and sold for taxes by Oswego County in 2002. Due to neglect, it was burned. Eliza Ann (Gregg) Sutton and that house became local folklore. After being warned not to look out the window at an eclipse of the sun because of the old superstition of bringing harm to the viewer, she did so anyway and immediately fell dead on the floor.

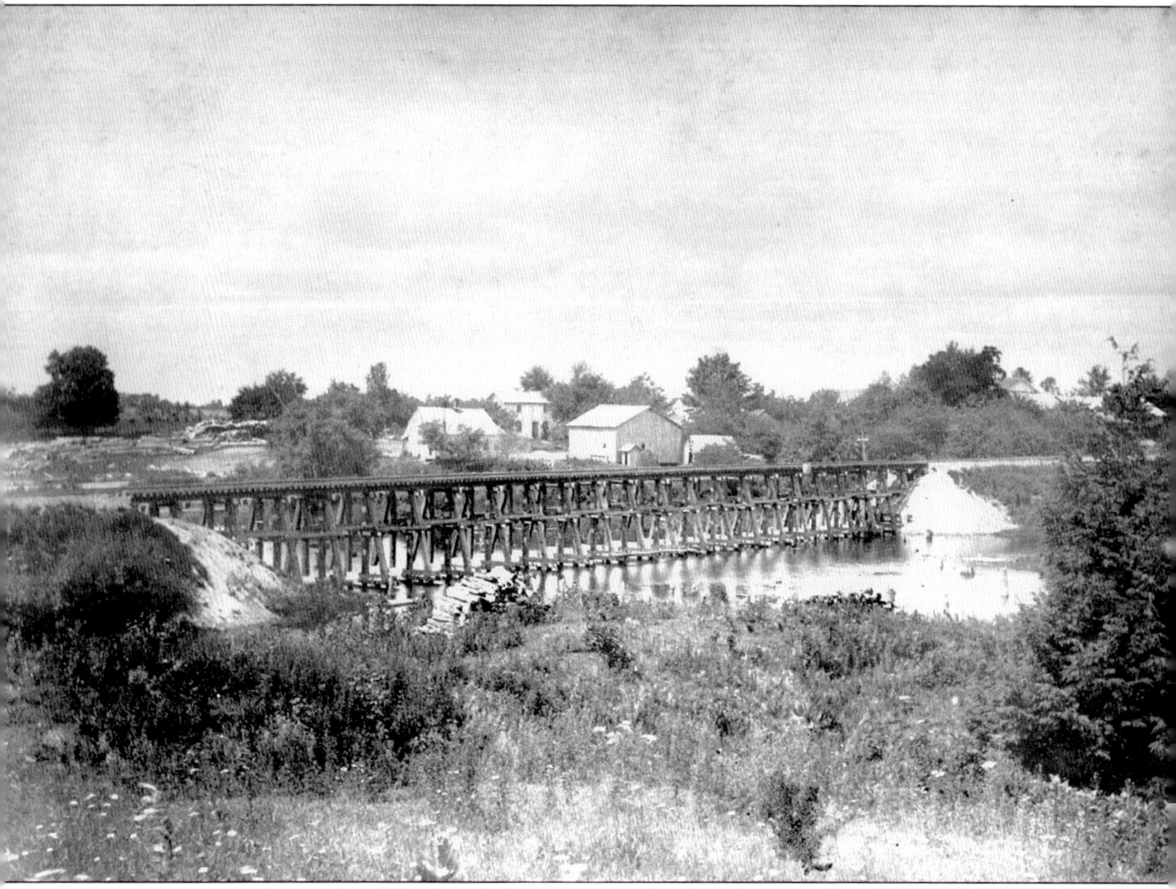

This early wooden railroad bridge, believed to be the Midland Railroad Bridge, crosses the Pennellville Pond. This view is from the east side of the pond on the side of the tracks away from the village, which was the rear lot of Cady Clark's farm. This is the area where Pennellville's Ku Klux Klan held a recruitment rally *c.* 1923. The point to the far right is where Cady Clark rented flat-bottomed rowboats for fishing for $1 a day in the 1950s.

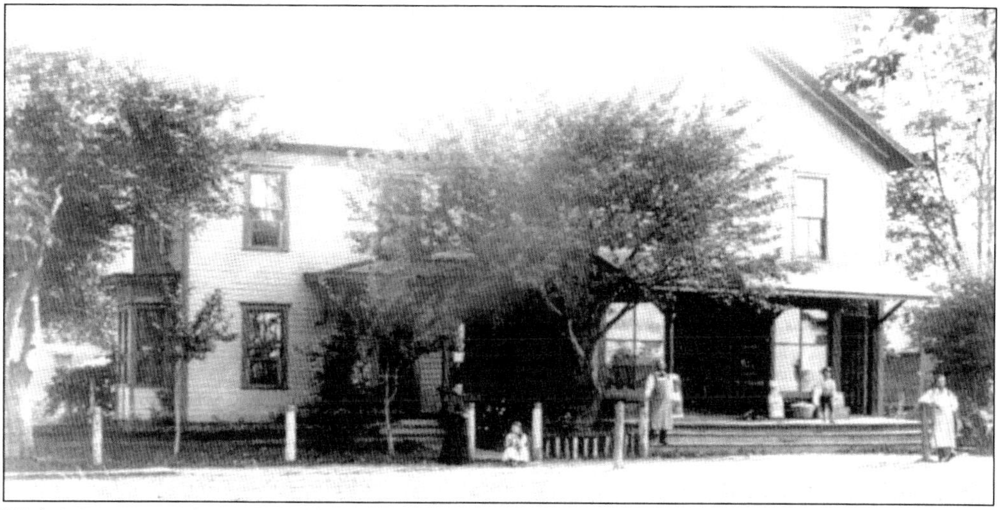

Walt Merriam and Grant Cable stand in front of Merriam's store in Pennellville. The Merriam brothers built the store after buying a lot from A. Gregg in 1889. Others who owned the store over the years included Ed Griffin and Jake and Lena Dreher. Also, Garfield and Florence Gridley operated the business for many years, and the post office was located in this building at one time. Not long ago the store was converted to apartments, which were rented out by Bill Graff, and later, it was bought by Rodney Trask.

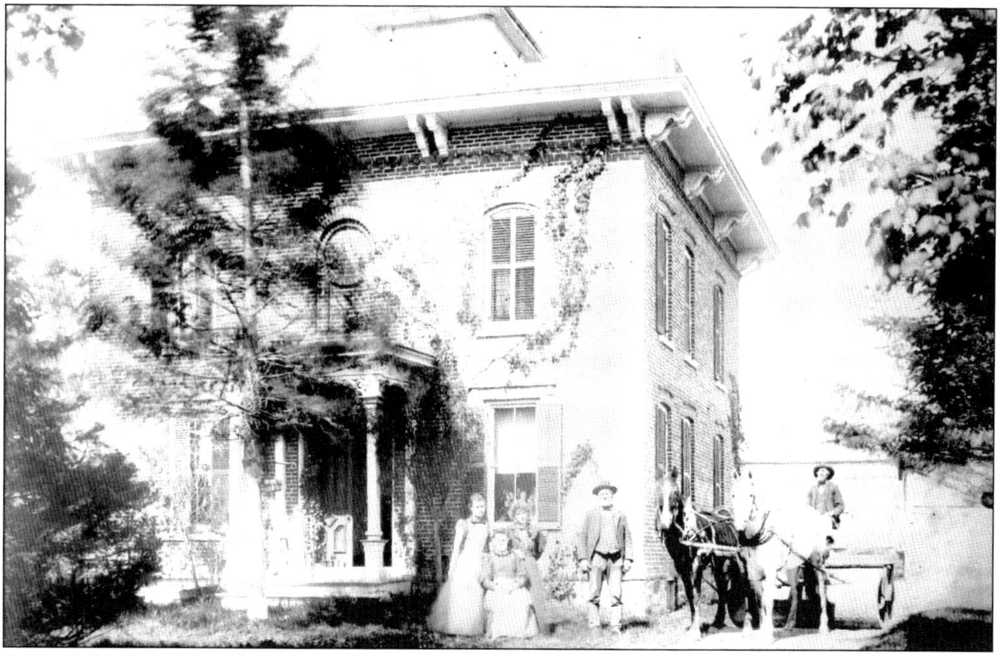

Peter A. Parker, his wife, Margaret, and daughters, Florence and Frances, lived in this home, on what is today Route 54 in Pennellville. The team is pulling a roller used to pack snow on the roads in winter for sleighs and to smooth roads in the spring. Erected in the 1870s, the house is believed to have been built with bricks from the Pennellville Brick Yard, owned by Parker. Previously, there was a wood frame house on the property. In the 1950s, the Parker house was owned by Mr. Dygert, who raised jumping Morgan horses and, after leaving Pennellville, opened Dygert's restaurant next to the Regional Market on Park Street in Syracuse.

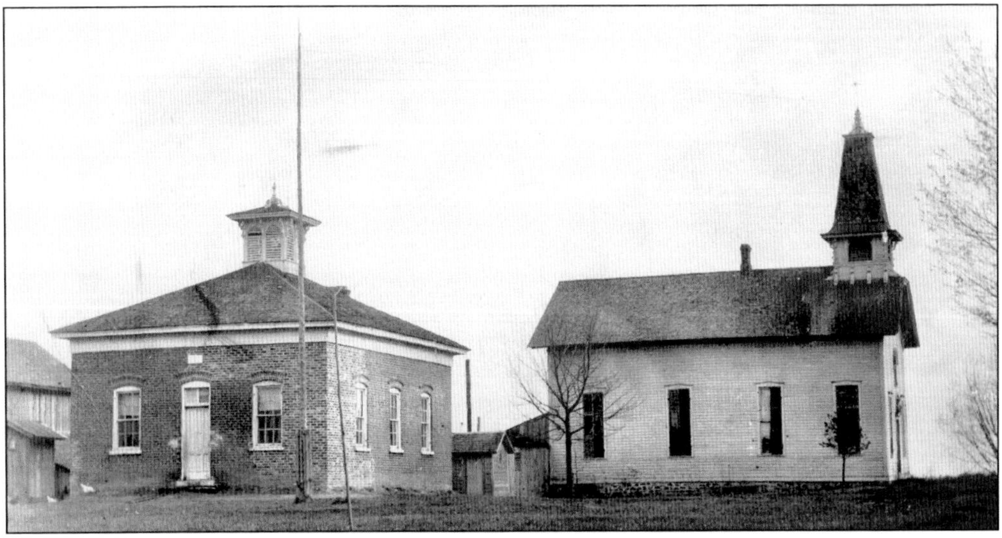

This brick schoolhouse and Methodist Protestant church were located on the Phoenix–Pennellville Road (Route 54) in Pennellville. A home and the Pennellville garage are on this site today. The church was built in 1871 by the First Universalist Society of Gilberts Mills and was a Universalist church for most of its existence. It was rented by George Simons, a spiritualist, on December 5, 1877, and the building was used for séances and spiritualist meetings when not in use by the Universalist Society. (Courtesy of Richard Huntley.)

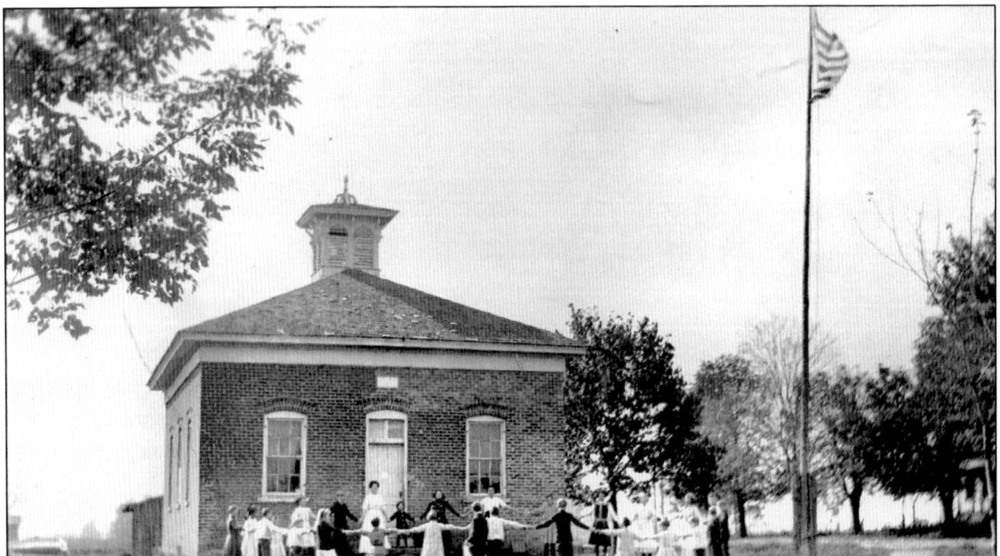

This brick schoolhouse was built after the nearby Checkerboard School burned. It was located on the corner of Route 54 and Godfrey Road. This was one of the schools that was replaced by the Three Room School in Pennellville. This building was heavily damaged by the 1920 tornado, and classes were held in the Grange hall until the new school was completed. "Gus" Soene and Henry Saarie bought the property and made it into a garage with living quarters.

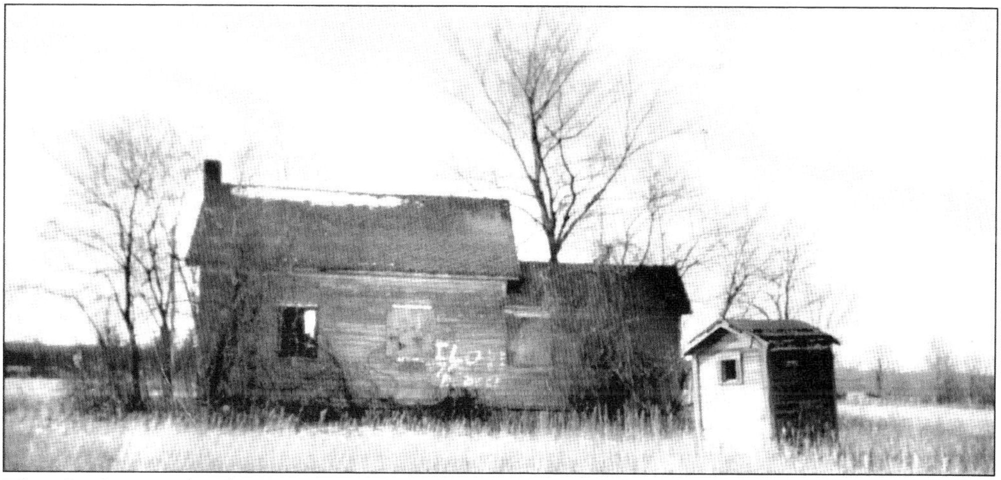

The Seafring School, on Middle Road (Center Road) in Pennellville, was a one-room schoolhouse that was on the farm of Adam Seafring, from whom it got its name.

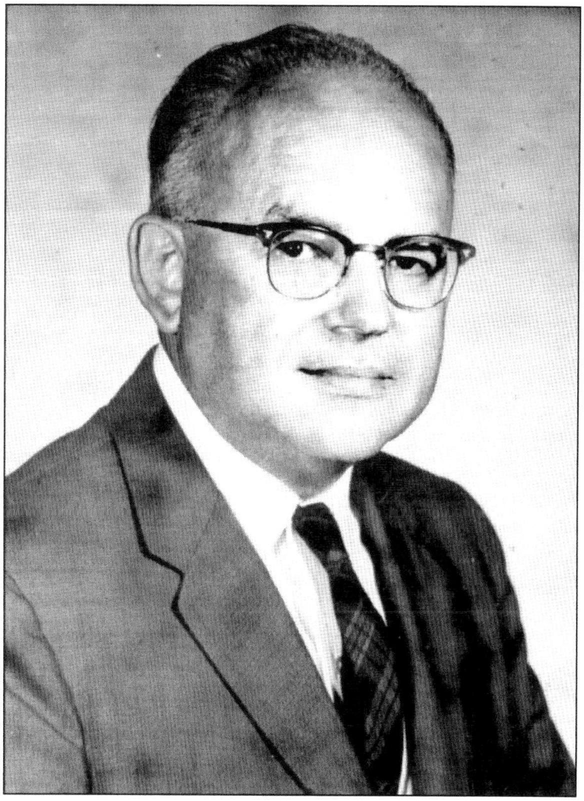

Renowned physicist Dr. Roy Clarence Spencer lived on Oneida River Road in Pennellville. He attended the Seafring School (1907–1914) and went on to graduate from Phoenix High School (1918) and Cornell University (1922). He earned his Ph.D. in physics from Columbia University (1932). Spencer was a pioneer in the application of optics and Fourier method to designs of microwave antennas, worked in research on x-rays with double x-ray spectrometers, and was one of the early scientists to work with the U.S. space program. He is listed in *Who's Who in the East*, *Who's Who in Engineering*, *Who's Who in Science–1700 to 1966*, *American Men of Science*, and *Leaders in American Science*. (Courtesy of Richard Huntley.)

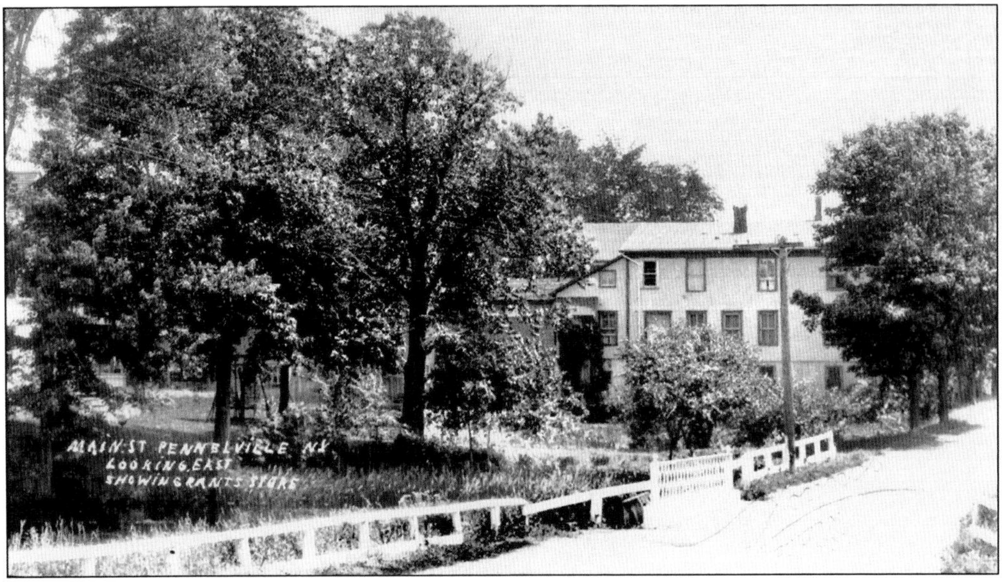

This view looks east on Main Street (Route 54), which crosses the pond in Pennellville. Grant's store is on the corner in the background. (Courtesy of Richard Huntley.)

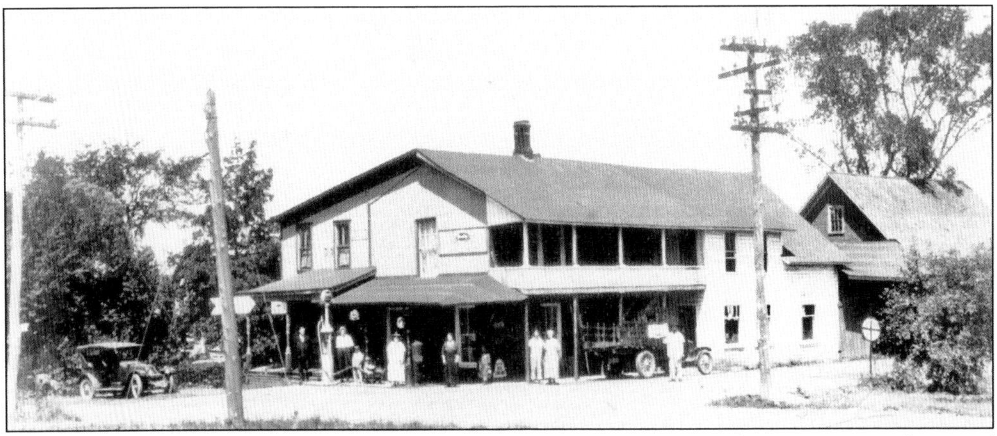

Grant's store in Pennellville was earlier known as Sherwood's store when Amos. B. Sherwood & Son ran it. It was one of the locations of the Pennellville post office over the years. The store sold groceries and had a bar and a pool table in the back. It had a creek running through the cellar that emptied into the pond. When industry was in the area, the building became a hotel with some 11 upstairs rooms that were rented out. The hotel closed in 1955 and was then privately rented. It burned on January 6, 1959, in a fire caused by a faulty stove. (Courtesy of Richard Huntley.)

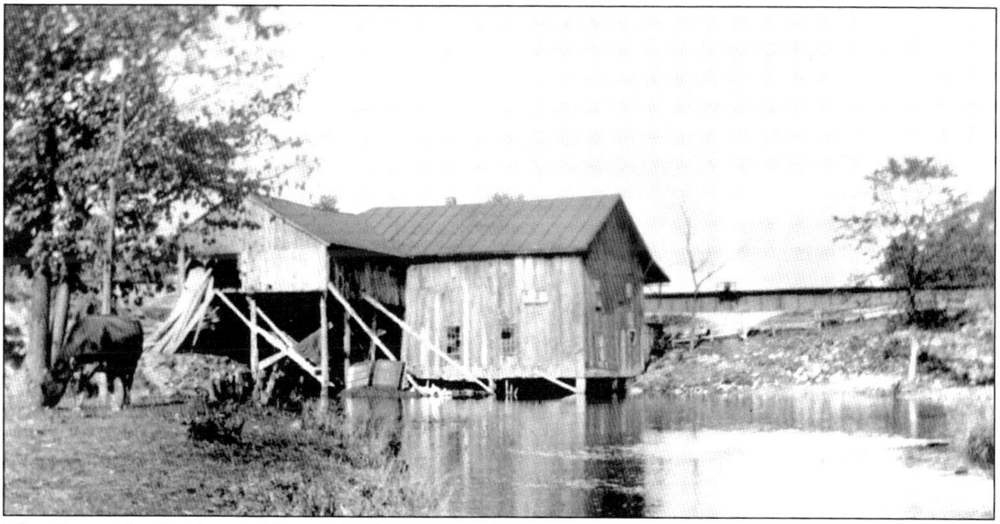

The Pennellville Saw Mill was built in 1833 by Lauren Seymour, who was hired by Richard Pennell. The village's original name was Pennell's Mill, named after this mill. In 1836, Hugh Gregg bought the mill for $3,500. In the early 1900s, there was a cider mill under the sawmill. Other owners were Hosea Ross (1883), Bowering, and Silas Godfrey. The mill was acquired by the Godfrey family in 1917, and the mill and the water rights are still owned by the family today. A waterwheel was added in 1918. An oil painting was done of this mill by renowned landscape artist Max W. Mason.

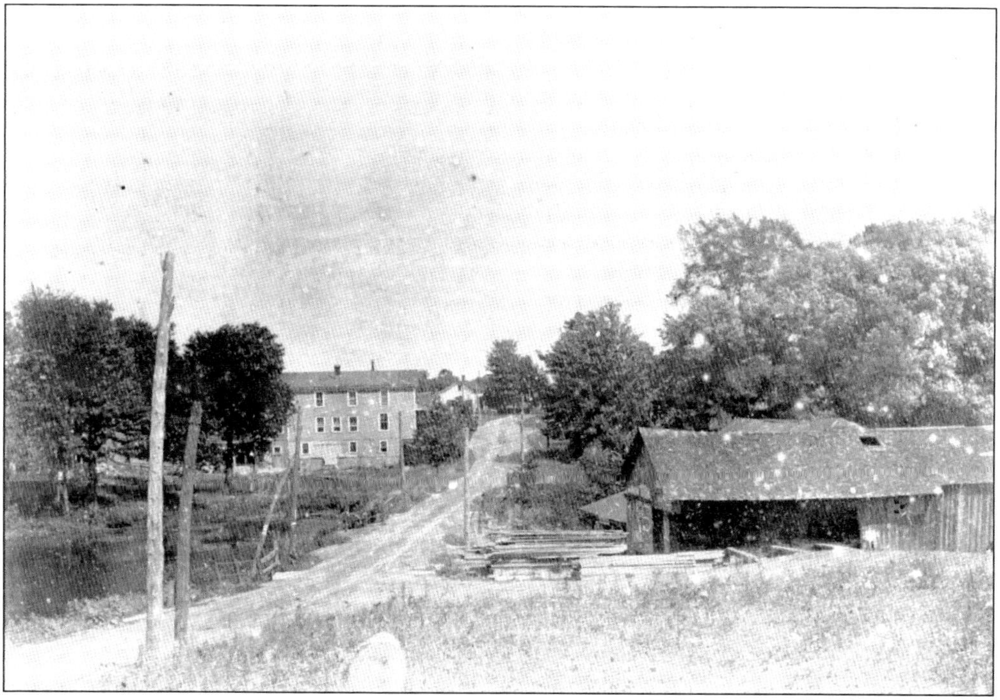

The Pennellville Saw Mill stands in the foreground, with Grant's store in the background on what is Route 54 today.

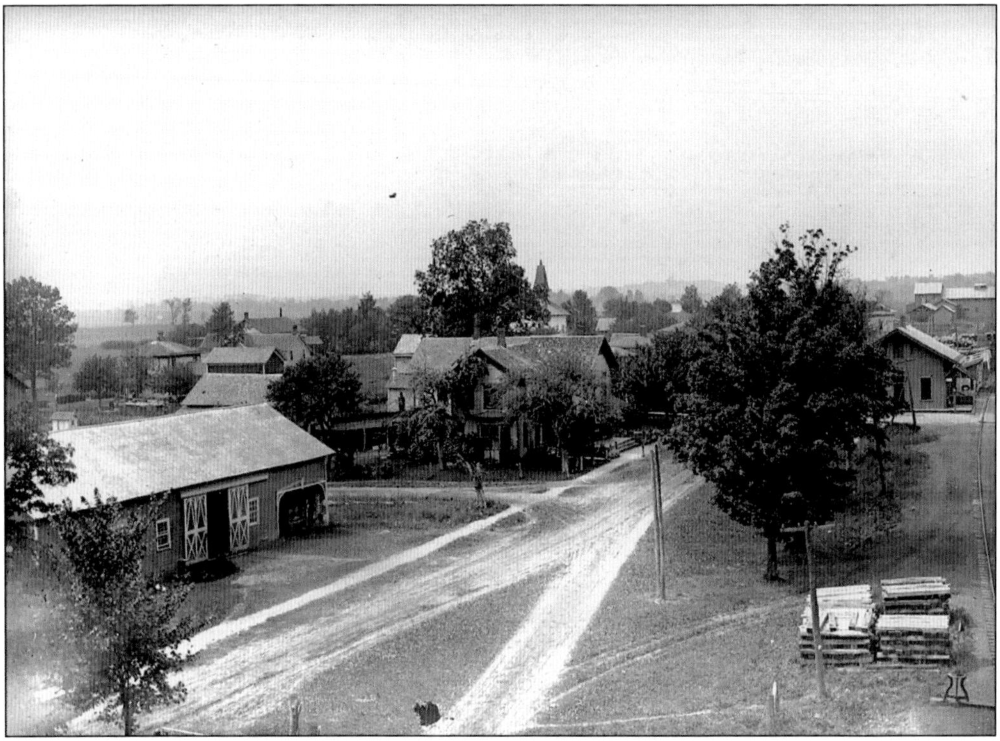

This view of Main Street (Route 54) is believed to have been taken from the water tower of the Ontario & Western Railroad. It shows the Pennellville Hotel Stables, Gridley's store, the train depot, and the old canning factory (upper right).

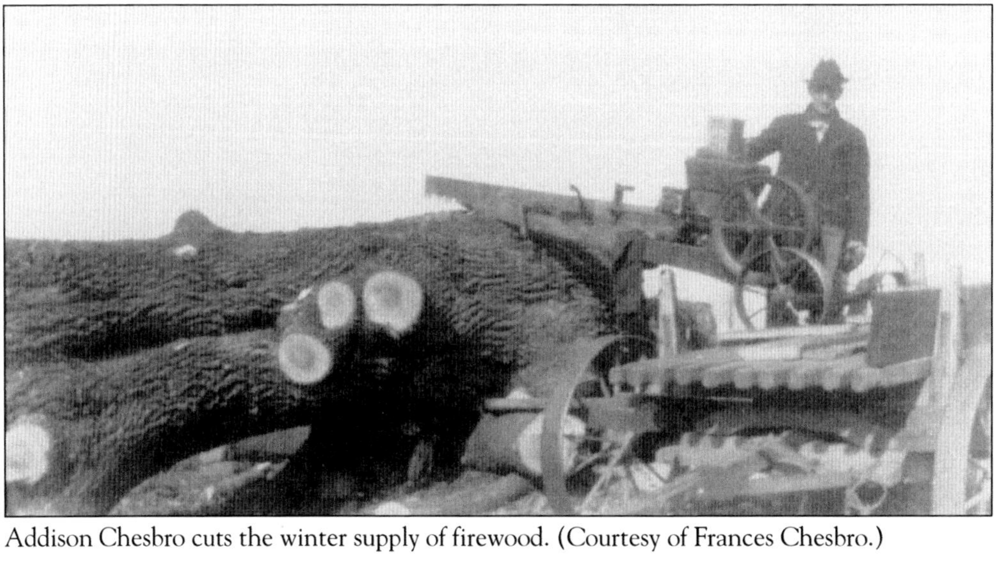

Addison Chesbro cuts the winter supply of firewood. (Courtesy of Frances Chesbro.)

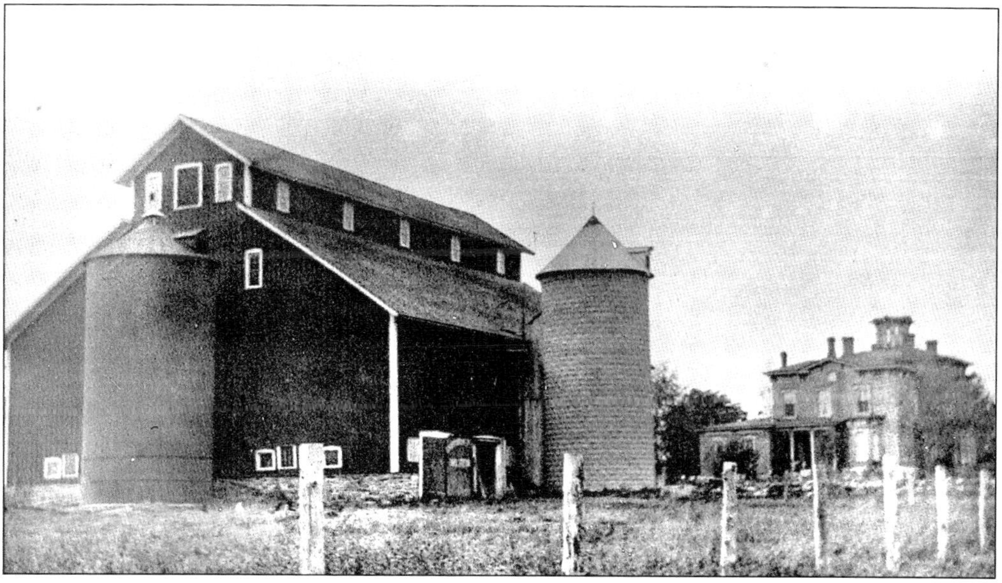

This farm was traded in 1894 to O.J. Godfrey by Calvin Corey for the Godfrey farm in the town of Theresa. It was on this location that David Perry built his log cabin in the 1820s, in which local hunting parties of Native Americans would sleep by the fireplace in cold weather. Perry Road, to the north, is named after David's brother Daniel Perry, whose log cabin was located there. The farm is being subdivided for housing today. The Coreys returned to Pennellville in 1900 and purchased another farm.

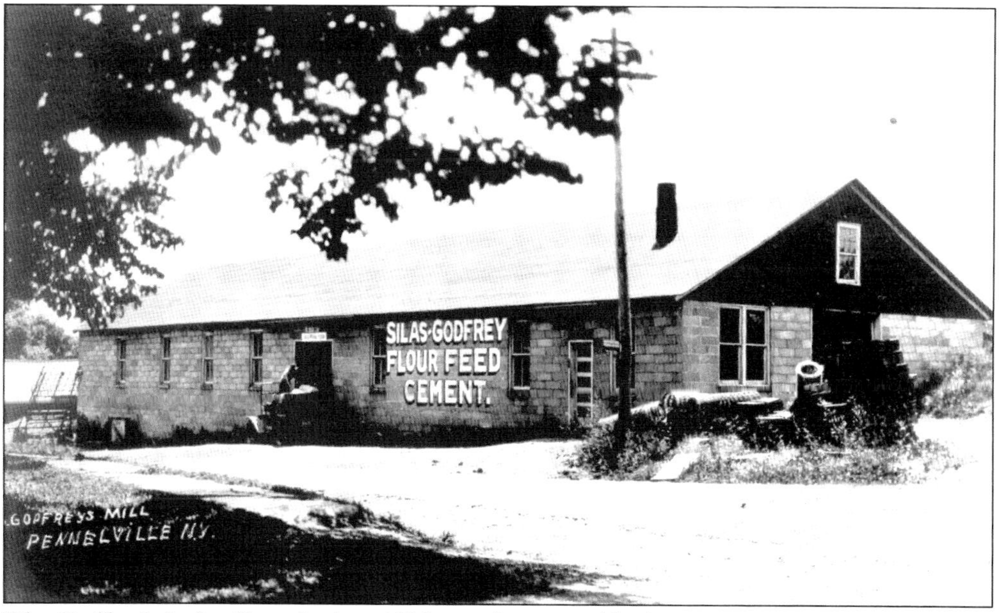

Silas Godfrey's feed mill was built in 1925 out of concrete blocks on Main Street in Pennellville. The next owners were Moses-Cronk. (Courtesy of Richard Huntley.)

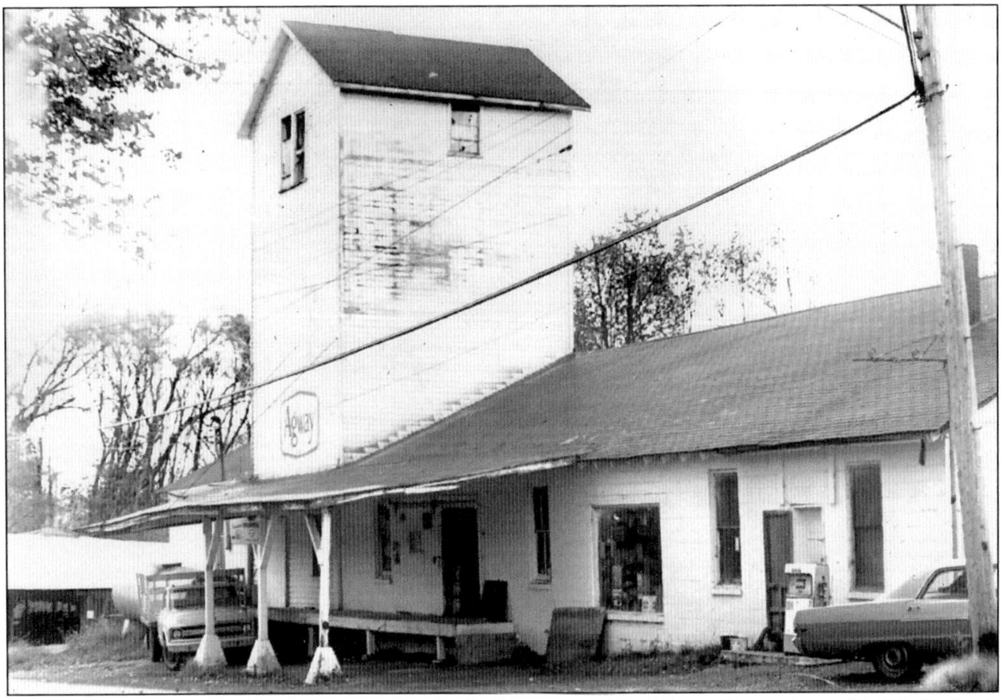

Silas Godfrey's feed mill appears as it looked when owned by Norm Dix, who sold G.L.F. feed. Godfrey's sawmill (the old Pennellville Saw Mill) is in the background.

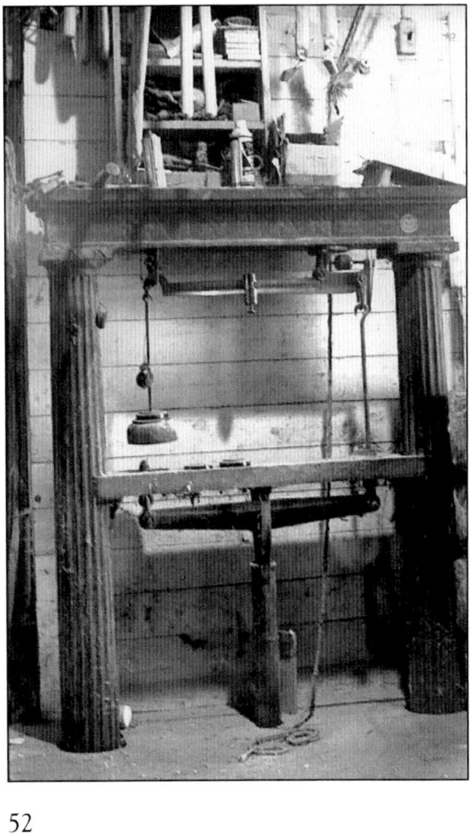

This is the Fairbanks scale in the Pennellville feed mill in the early 1900s.

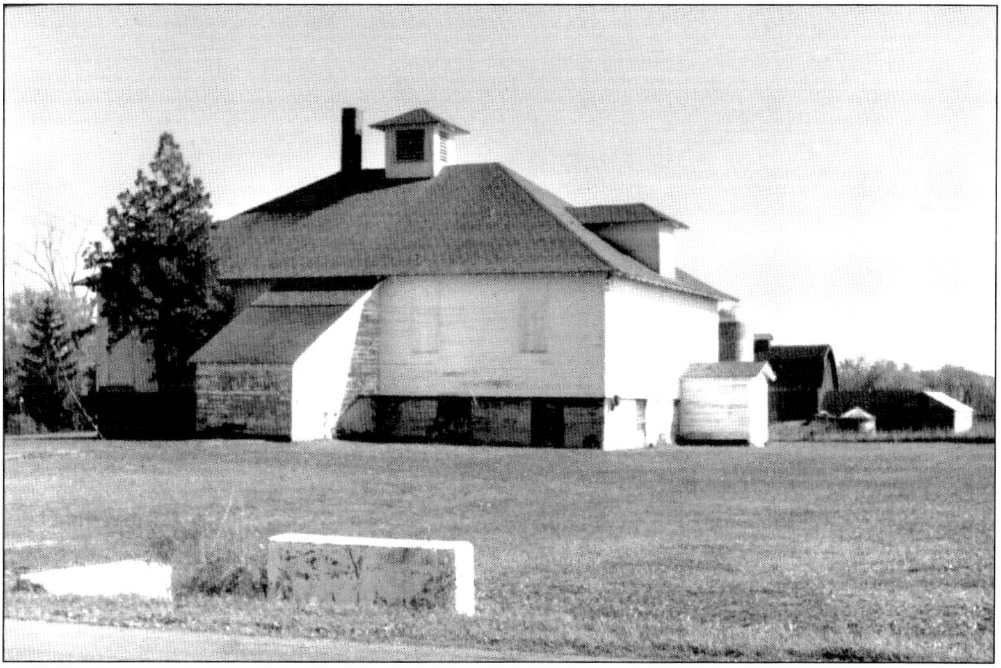

The Pennellville Three Room School was located on Route 54, next to where the new elementary school was built. On May 18, 1974, this building was burned by the Pennellville Fire Department at the request of the school district. Teachers in the school in 1951 were Mildred Caines (kindergarten, first, and second grades), Vivian Burton (third, fourth, and fifth grades), and Pauline Eckstedt (sixth, seventh, and eighth grades).

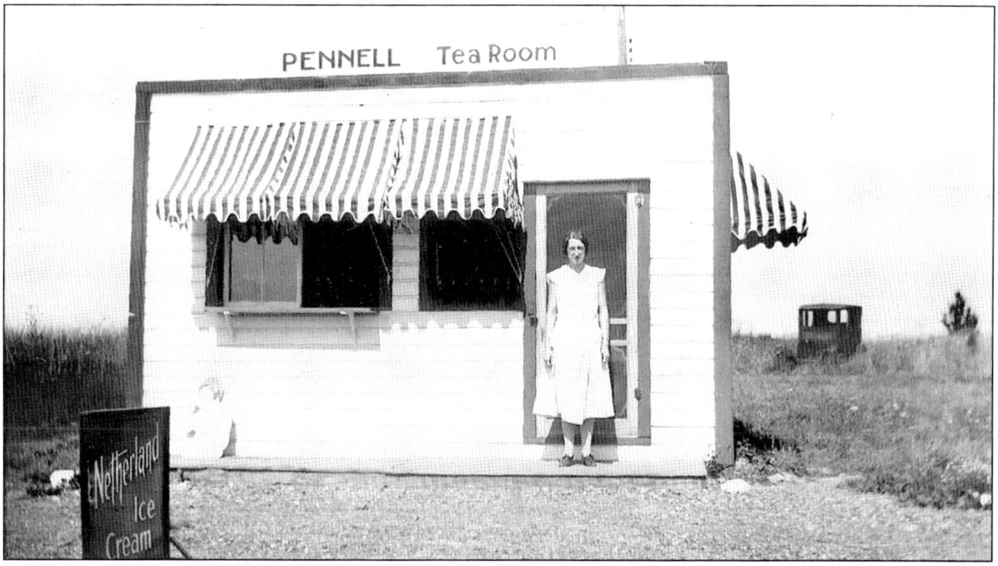

The Pennell Tea Room was across from the Three Room School. It was run by Margaret Cable (standing in the doorway) and Florence S. Huntley. (Courtesy of Margaret Straight.)

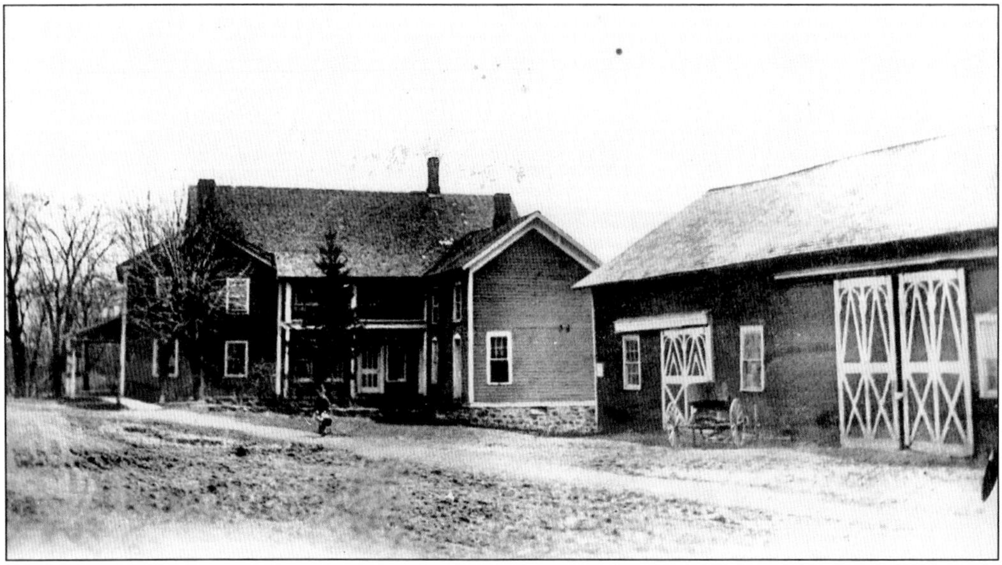

The Pennellville Hotel and Stable building was the site of the Pennellville post office in 1867. The original tavern was built by Rodney S. Gregg in 1836 and was run by his son Ambrose Gregg for many years. William Freeman was captured here in 1846. At his trial, his lawyer William Seward (Pres. Abraham Lincoln's future secretary of state) was the first to use insanity as a defense in court. The hotel was also the site of the capture of "Pitch Fork" Johnson of the locally famous Loomis Gang. The 88th regiment, 24th Brigade, Company G of the New York National Guard was stationed here during the Civil War.

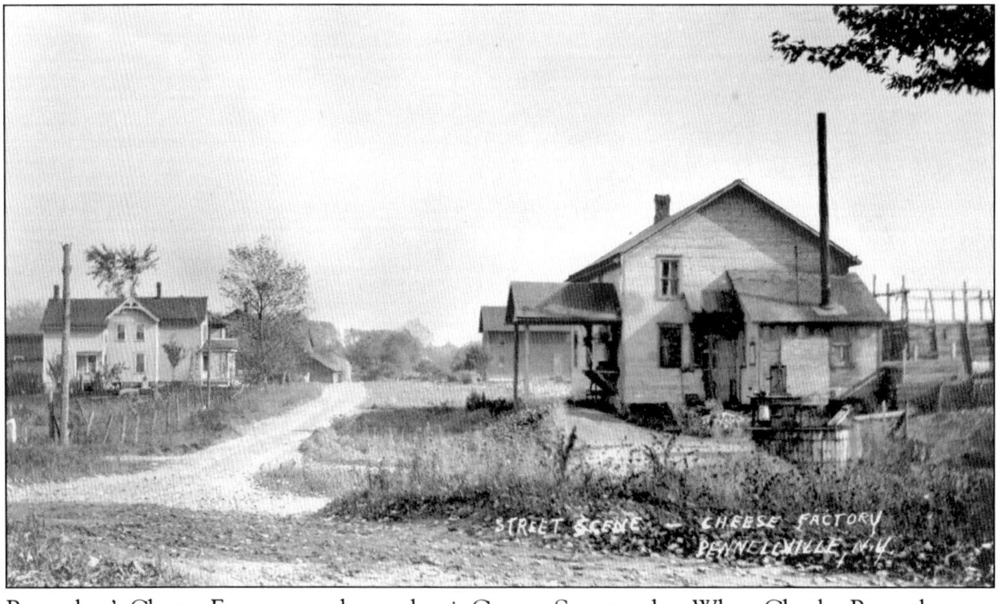

Barnaskey's Cheese Factory stands on what is Grange Street today. When Charles Barnaskey ran the factory, he lived in the Foster house, which was the first house on Grange Street. In 1894, Ardie Hinckley ran the factory for Barnaskey. In 1906, Anthony Pepper's horses ran away while he was unloading and spilled 23 cans of milk. Charlie Pluff used to throw turtles in the whey vat to fatten them up. The property contained an artesian well that was filled in when the new Three Room School was built. Pennellville's school bus garage was located near this site.

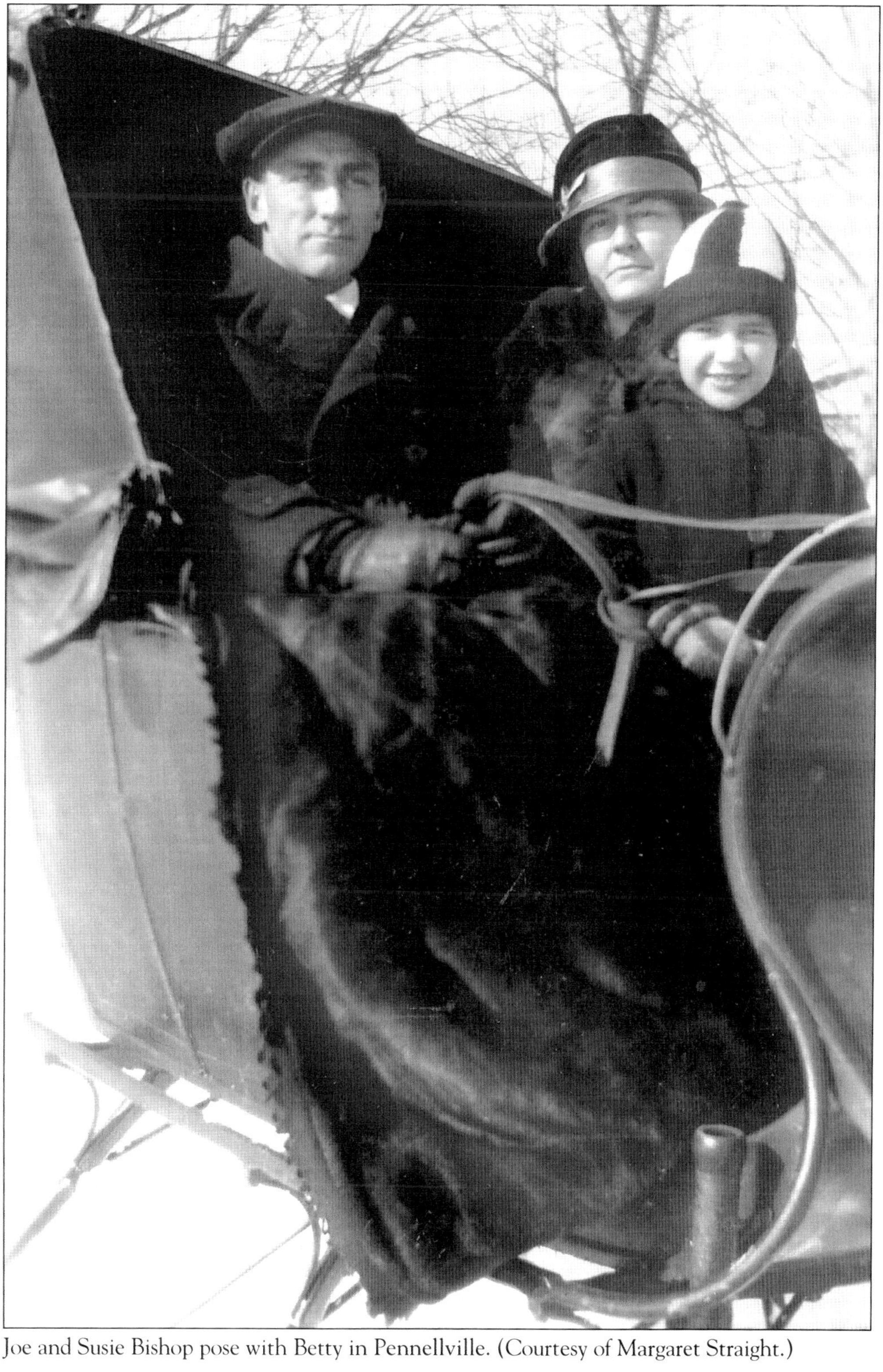

Joe and Susie Bishop pose with Betty in Pennellville. (Courtesy of Margaret Straight.)

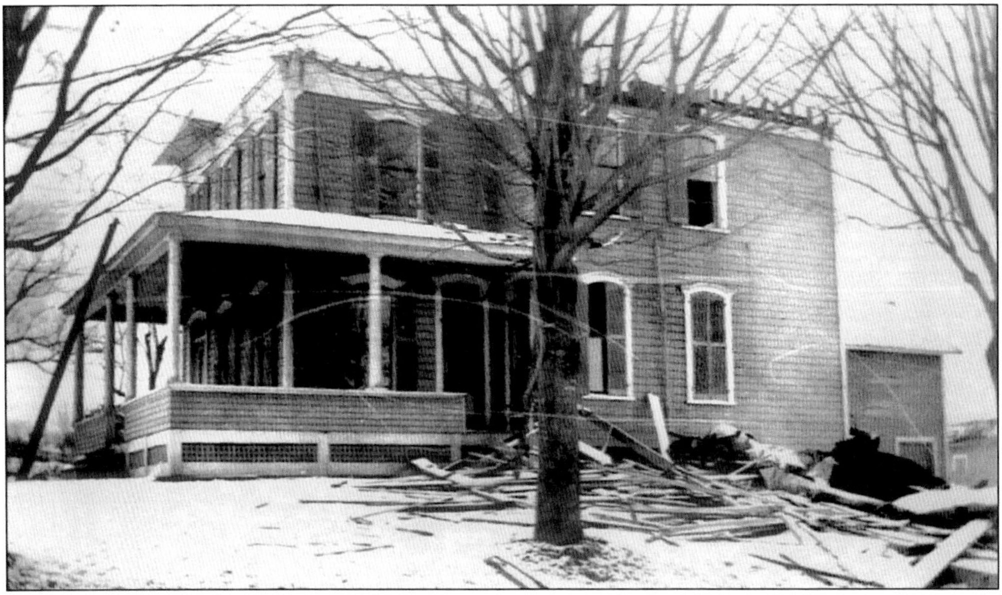

Shown is the Fred Biddlecum house on Biddlecum Road after the December 1920 tornado. (Courtesy of Roy Huntley.)

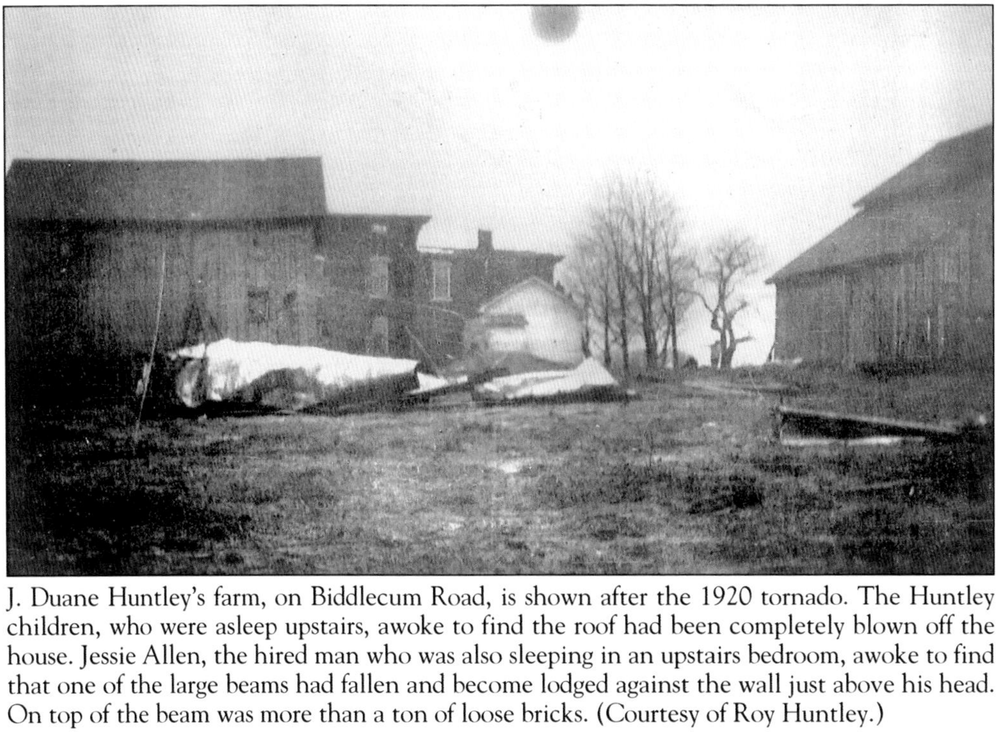

J. Duane Huntley's farm, on Biddlecum Road, is shown after the 1920 tornado. The Huntley children, who were asleep upstairs, awoke to find the roof had been completely blown off the house. Jessie Allen, the hired man who was also sleeping in an upstairs bedroom, awoke to find that one of the large beams had fallen and become lodged against the wall just above his head. On top of the beam was more than a ton of loose bricks. (Courtesy of Roy Huntley.)

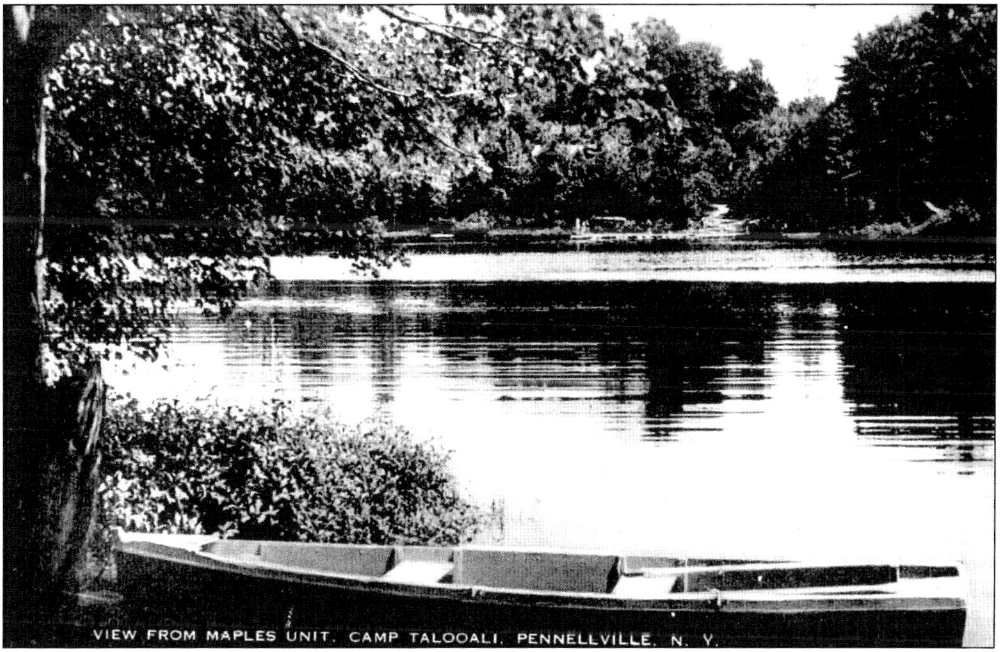

The Onondaga Council of Camp Fire Girls operates Camp Talooli on Lake Tawikoma in Pennellville.

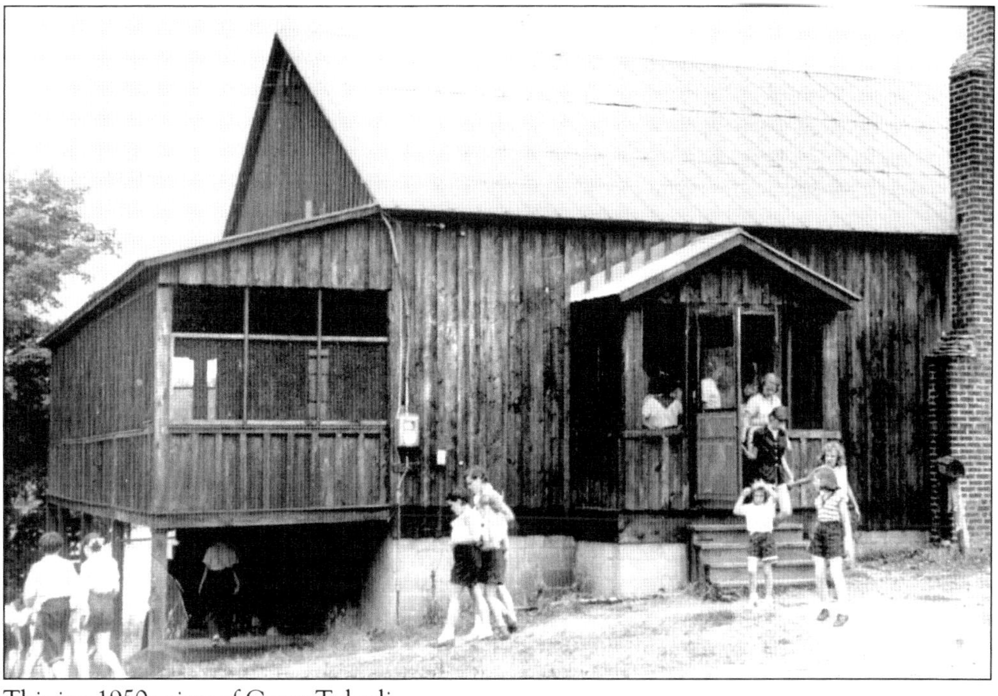

This is a 1950s view of Camp Talooli.

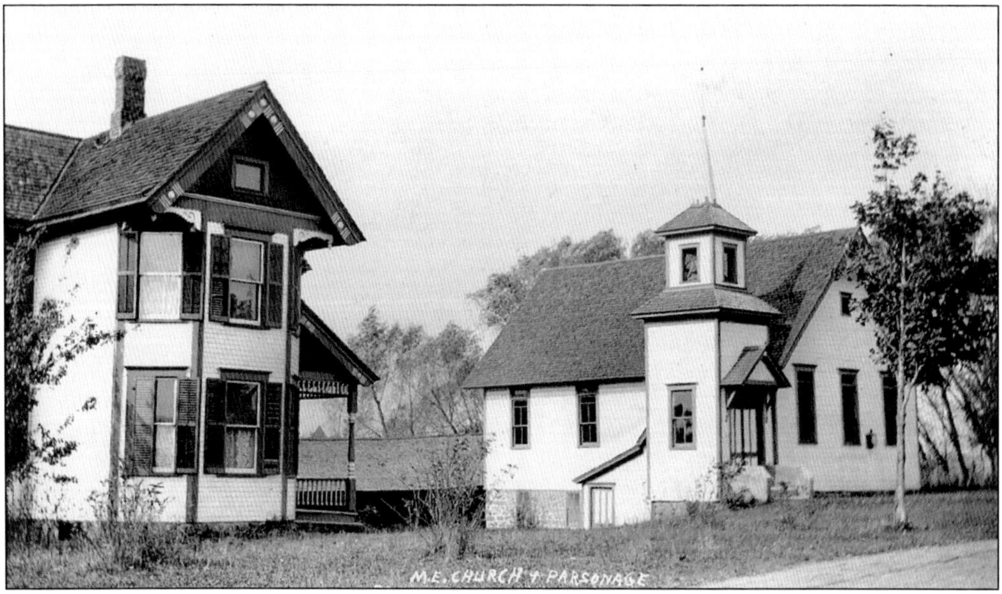

The Methodist church, with a horse stable and parsonage, was located on Sutton Road in Pennellville. The church was destroyed on April 27, 1962, in a fire caused by sparks from a neighbor's burning rubbish pile.

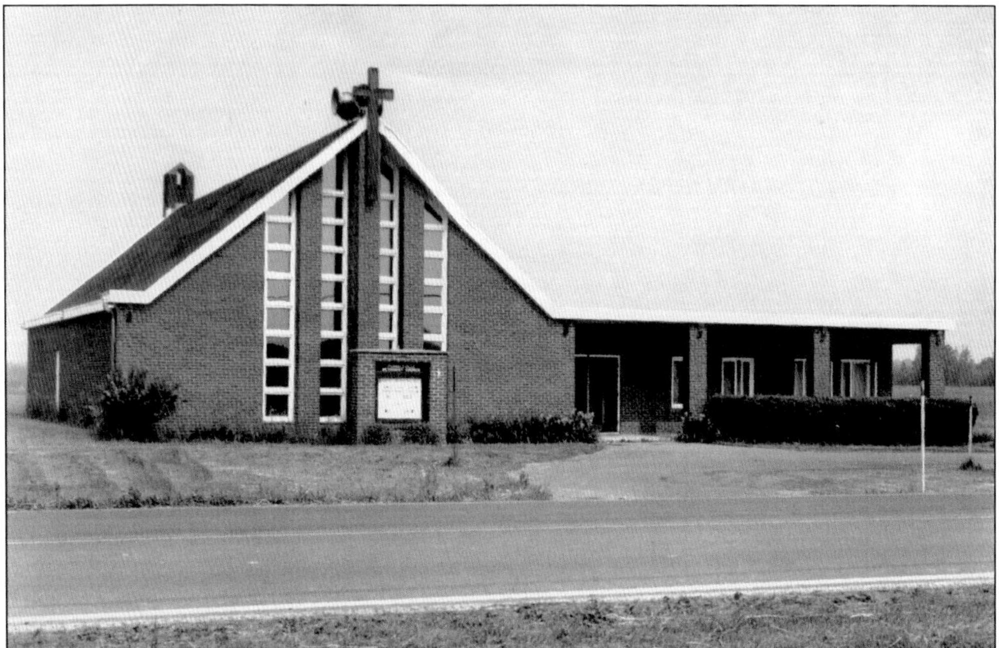

This is the New Pennellville Methodist Church on Route 54. The consecration service was held on December 8, 1963. The service of dedication and burning of the mortgage was held on May 18, 1975.

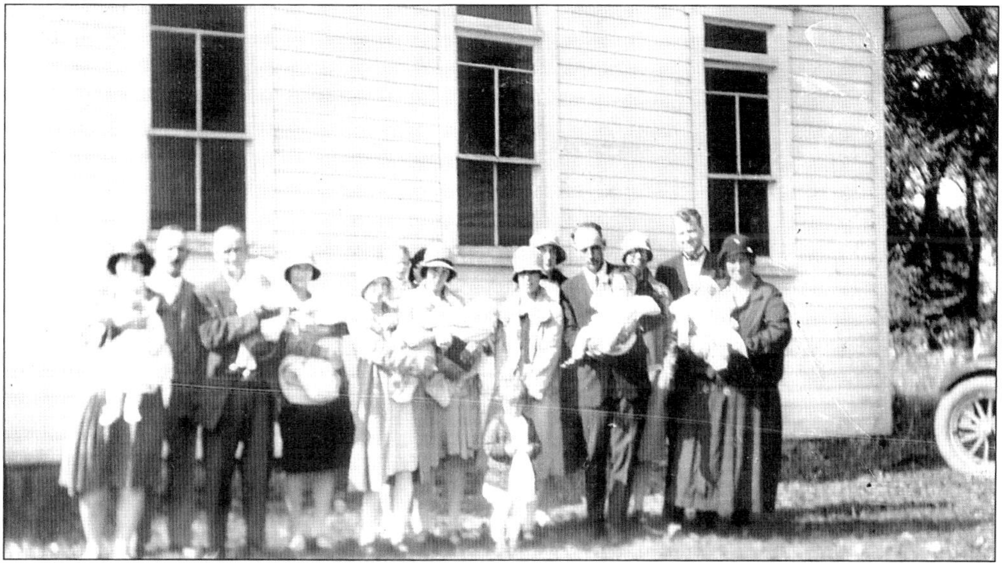

Outside the old Pennellville Methodist Church are parishioners and their children who are on the "cradle roll," the list of newborn members of the Pennellville Sunday school. The photograph was taken on October 6, 1929. (Courtesy of Margaret Straight.)

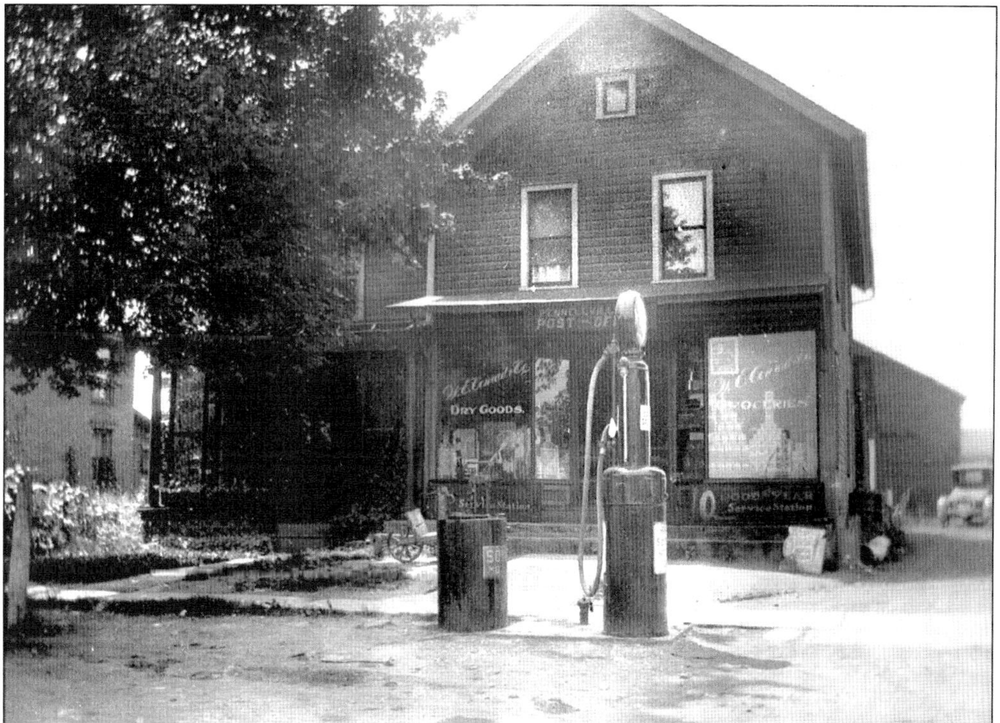

An early photograph shows Conrad's dry goods store in Pennellville. Edward Conrad dissolved his partnership with Omar Gregg in the Gilberts Mills store in 1907 and built this grocery store in Pennellville. For many years Conrad's daughter, Cora (Nelson) McMahon, was postmaster, and the Pennellville post office was located in the store at one time.

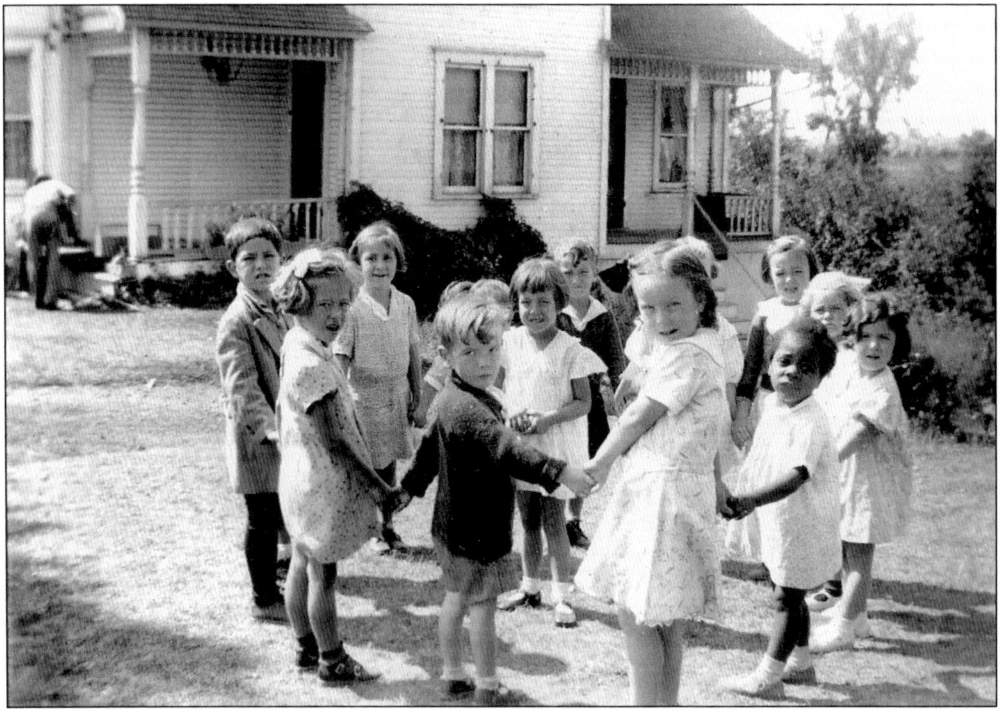

Shown are students attending vacation Bible school at the old Pennellville Methodist Church. (Courtesy of Margaret Straight.)

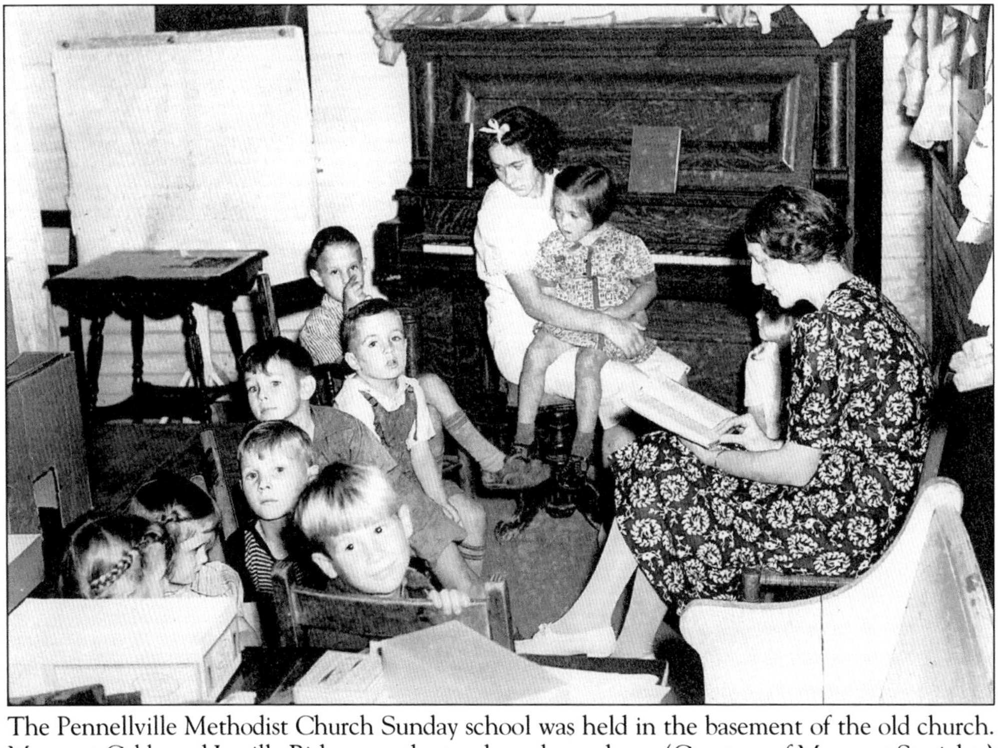

The Pennellville Methodist Church Sunday school was held in the basement of the old church. Margaret Cable and Lucille Bishop are the teachers shown here. (Courtesy of Margaret Straight.)

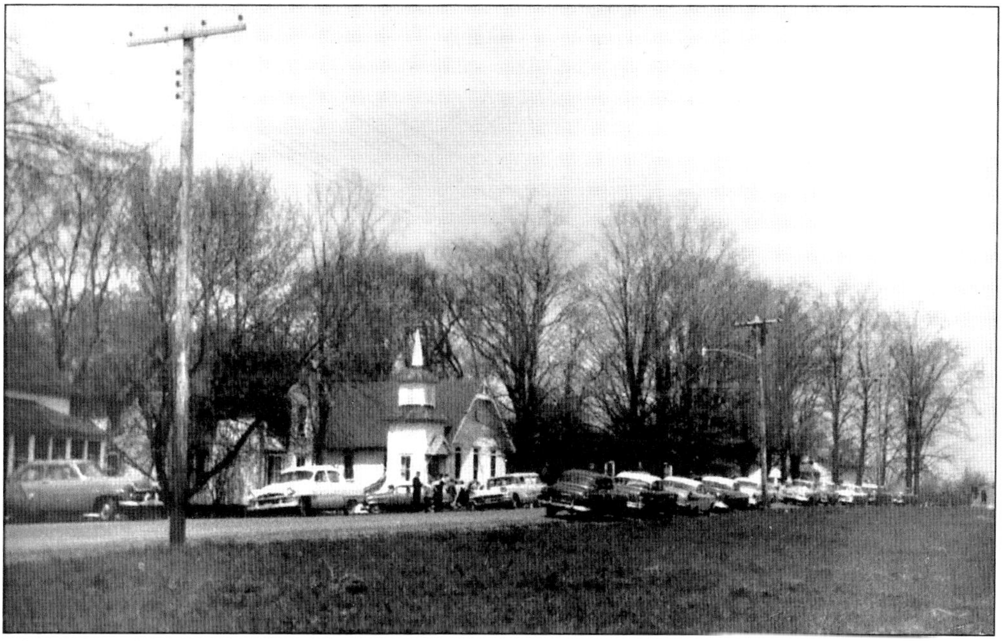

This image shows a typical Sunday morning in front of the old Pennellville Methodist Church during the 1950s. (Photograph by John Hyvonen, courtesy of Marian Creamer.)

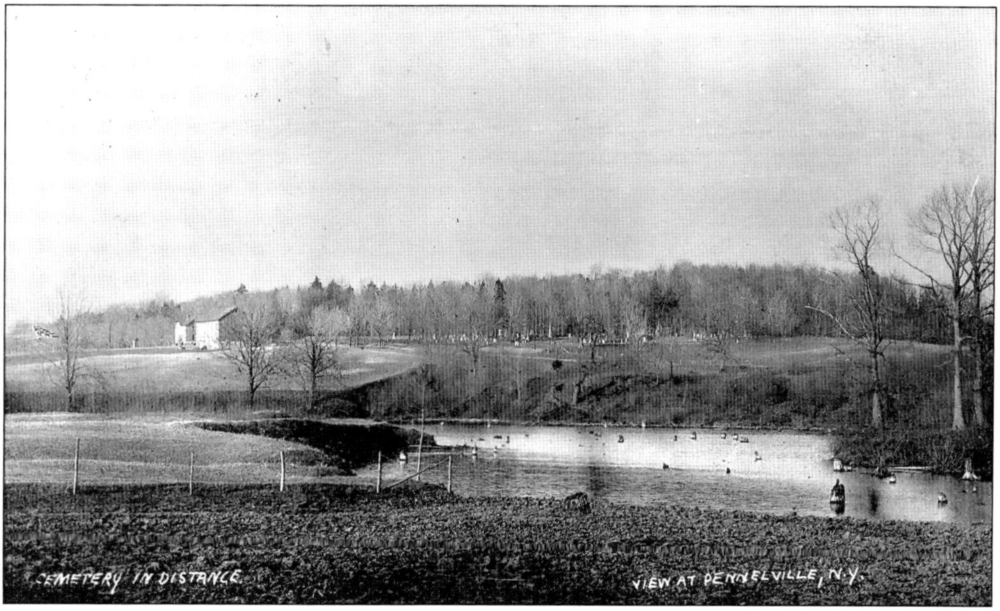

This is a long-range view of the Pennellville Cemetery from the village of Pennellville. The Pennells conveyed land to the trustees of District School No. 7 for a burial ground and Episcopal church on November 25, 1843. A group of residents met at the schoolhouse on December 10, 1875, and formed the Pennellville Cemetery Association. Among those buried in Pennellville are George Casper Schroeppel, Dr. Richard and Mary Pennell and other Pennell family members, Revolutionary War veteran Cornelius Wallis, and an early woman doctor named Mary Potts. Merrick Corey's body was stolen from the cemetery by graverobbers. It is believed to have been stolen for medical research.

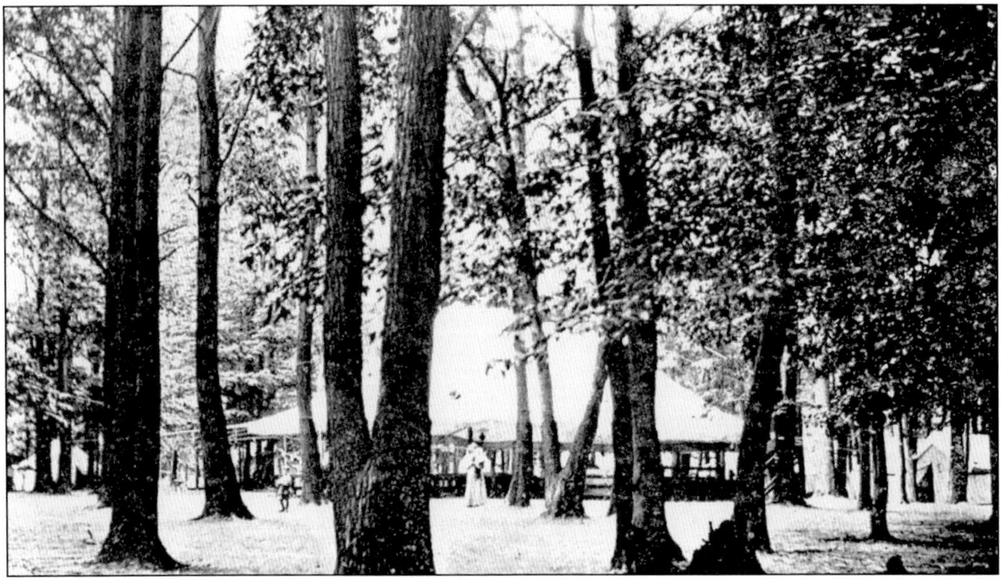

This page contains photographs of the Methodist-Protestant campground, Edgewood Park in Pennellville. The campground was located in the area of Sutton and Evans Roads in the early 1900s and was a popular religious retreat that drew people from far and wide. Some even came from as far away as Hornell via the Ontario & Western Railroad. For those who came by horseback or drove a horse and wagon or buggy, there were spikes in the trees to tie the horses to. (Bottom photograph courtesy of Richard Huntley.)

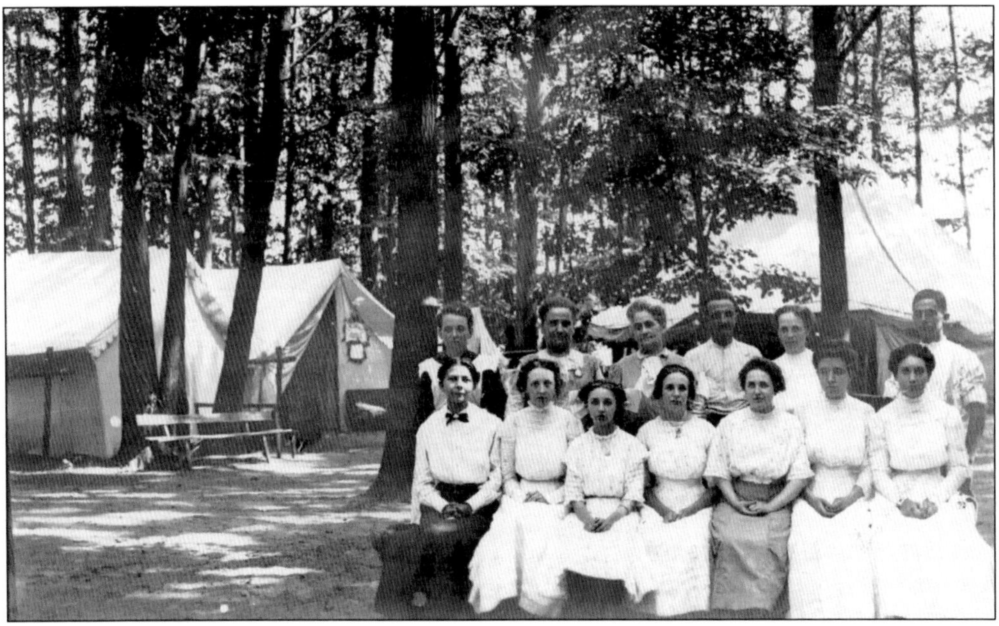

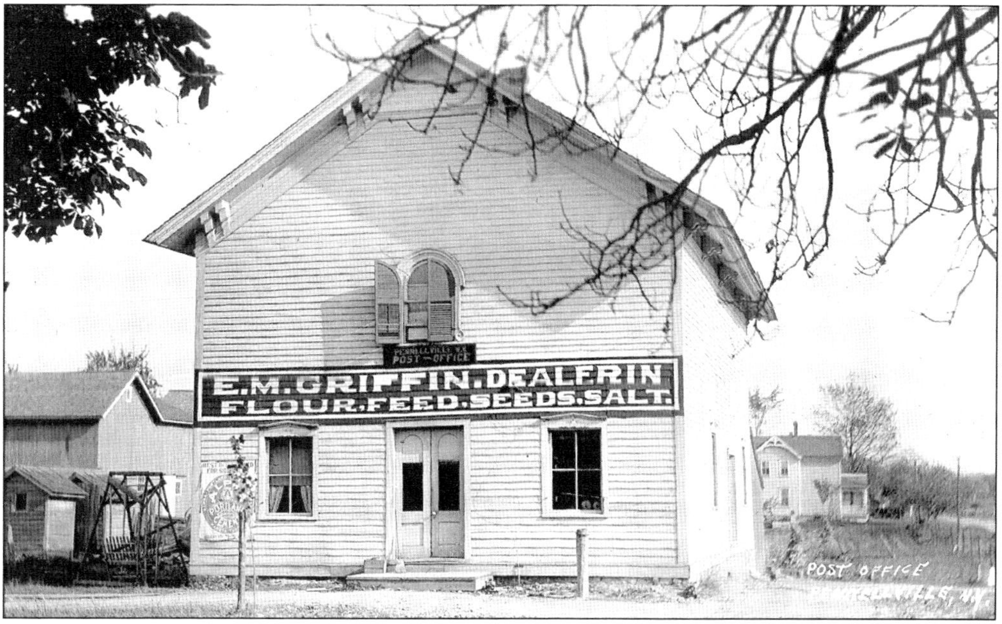

The E.M. Griffin feed store and the post office were located in what was the old Universalist (Methodist-Protestant) church building. The building was sold on a mortgage foreclosure on January 18, 1901, to Ed Griffin, after which it was vacant for many years. It was then rented by a local trapper who used it as his home and hung many hides outside to dry. The building was later used by Olin Snyder as a garage, and eventually, it burned in a fire that was started by a faulty stove.

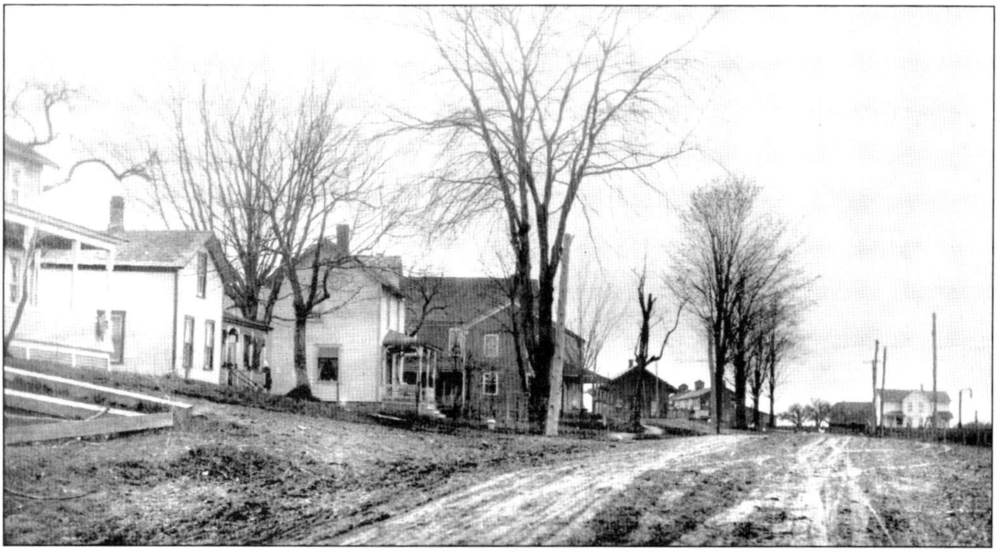

This view looks west along Main Street in Pennellville. The fourth building from the left is the Pennellville Hotel. The railroad depot and cheese factory (later the railroad icehouse) are in the background.

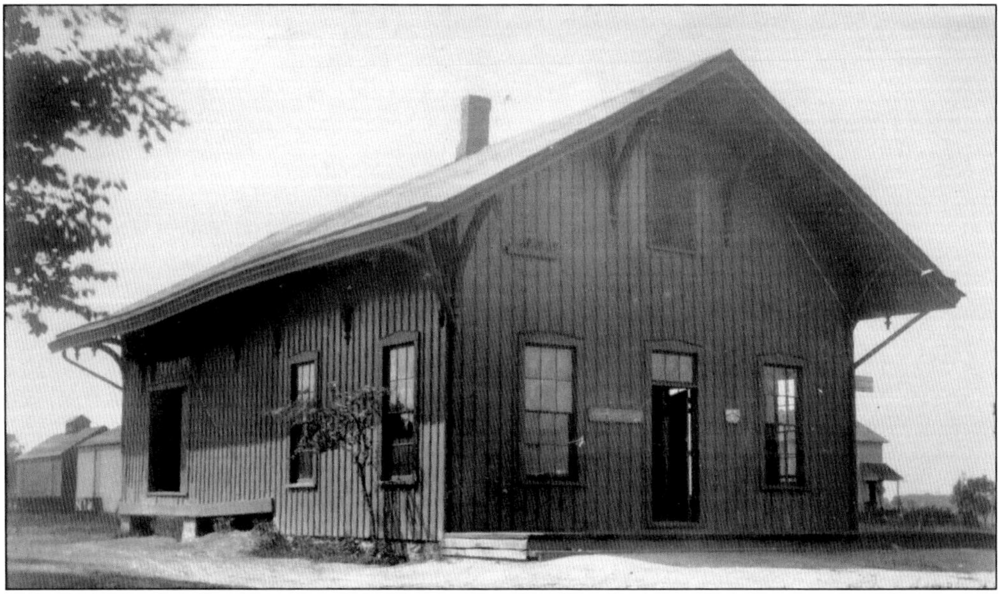

This is the Ontario & Western station on Main Street in Pennellville.

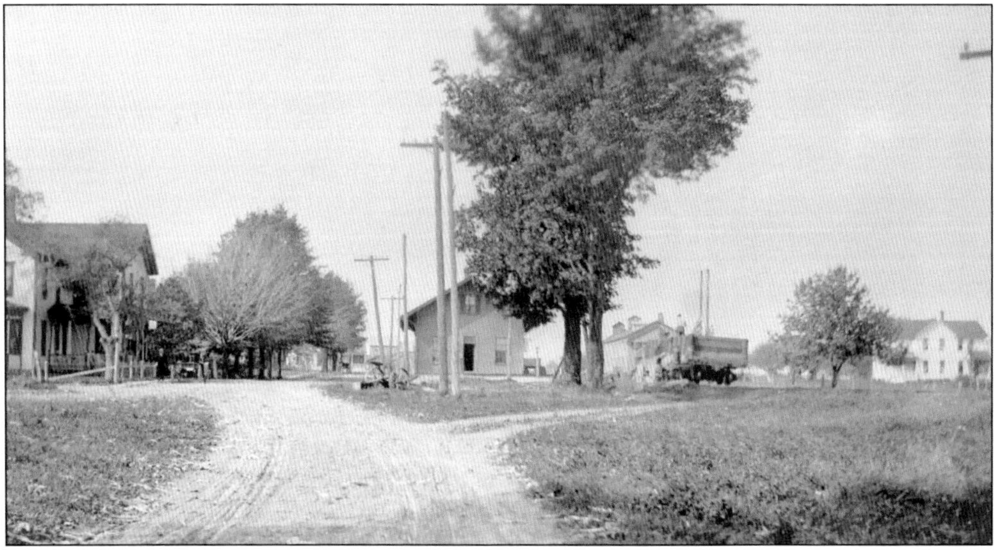

This view looks west toward Main Street (Route 54) and the Ontario & Western Railroad station. The home to the far right is near the location of the early apartments known as the Bee Hive that were made from half of Dr. Richard Pennell's summer home. Gridley's store is on the left.

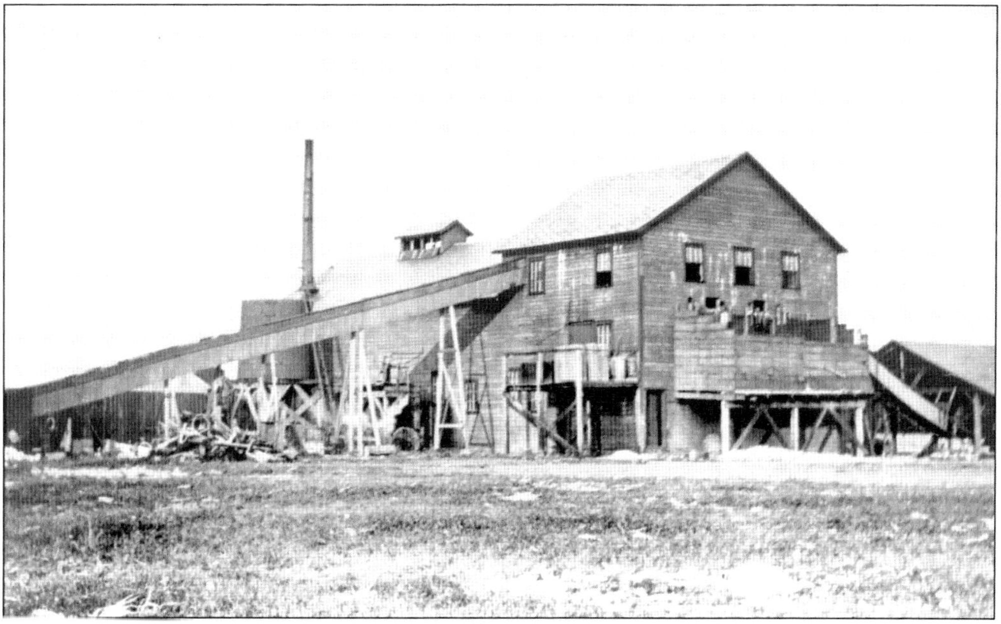

This is the original canning factory in Pennellville in the mid-1800s. At that time, it processed pickles, sauerkraut, and corn. An addition to the factory was built in 1918. The New Hartford Canning Company was one of the main companies to use the factory. Canning at Pennellville was done for various companies, whose labels were placed on the cans. None of the canned goods processed in Pennellville had a Pennellville label.

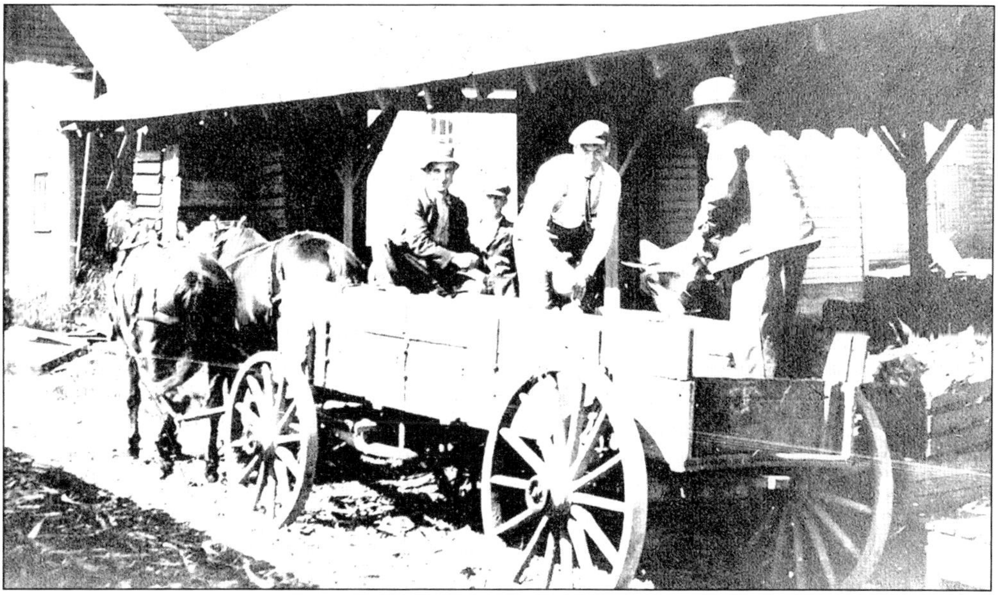

A wagonload of corn is unloaded at the Pennellville canning factory in the early 1900s.

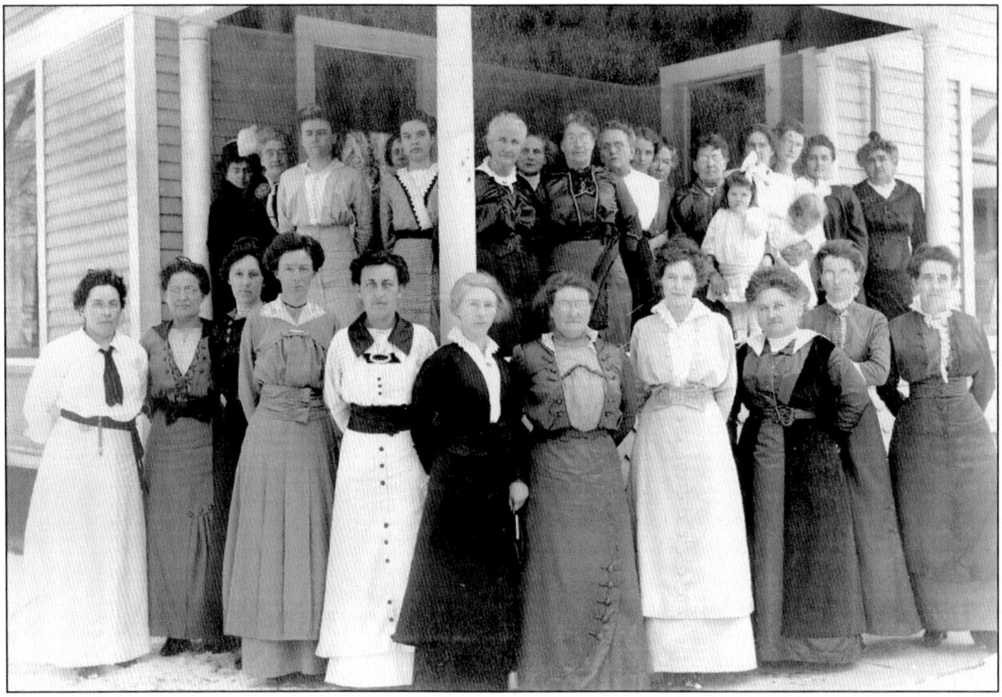

Women of Pennellville pose for a photograph. From left to right, are the following: (front row) unidentified, Lena Dreher, Lena Bishop Godfrey, Emma Parker, Estelle Nelson, Cora Nelson McMahon, Annie Nelson, Eunice Sherwood, Sofia Morrell, Nina Pierce, and Lillian Washer; (back row) two unidentified people, Alice Stevens, unidentified, Evadna Washer, ? Godfrey, ? Page, Adeline Hinckley, Sarah TenBroeck, Olive Griffin, Hattie and Dorothy Sherwood, Clara Kline and child, Garnet Stevens, Blanche Hirt, and Ditte Beardsly.

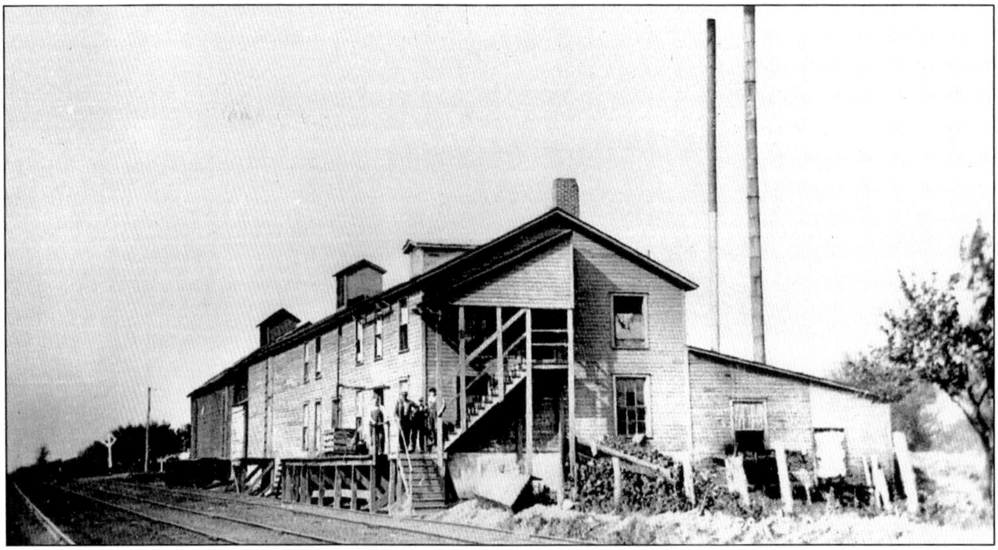

One of Pennellville's cheese factories was later used as an icehouse by the Ontario & Western Railroad. It was located along the railroad just north of the depot, near to what today is Godfrey Road. Vaughn Parker ran the factory for a while, and during that time he and his family lived in part of the building and his daughter, Helen Parker (Nelson), was born here.

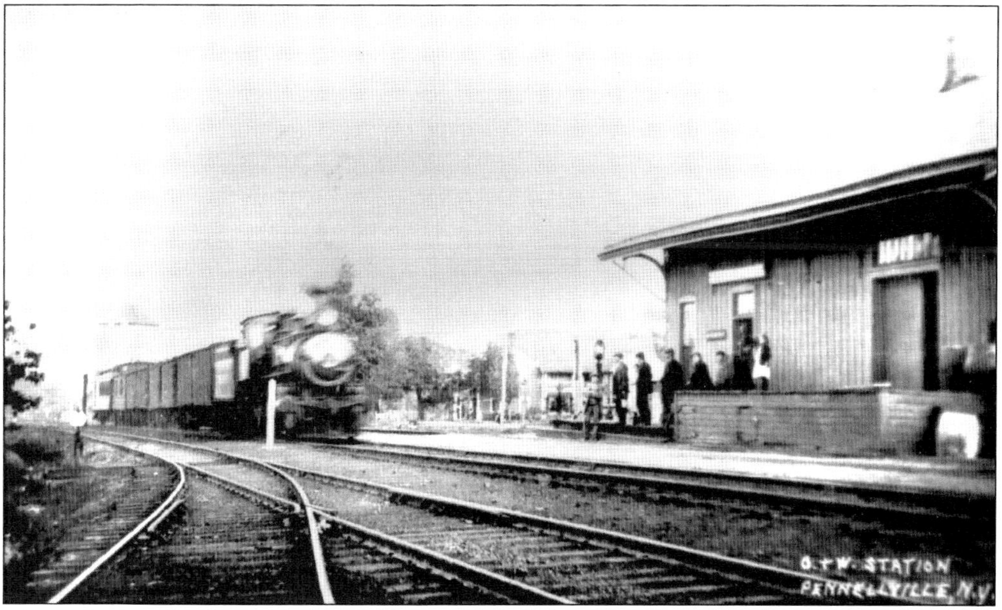

This is the Ontario & Western Railroad station in Pennellville.

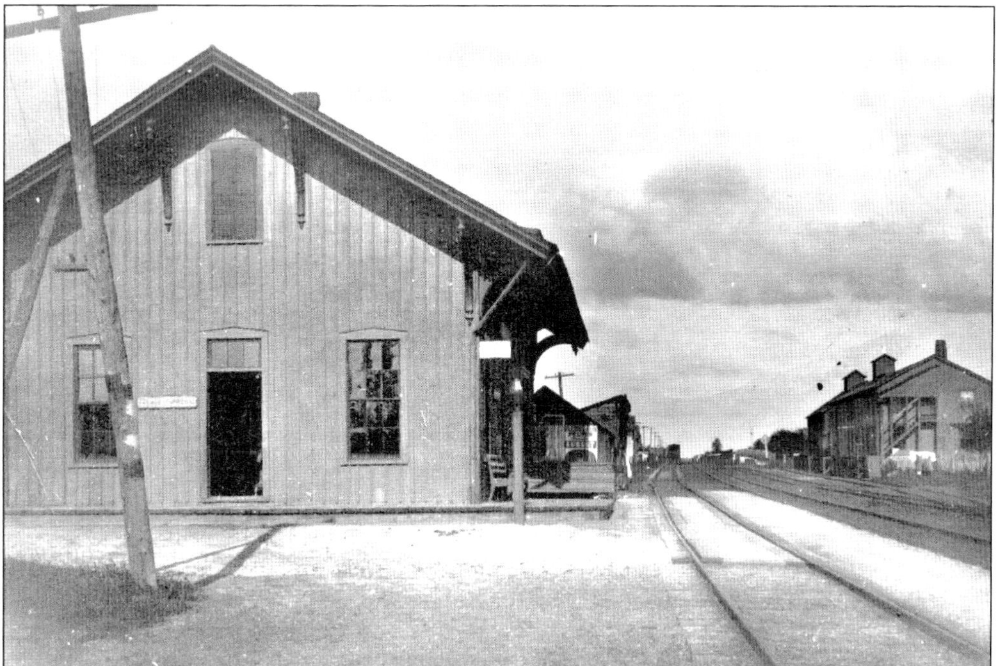
The Ontario & Western Railroad station is shown in a view looking west. The cheese factory (right) was later used by the railroad as an icehouse.

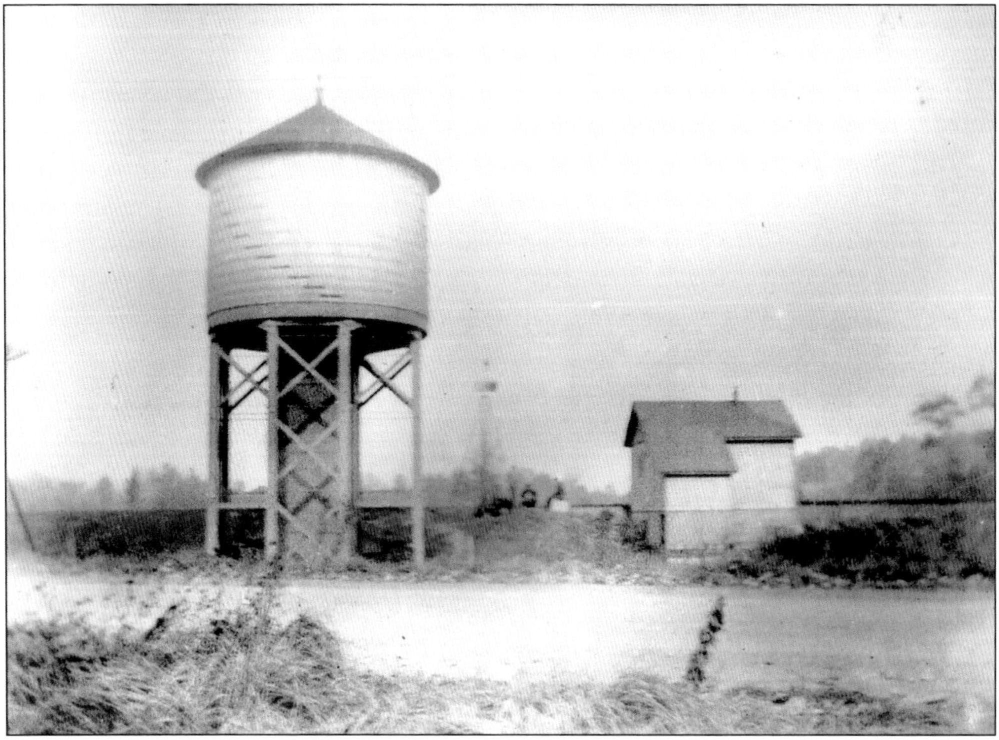

The Ontario & Western Railroad water tower and tool shed in Pennellville are shown here.

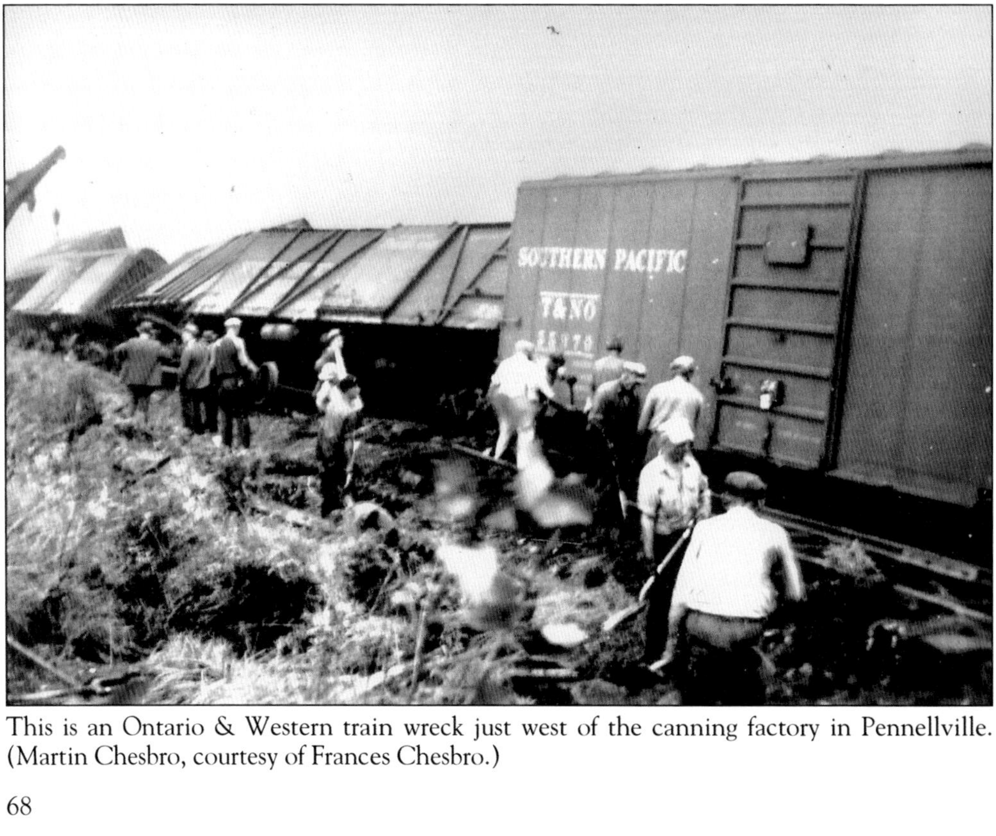

This is an Ontario & Western train wreck just west of the canning factory in Pennellville. (Martin Chesbro, courtesy of Frances Chesbro.)

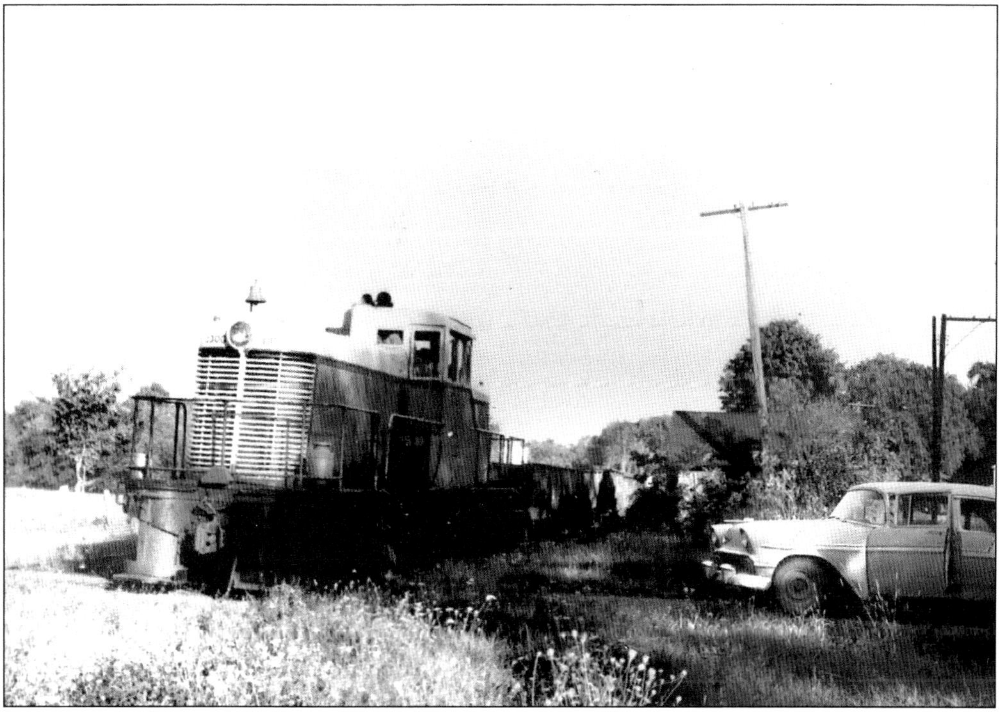

In July 1957, the Ontario & Western Railroad was auctioned off piecemeal for $10 million. Shown is the last engine to go over the tracks through Pennellville. The track, bridges, and anything of value was taken up behind the engine by scrap dealers. The iron bridge (below) across the Pennellville pond is being removed. (Photographs by John Hyvonen, courtesy of Marian Creamer.)

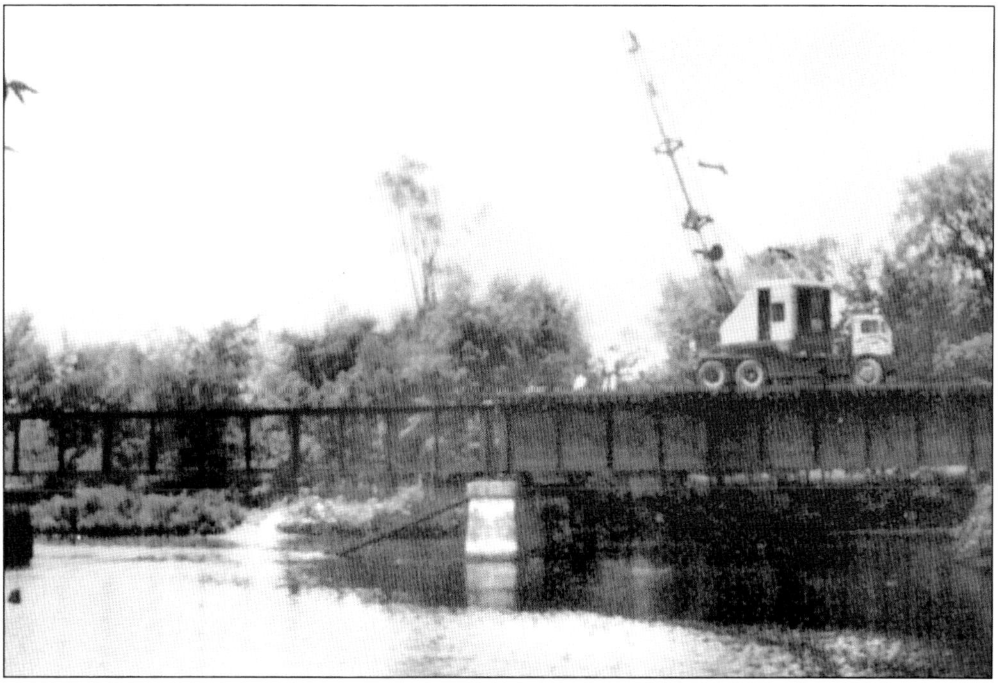

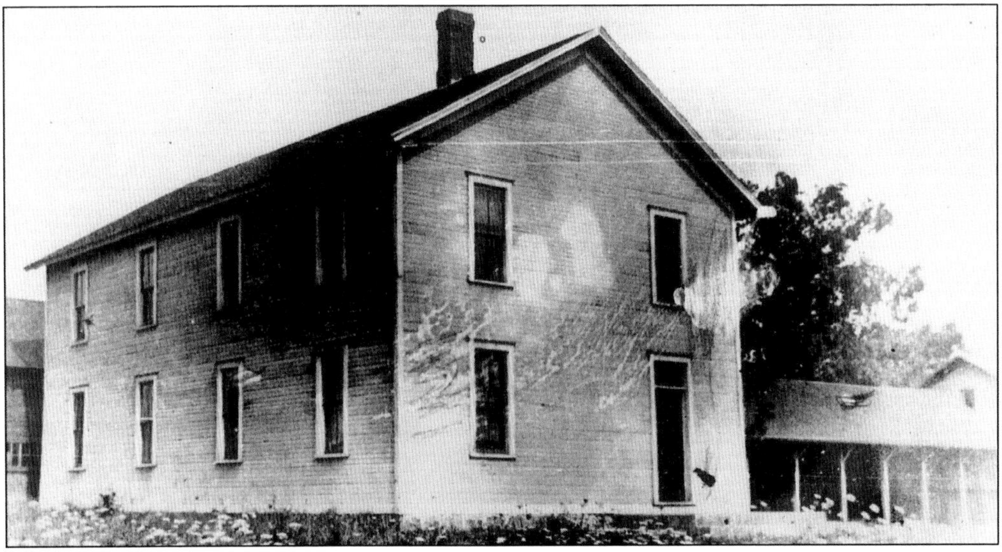

This is a photograph of the Pennellville Grange Hall and horse barn. In the dining room of Ambrose Gregg's home on January 9, 1891, 36 farmers from the Pennellville vicinity met and organized the Pennellville Grange. In May 1891, they purchased the building known as Gregg's Hop House and the lot for $250. In 1904, this new building was dedicated. The old building where meetings were held was moved across the street and used as a home. (Photograph by Royce Huntley.)

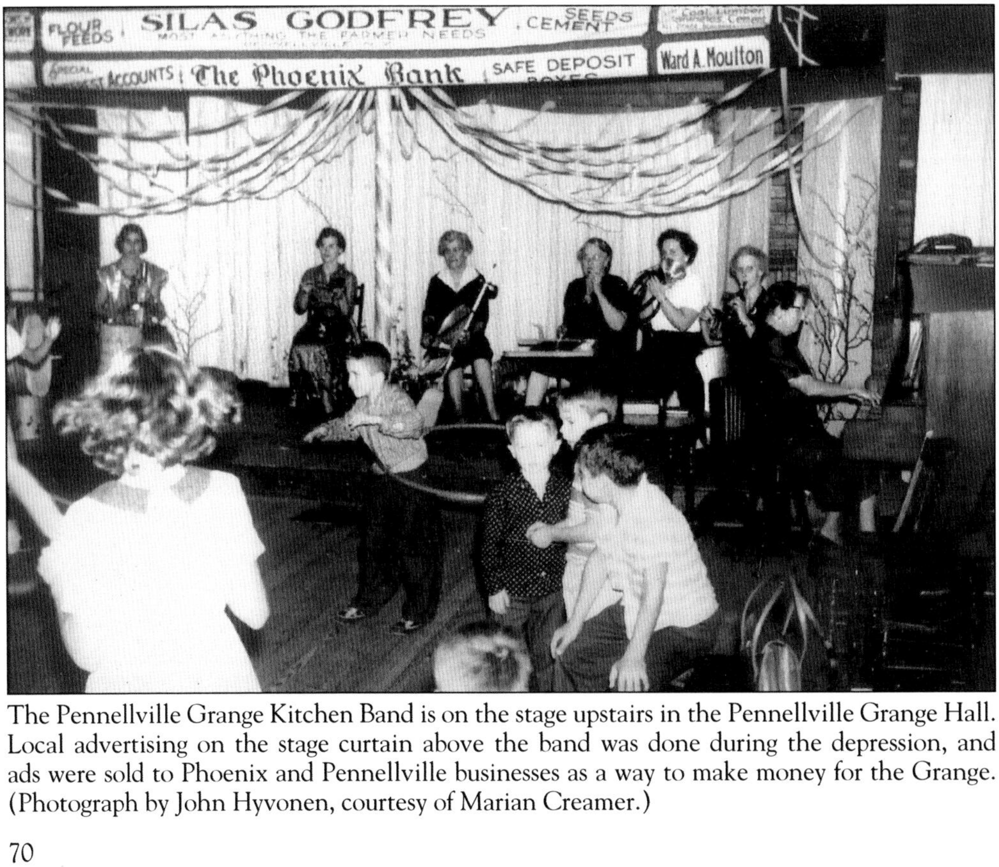

The Pennellville Grange Kitchen Band is on the stage upstairs in the Pennellville Grange Hall. Local advertising on the stage curtain above the band was done during the depression, and ads were sold to Phoenix and Pennellville businesses as a way to make money for the Grange. (Photograph by John Hyvonen, courtesy of Marian Creamer.)

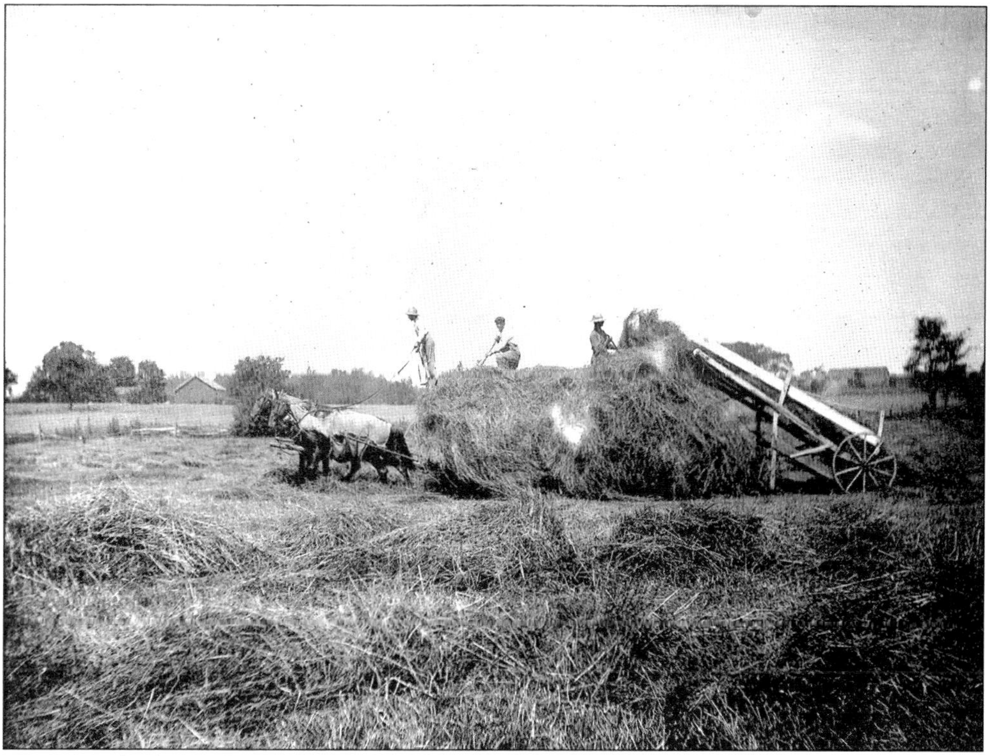

Haying at the farms along Oneida River Road takes place *c.* 1917.

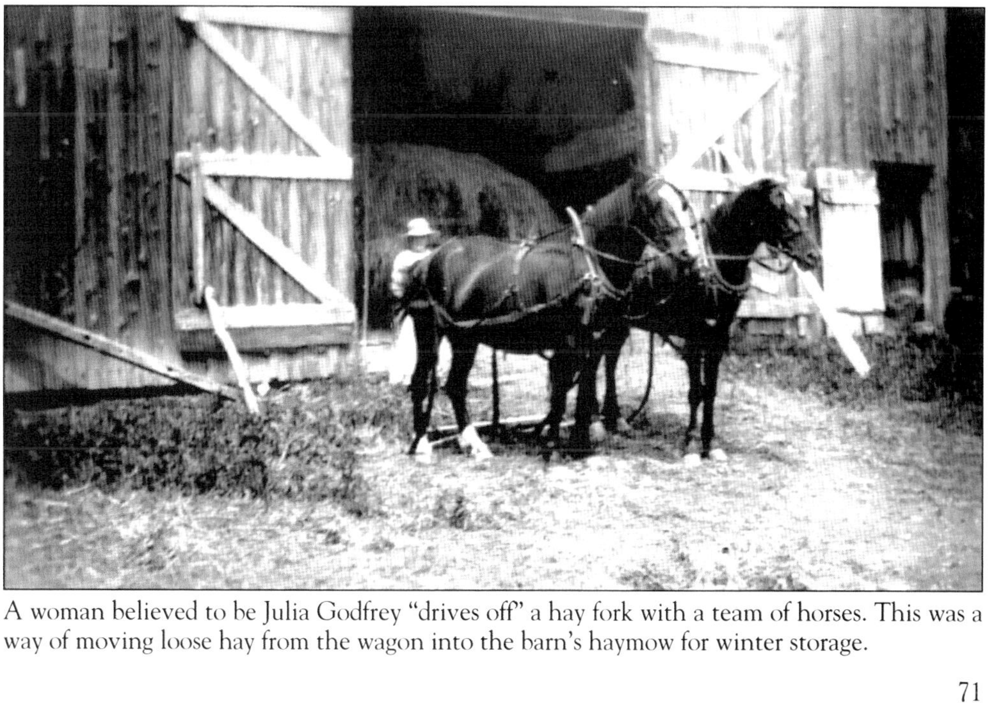

A woman believed to be Julia Godfrey "drives off" a hay fork with a team of horses. This was a way of moving loose hay from the wagon into the barn's haymow for winter storage.

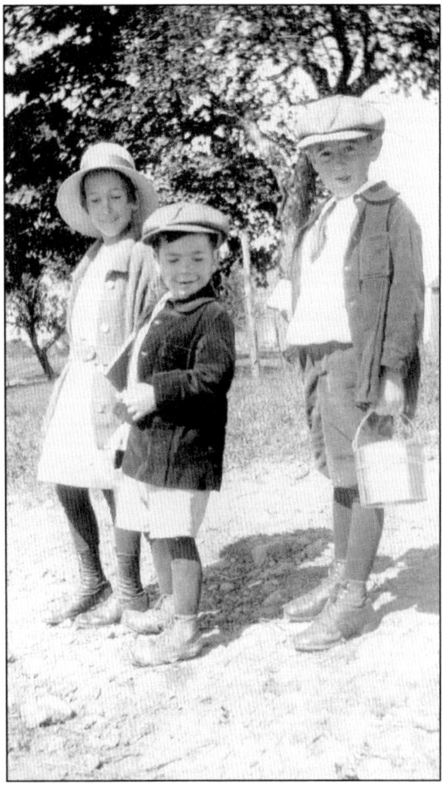

Julia, Roy, and Wayne E. Huntley begin their milelong walk down Biddlecum Road to the one-room brick school in the early 1900s.

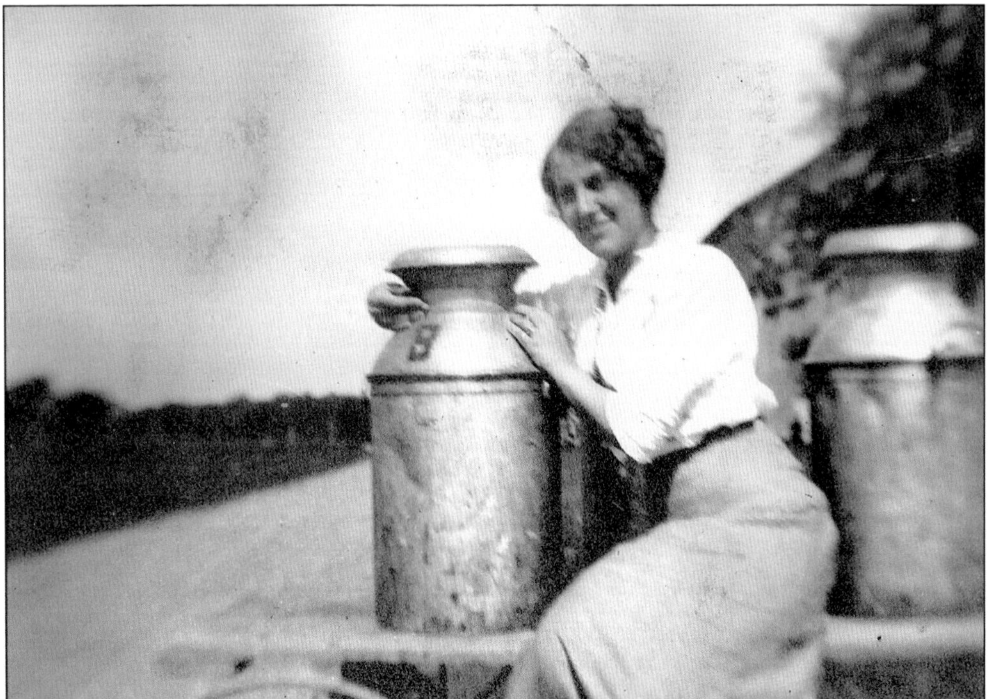

Irene Tusang poses for a picture before unloading the milk cans from a wagon in Pennellville.

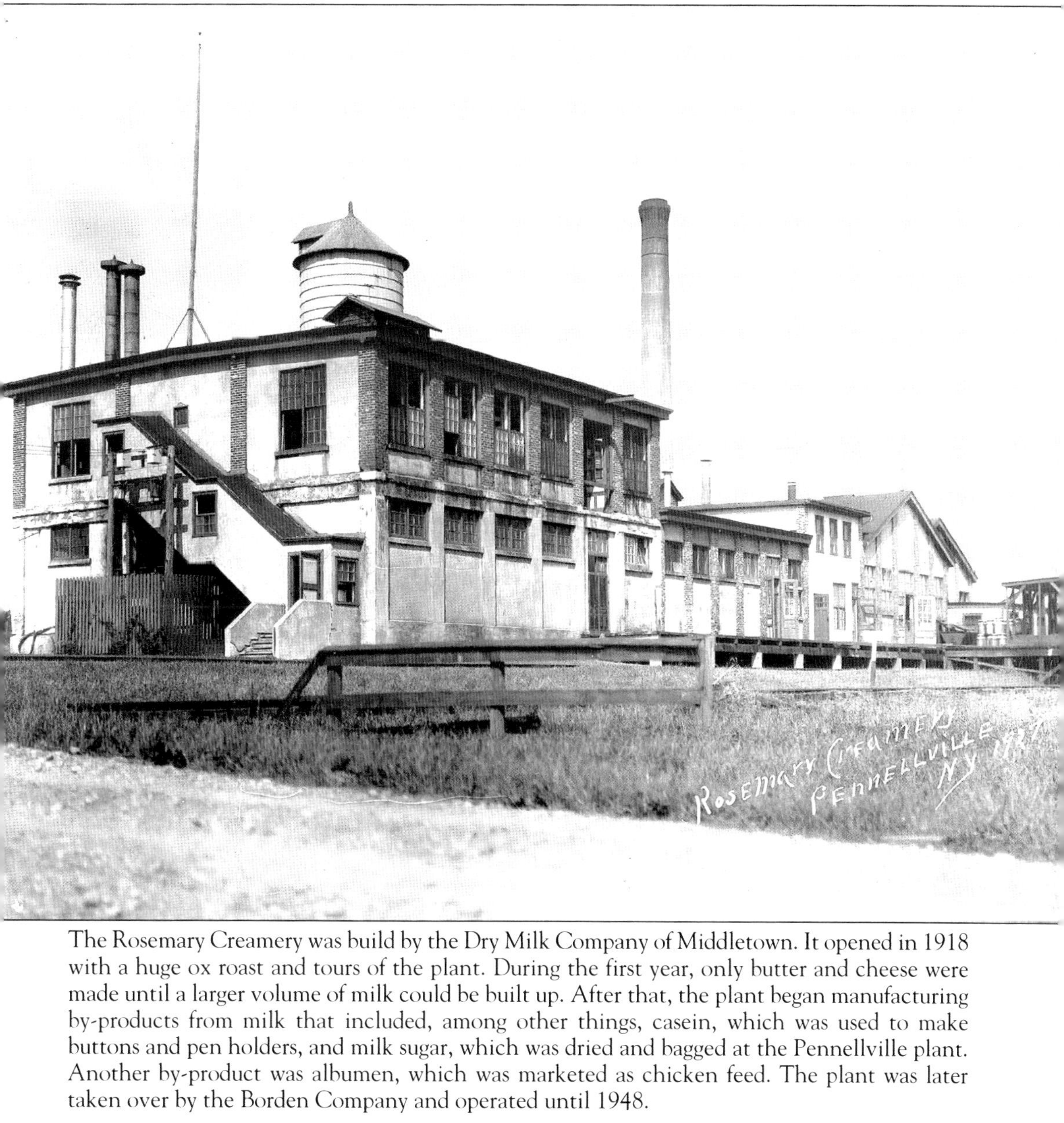

The Rosemary Creamery was build by the Dry Milk Company of Middletown. It opened in 1918 with a huge ox roast and tours of the plant. During the first year, only butter and cheese were made until a larger volume of milk could be built up. After that, the plant began manufacturing by-products from milk that included, among other things, casein, which was used to make buttons and pen holders, and milk sugar, which was dried and bagged at the Pennellville plant. Another by-product was albumen, which was marketed as chicken feed. The plant was later taken over by the Borden Company and operated until 1948.

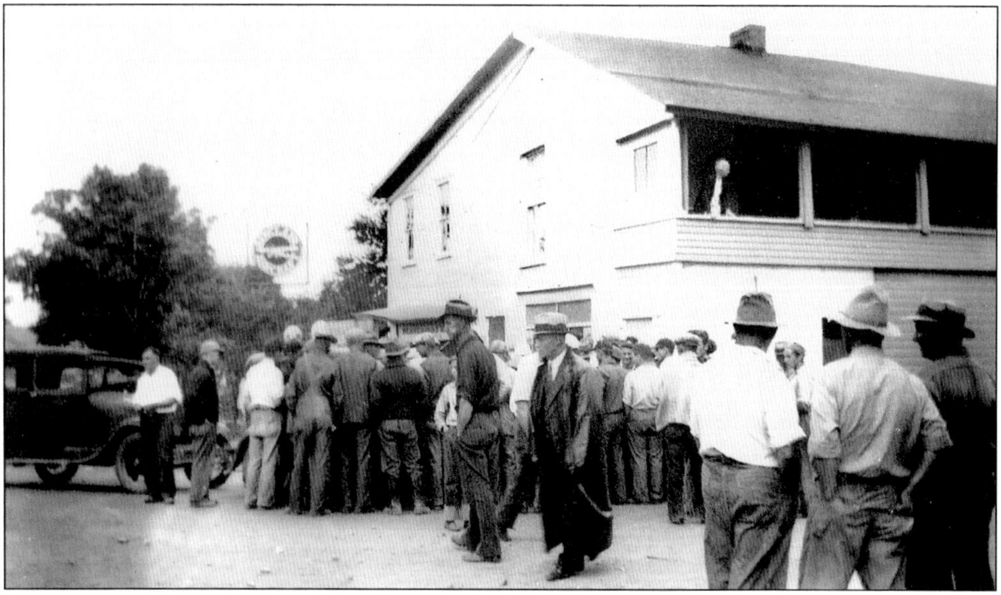

Milk strikers gather in front of Grant's store in Pennellville in 1939. During the Depression, farmers found that there were only very few markets where they could sell their milk for cash. Big business and the individuals who ran them used the desperate economic situation to their advantage and would pick and choose from whom they would purchase milk and when. They often rejected a farmer's milk for no other reason than to keep the farmers in line. For the most part, the farmer had no other place to sell his rejected milk and it would spoil. This treatment escalated into the milk strikes of the 1930s by farmers across New York State. The Rosemary Creamery in Pennellville was one of the many milk plants struck. Farmers from other areas came to Pennellville and joined local farmers in the strike. The strike at times was violent. Farmers bringing their milk to the plant would be stopped and their milk dumped. Sometimes shots would be fired into the side of milk cans and milk trucks. Usually, the striking farmers would just make the milk worthless. This was often done by throwing bottles of kerosene where the milk was. The fumes would get into the milk even through closed cans. Two young men from Pennellville were killed during the 1939 strike.

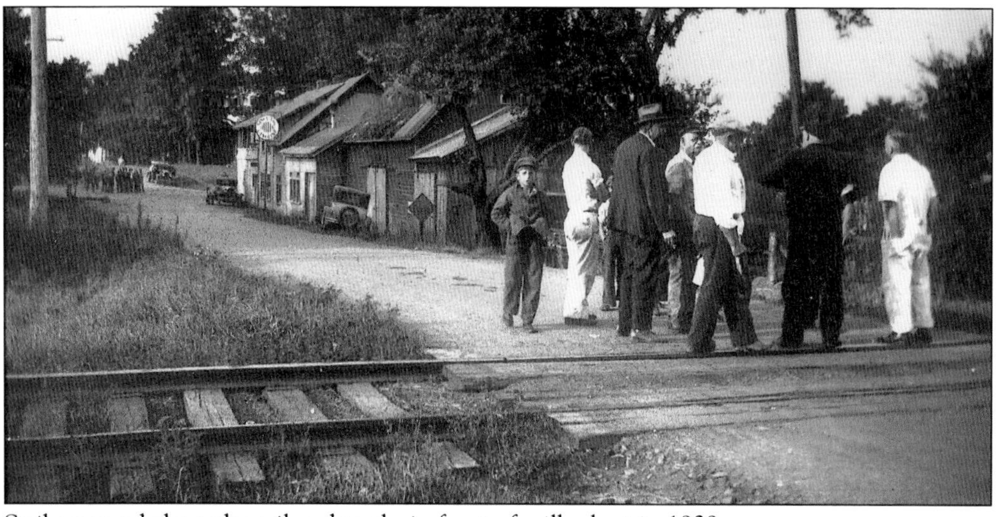

Strikers stand along the railroad tracks in front of milk plant in 1939.

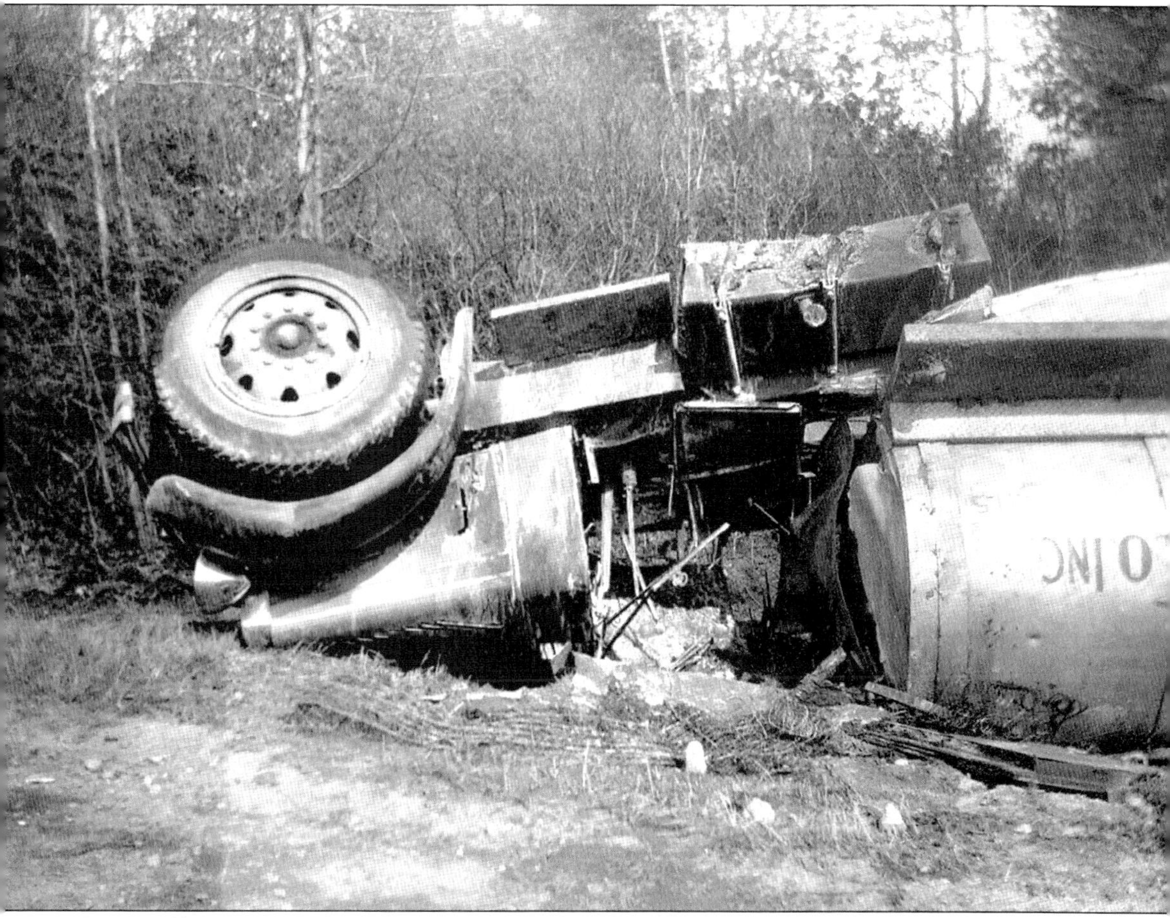

On a milk run to New York City during the 1939 strike, two Pennellville men were killed when their truck left the road and overturned three times. This photograph is believed to be the accident in which Carl Washer and Glen Clark of Pennellville were killed on August 18. Clark, 28, was the regular driver for the C.A. Terpenen Company of Solvay, and Washer, 30, was a Rosemary Creamery employee and alternate driver. Although ruled an accident, there were rumors around Pennellville that the truck's brake lines had been cut. (Barney Clark, courtesy of Marge Godfrey.)

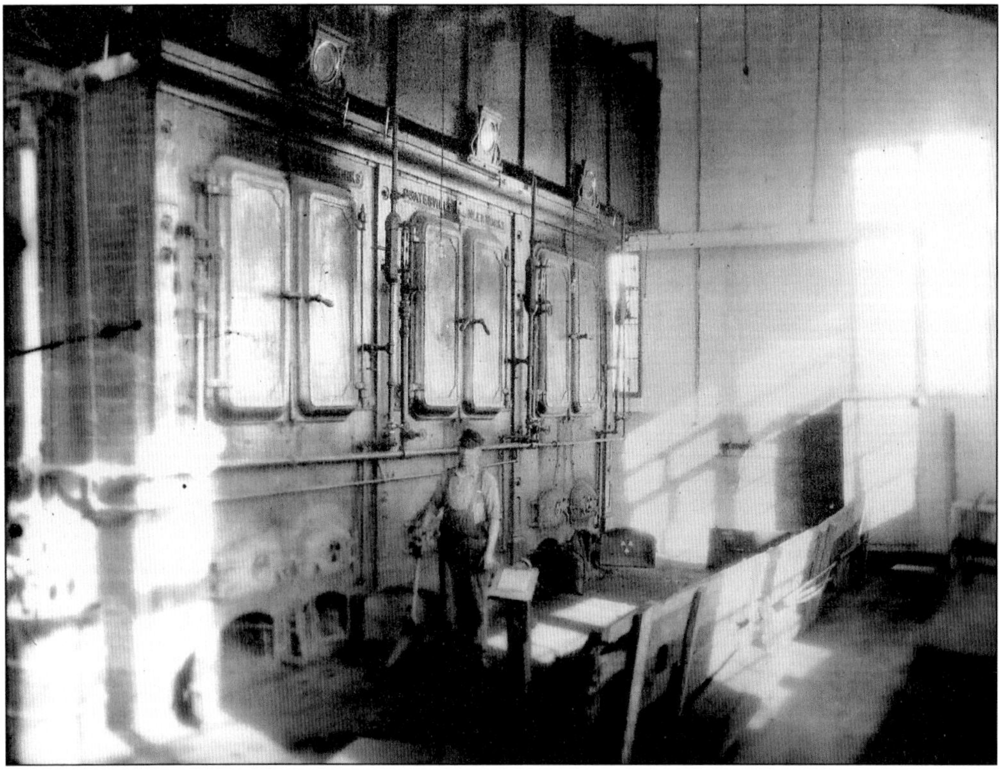

These are interior views of the Rosemary Creamery.

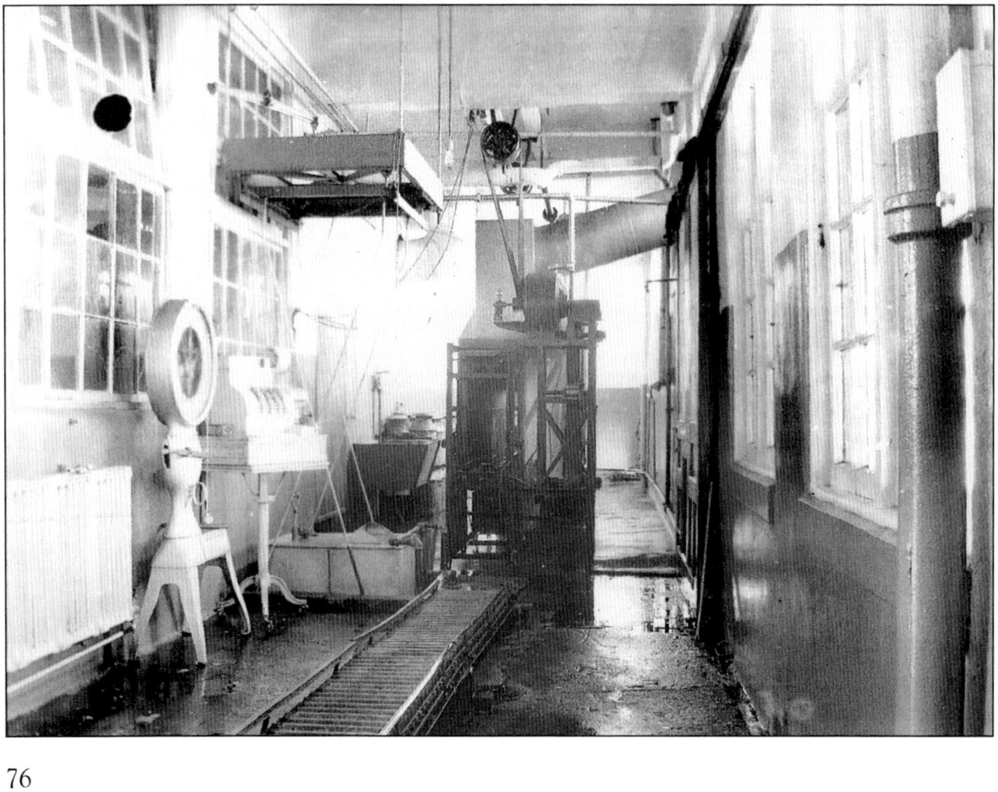

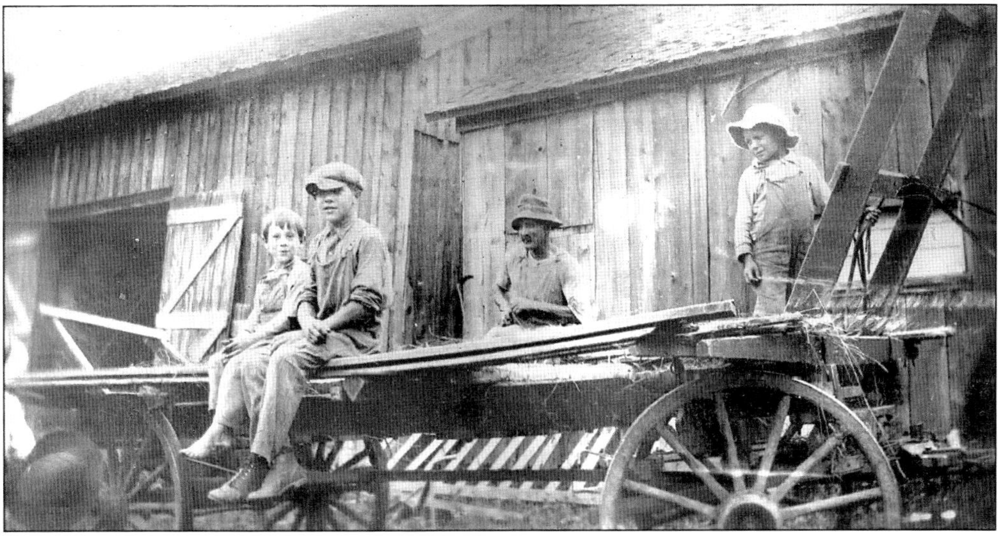

Pictured on Duane Huntley's farm, from left to right, are Wayne E. Huntley, Cecil O'ree, Harvey O'ree, and Paris O'ree. Harvey O'ree worked area farms on shares, among them the Huntley farm on Biddlecum Road in Pennellville. The O'ree family lived on Huntley's tenant farm, just west of the corner of Biddlecum Road and Route 264. Today, that area is just a field, as all the barns and the house are gone. In the 1920s, the O'ree brothers took up professional boxing as a means of making money. They all fought under the name of Williams to hide their Irish heritage. Harold O'ree was the most famous locally. He fought under the name of Bobby Williams. Among his bouts, he fought Johnny Haystack six times, winning five of those fights, and he knocked out "Cave Man" Fisher in five rounds. Fisher fought five world champions.

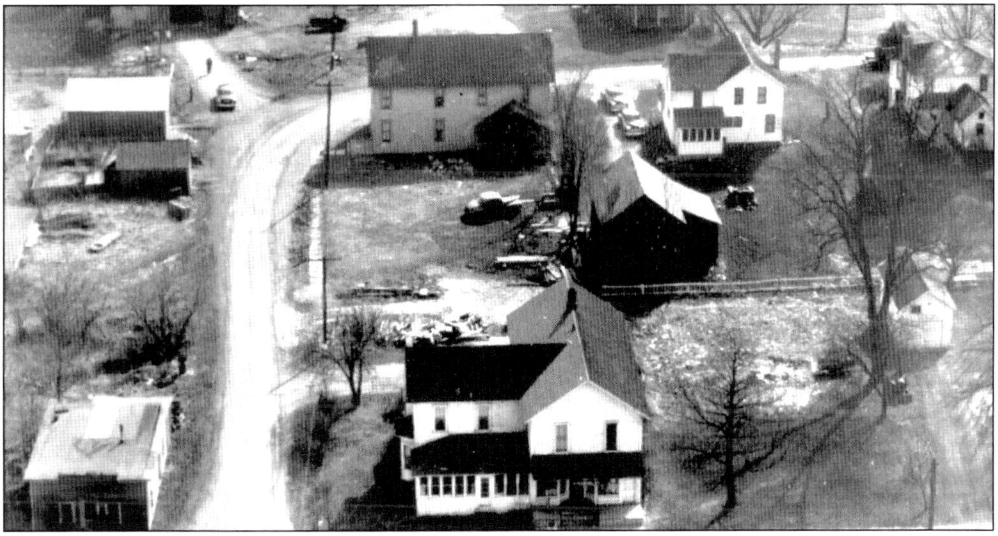

This is an aerial view of Second Street (Grange Street) and Main Street (Route 54). In the foreground, the Pennellville Pool Hall (opened in 1918) is on the left and Garfield Gridley's store is on the right. The Grange hall is on the far inside corner, and Gregg's farm is on the outside corner. The house behind the Grange and the building between the store and the Grange belonged to Herbert Rupracht, one of Pennellville's blacksmiths whose shop used to be between the Grange and his home.

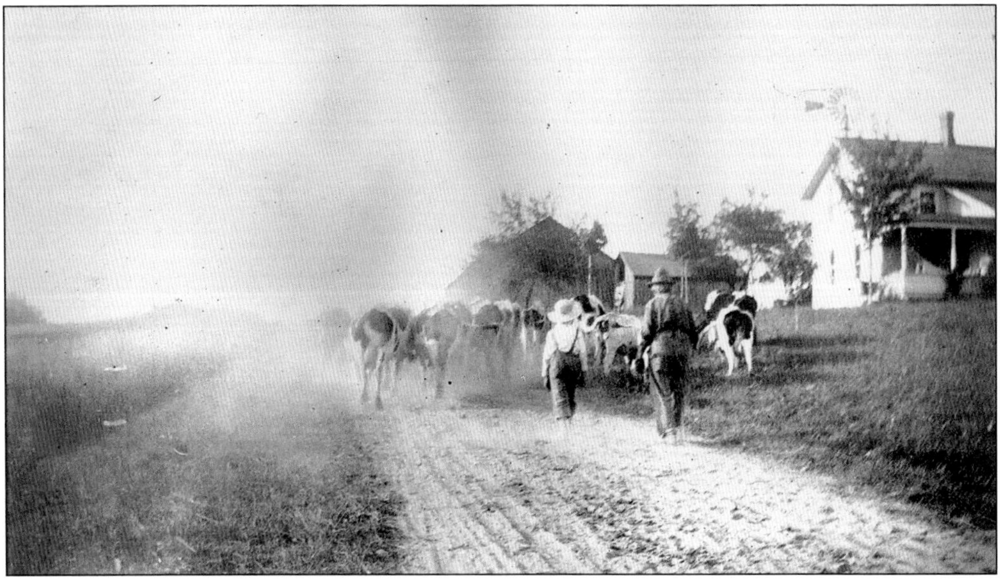

Wayne Huntley and Ferrand Huntley are on one of their twice-a-day rituals of driving the cattle to the barn to be milked by hand. The dirt road is Swamp Road, which today is called Peter Scott Road and lined with many homes.

The Swamp Road School, or Huntley School, was located on the farm of Hugh Huntley (later owned by his son Wayne) on Swamp Road (Peter Scott Road) in Pennellville. The school was located on the east side of the road, just south of Hoyt Road. Wayne Huntley's daughter Lula was one of the teachers here, as was Janet Wilson Foster, who started teaching in Schroeppel schools at the age of 14.

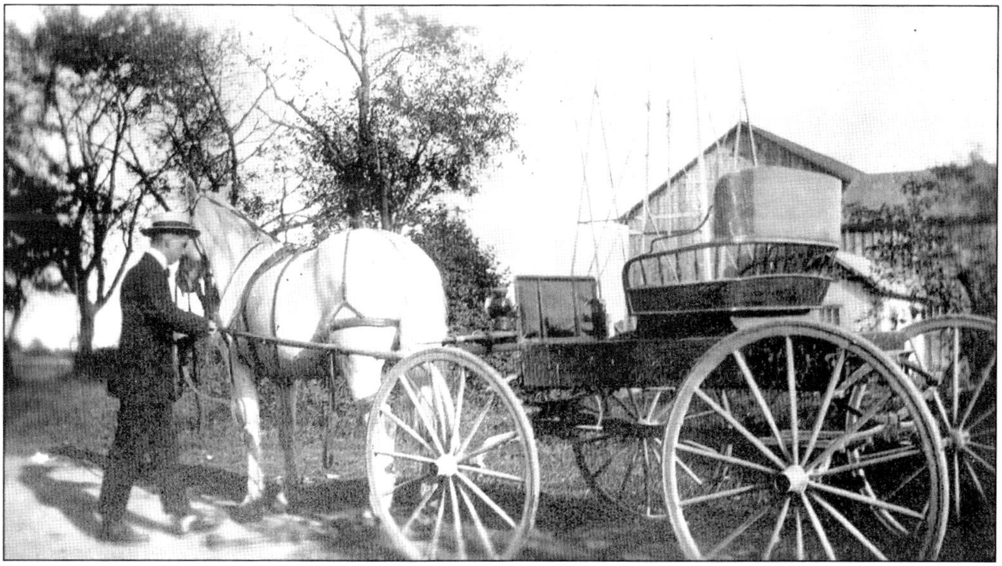

Clayton Ellis is seen at the Wayne Huntley farm on Swamp Road in Pennellville. The Ellis family was living on the farm and working it on shares. During Prohibition, the farm was raided and a still was confiscated from the grain shed, which is still standing today. The still was put on display at the sheriff's office in Phoenix, where crowds of people stopped by during the day to view the evidence. Local moonshiners knew a still was not a museum piece. It was stolen from the sheriff's office that night.

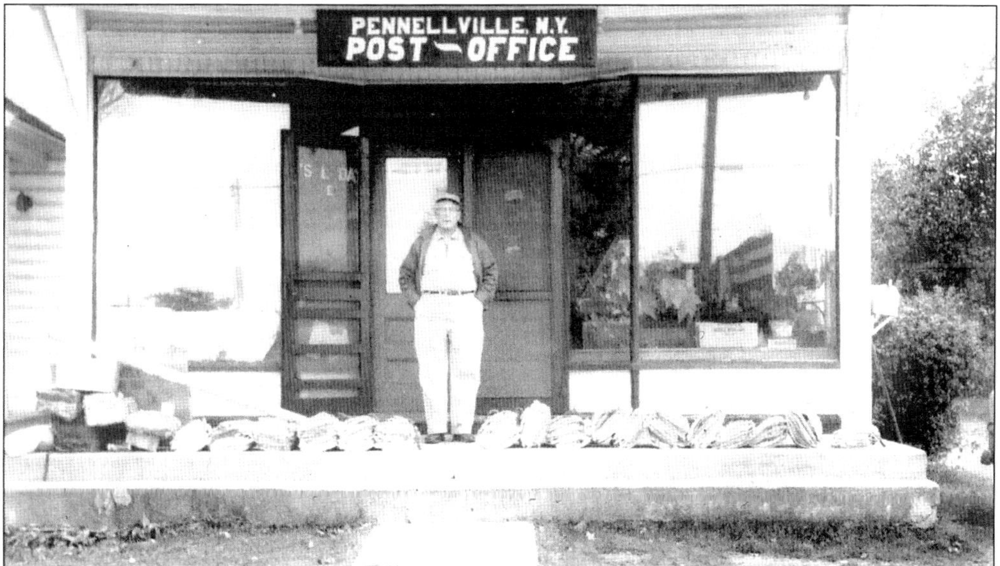

John Hyvonen is shown on his last day at work in 1961 after 29 years as Pennellville's only mail carrier. Hyvonen spent some of his spare time taking pictures and home movies of the Pennellville area. Some of his photographs are included in this book. The post office occupied Conrad's store (no longer a store) when this picture was taken, and Cora McMahon was postmaster. Before Hyvonen, the route carrier was Tim Stevens, a man of Native American descent, who started in 1903. He delivered mail, first, by horse and buggy and, later, in an old car he had equipped with skis, as the roads were not very well plowed.

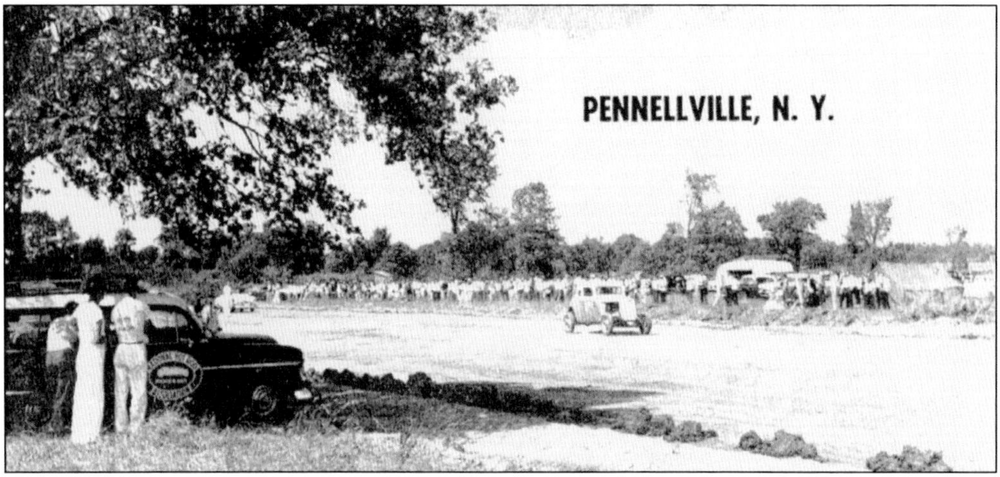

The Pennellville Drag Strip, a National Hot Rod Association dirt track, was owned by Barney Clark and located on his property along the west side of Sutton Road. The Pennellville track was featured in an article on East Coast tracks in the November 1954 issue of *Hot Rod* magazine. (Photograph by Rick and Fred Horsley, *Hot Rod* magazine, 1954, Trend Inc., Los Angeles, California.)

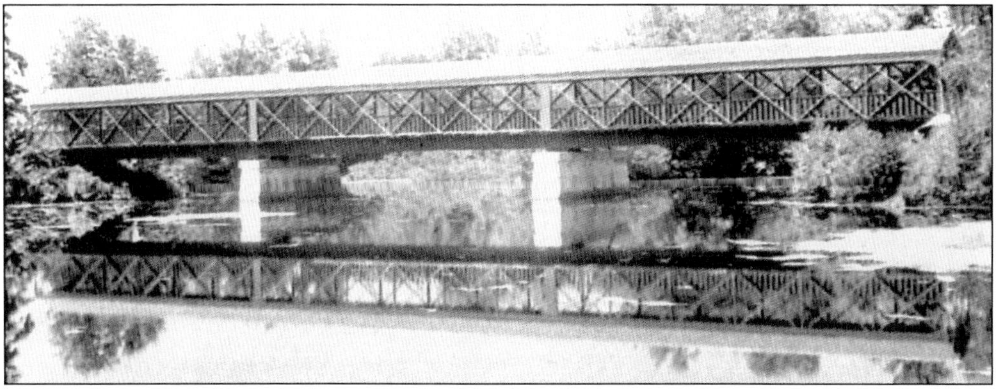

Pennellville's covered bridge was built in 1973 over the Pennellville Pond. The covered bridge, at 210 feet long, was the second longest in the state. It was constructed with steel supports, redwood trusses, a three-inch cherry hardwood floor, and a shake-shingle roof. The bridge was built along the old Ontario & Western Railroad bed, which is now used as a recreation trail for hikers, bike riders, snowmobilers, and others. The bridge was the idea of the then Oswego County Parks and Recreation director, Alan Foster. It cost $8,500, and the state and county each paid half of that amount. The bridge was totally destroyed by a violent wind storm on November 12, 1992. (Courtesy of Fulton Savings Bank.)

Seven

PHOENIX

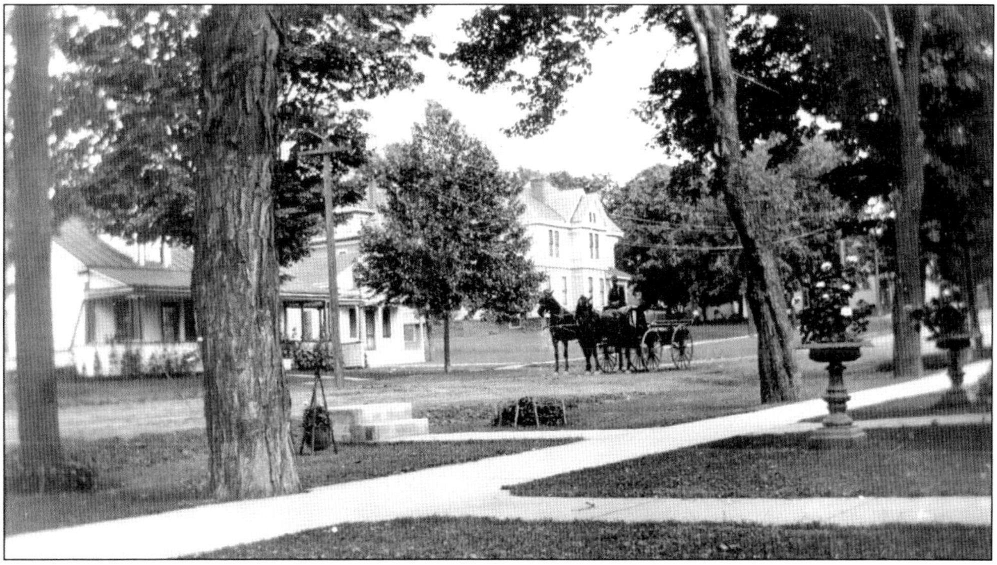

This is an early view of Main Street in Phoenix. Cement buggy steps (foreground) made it easier for women to get in and out of wagons and carriages. A few of these steps can still be seen along Phoenix streets today.

In 1792, Daniel Phoenix purchased a 1,200-acre tract of land from Ezra L'Hommedieu. It became known as the Phoenix Tract or Phoenix Patent. In 1828, the village of Phoenix took its name from the name of the tract in which it was located. At this time, the tract was owned by Alexander Phoenix (believed to be Daniel's son). Some historical material says the village was named after Daniel, while other material says the village was named after Alexander. In either case, these property owners never had a permanent residence here. Phoenix was laid out into village lots in 1836 and the first bridge across the river was also built that year. The village of Phoenix was incorporated in 1848.

Although the economic hub of the town of Schroeppel shifted over the years between Gilberts Mills, Pennellville, and Phoenix with the arrival of better forms of transportation, the village of Phoenix continued to hold an economic base and grow after the Oswego Canal system was completed in 1828. The most prosperous years of Phoenix's early development were said to be between 1850 and 1870. Before the canal, the river had shallow areas that could be walked across, it was deep in other sections, and there were areas of fast moving rapids, which made it unsuitable for the shipping of large amounts of cargo.

Phoenix business and manufacturing sections quickly outgrew those in other areas within the town after the completion of the canal. Even when larger markets and faster shipping were found through the Ontario & Western Railroad in Pennellville, the bulk of the actual manufacturing and stores stayed in Phoenix and only shipped and received goods through Pennellville. Shipping via the canal also continued to be an option, especially for markets like Syracuse that were bypassed by the railroad.

In many instances throughout its history, Phoenix as a community equaled or surpassed that of any other village or small city. Numerous products were manufactured in Phoenix—items like tools, jackknives, straight razors, paper goods, furniture, and even bologna. Delong motorcycles were made in Phoenix *c.* 1902. Over the years, Phoenix was known for having many prominent individuals, several of whom were inventors. Yet, Phoenix has also had more than its share of natural disasters and nearsighted visionaries. The largest disaster was the Phoenix fire of 1916 that destroyed the entire business section of the village. Today, Phoenix is a village with many problems, not the least of which is trying to compete with several malls and business centers located only a couple of miles away in the town of Clay.

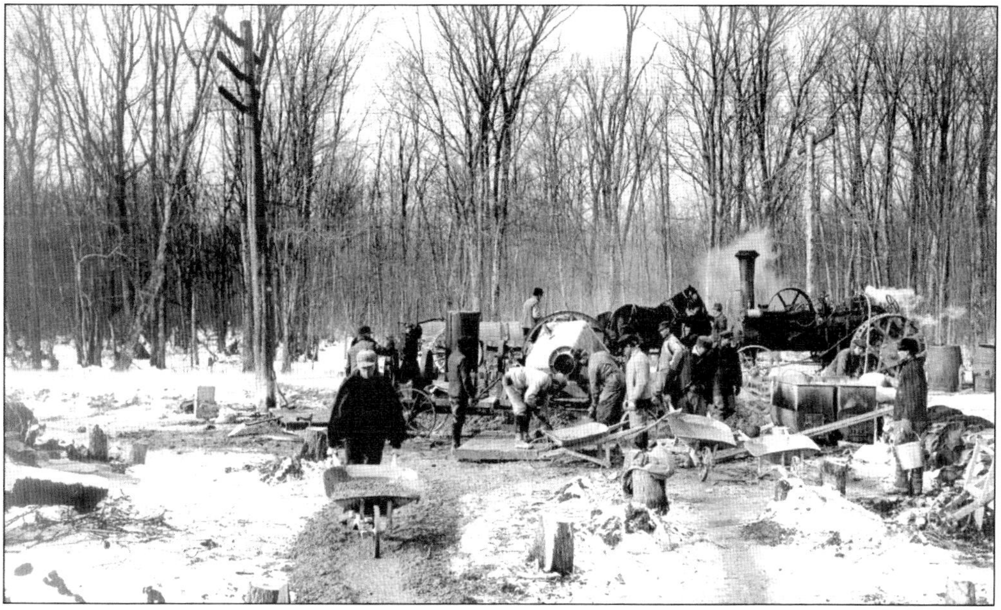

This photograph is identified as "concrete work at Sta F. 119 in swamp near Phoenix" and is dated February 13, 1907.

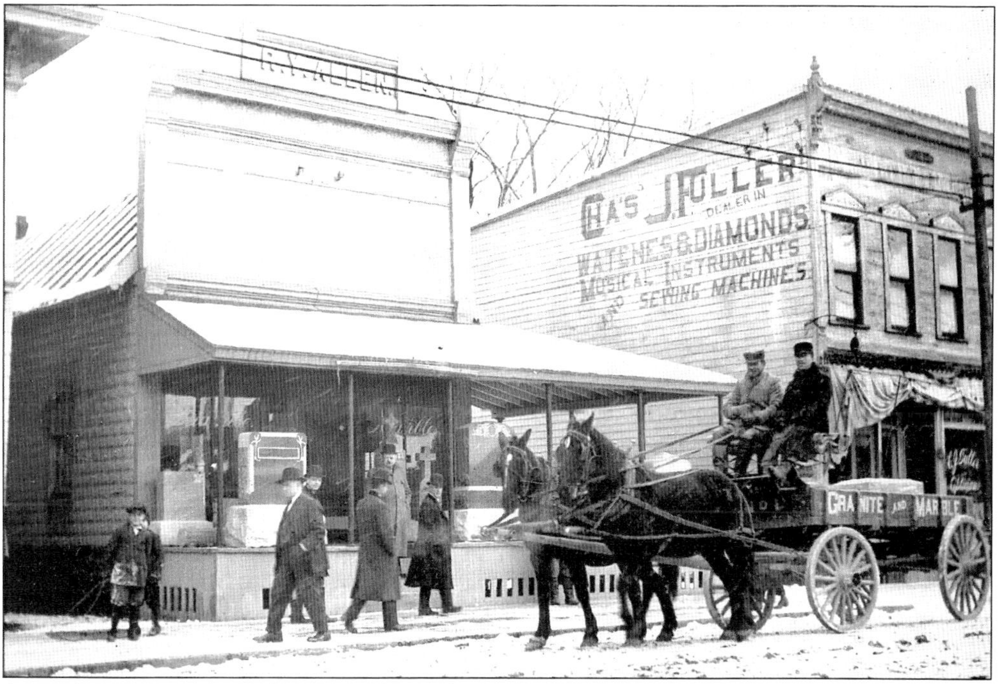

An early street scene in Phoenix is shown here.

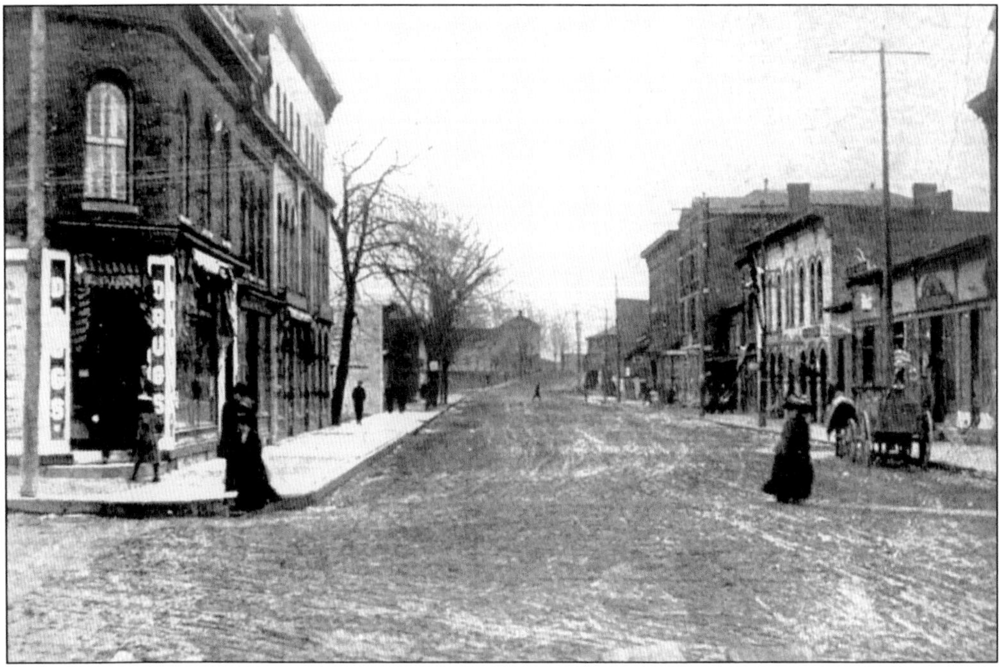

This early view looks south on Canal Street in Phoenix.

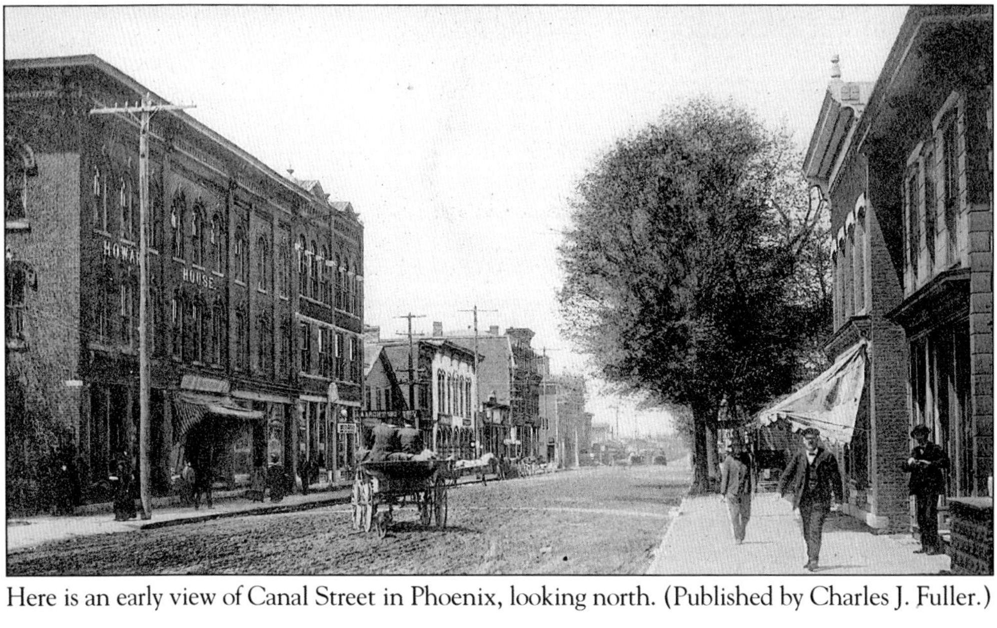

Here is an early view of Canal Street in Phoenix, looking north. (Published by Charles J. Fuller.)

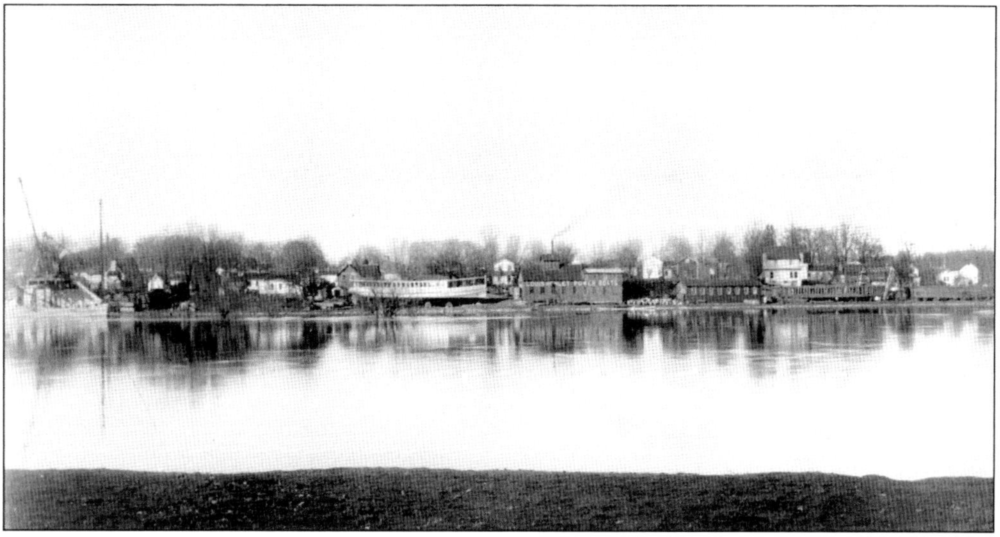

Although there were many boatyards in Phoenix, Henley's Boat Yard was the last and, thus, is the one most often seen in photographs. Lewis Henley, who reportedly designed various boat hulls, is often listed as one of Phoenix's many inventors. (Photograph by R.S. Kellar, courtesy of Richard Huntley.)

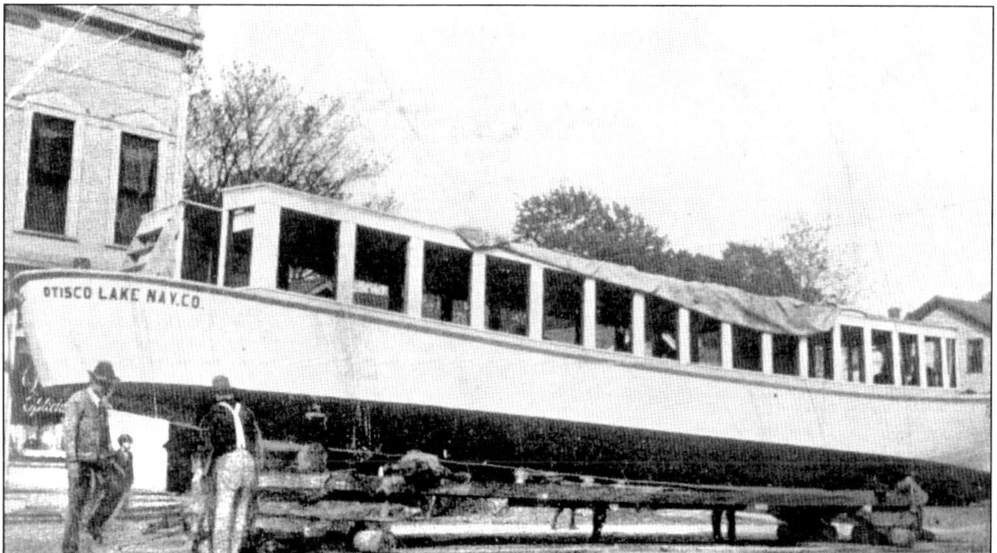

A boat built at the Phoenix Boat Yard leaves Phoenix via the trolley tracks through the center of Canal Street. The boat was being shipped to the Otisco Lake Navigation Company. (Photograph by C.J. Fuller, courtesy of Richard Huntley.)

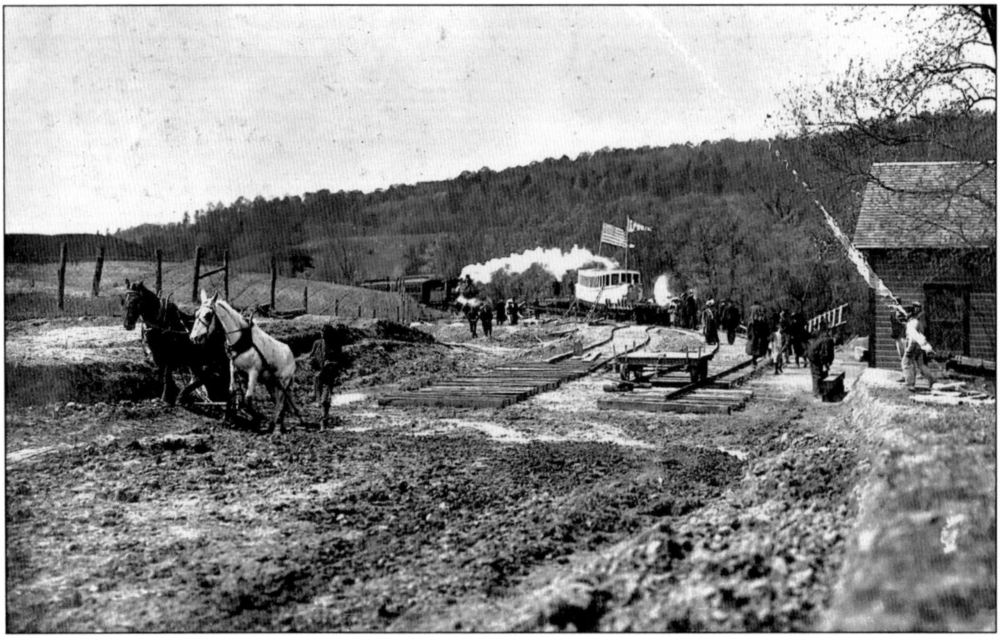

A recently completed boat from the Phoenix Boat Yard is being sent on its way.

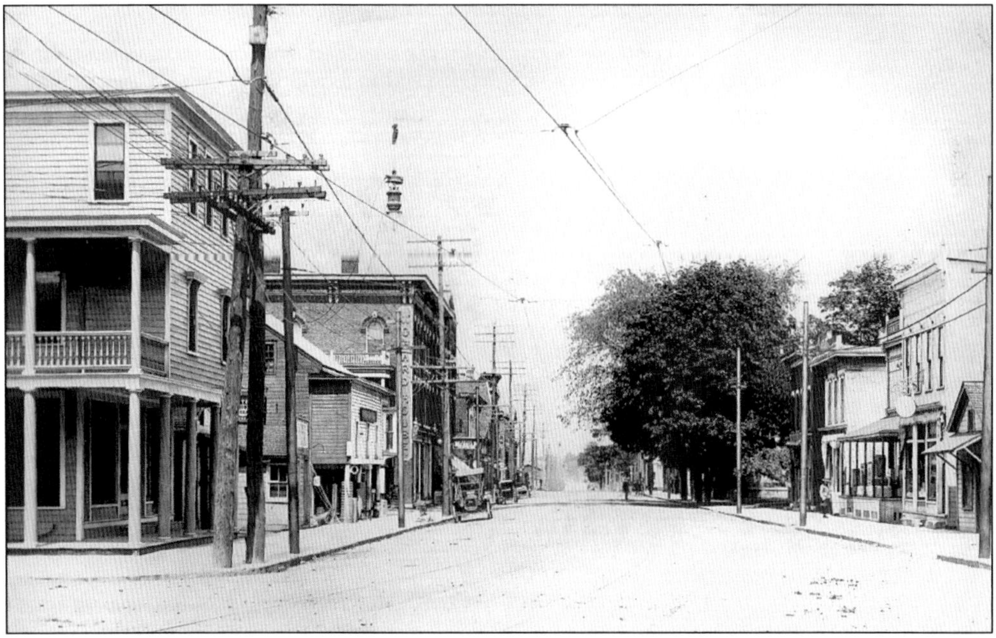

This is a photograph of business district before the 1911 Phoenix fire. In the left foreground is the Phoenix Hotel, which burned in that fire. It was rebuilt as a two-story structure.

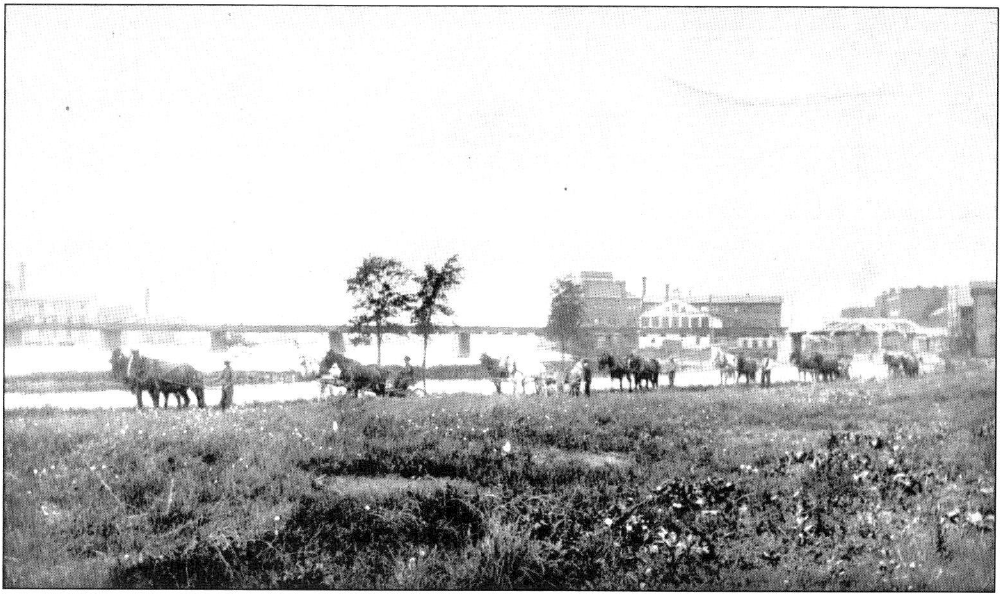

A towpath runs along the Oswego Canal in Phoenix. (Photograph by R.S. Kellar, courtesy of Richard Huntley.)

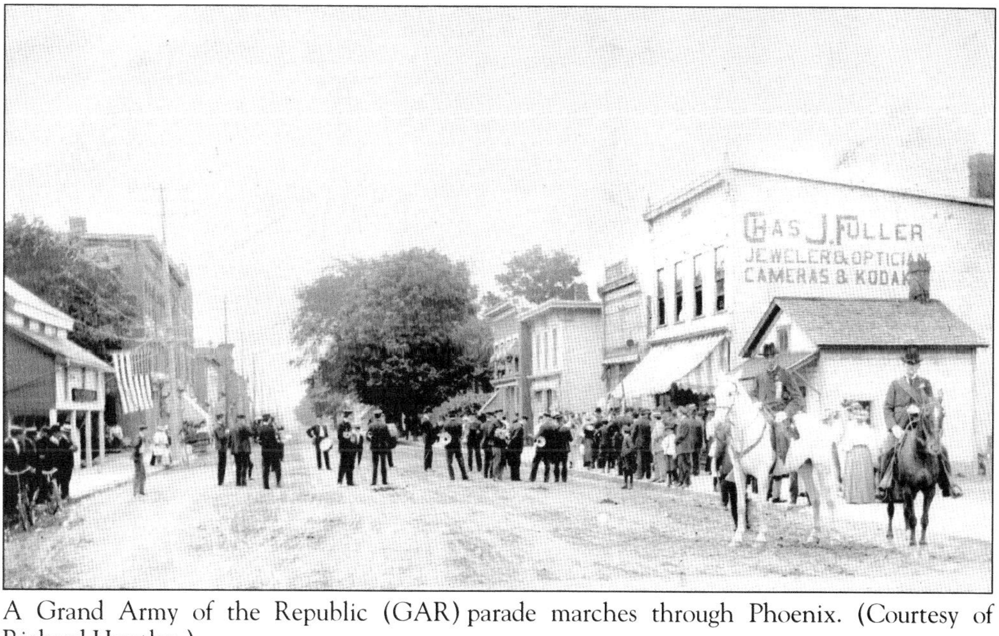

A Grand Army of the Republic (GAR) parade marches through Phoenix. (Courtesy of Richard Huntley.)

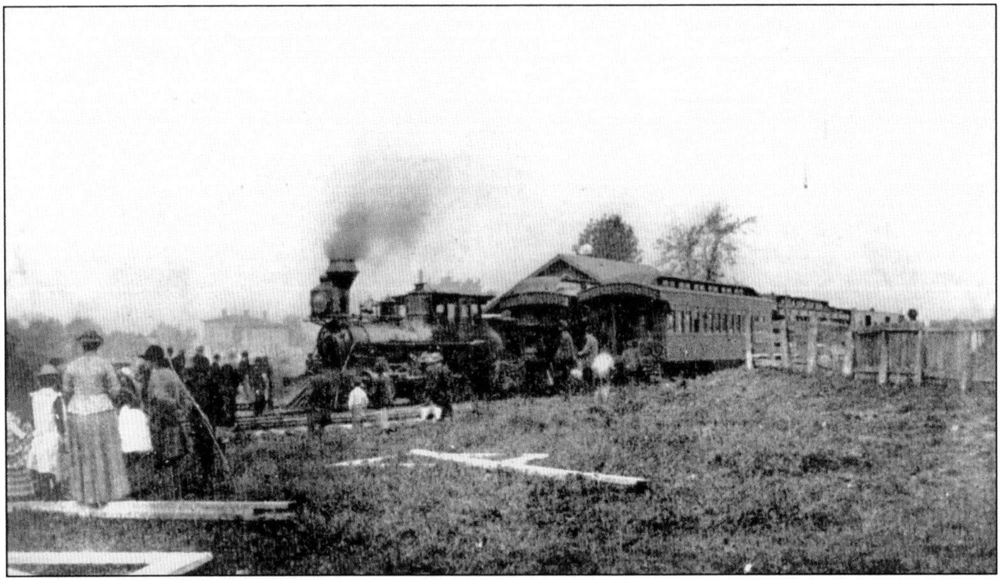

The first train came through the Phoenix railroad station on July 8, 1885. Originally known as the Syracuse, Phoenix & Oswego Railroad, this section was immediately taken over by the Rome, Watertown & Ogdensburg railroad upon the completion of the line. The Rome, Watertown & Ogdensburg was later taken over by the New York Central. On the day the Phoenix branch was opened, passenger trains left Syracuse and Oswego at the same time and met in Phoenix for a large celebration. (Photograph by C.J. Fuller, courtesy of Richard Huntley.)

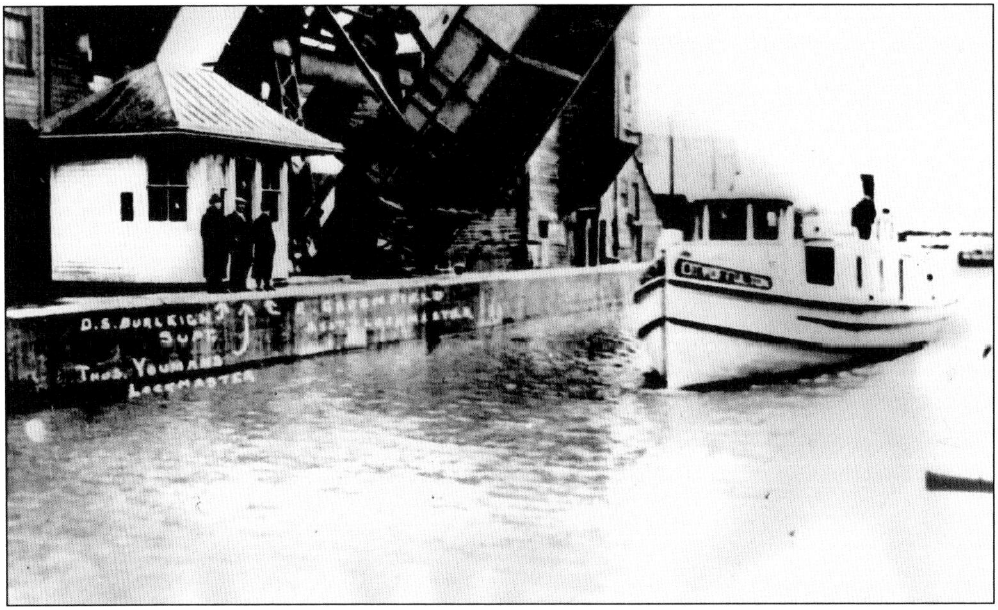

Shown is the lift bridge in Phoenix in 1909. The first boat through the new lock of the barge canal in Phoenix was the *City of Fulton*, owned by the superintendent of the Oswego Canal, David Burleigh of Phoenix. This boat was built in Phoenix. Burleigh's father, Joshua, came to Schroeppel in 1855 and built a log cabin near Pennellville. David Burleigh ran away from home at age 13 to drive horses on the Oswego Canal, and at age 20 he began work as a steersman. He became superintendent of Section 2 of the Oswego Canal on March 1, 1900, and served for 11 years.

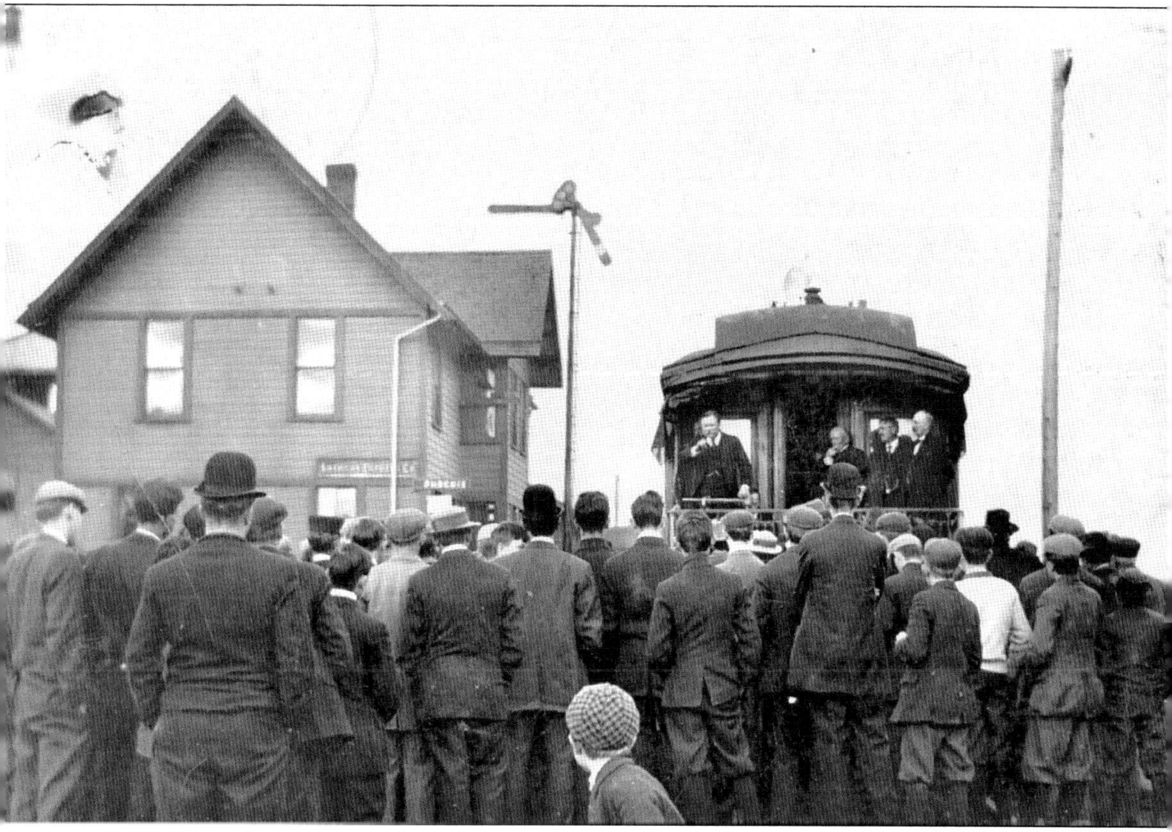

Col. Theodore Roosevelt speaks to Phoenix residents from the rear of a train at the Phoenix Railroad station in 1910. (Courtesy of Richard Huntley.)

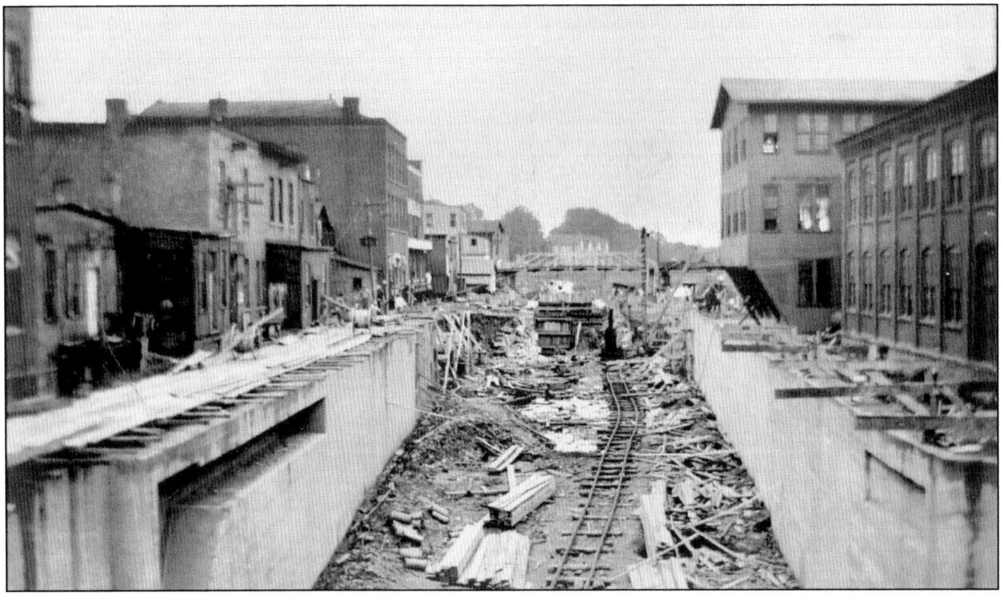

Construction work on the barge canal in Phoenix takes place c. 1909. Tracks at the bottom of the canal are for the narrow-gauge train that was used in the construction. A similar train was used in the construction of Swamp Road (Peter Scott Road today) and part of Sutton Road. (Courtesy of Richard Huntley.)

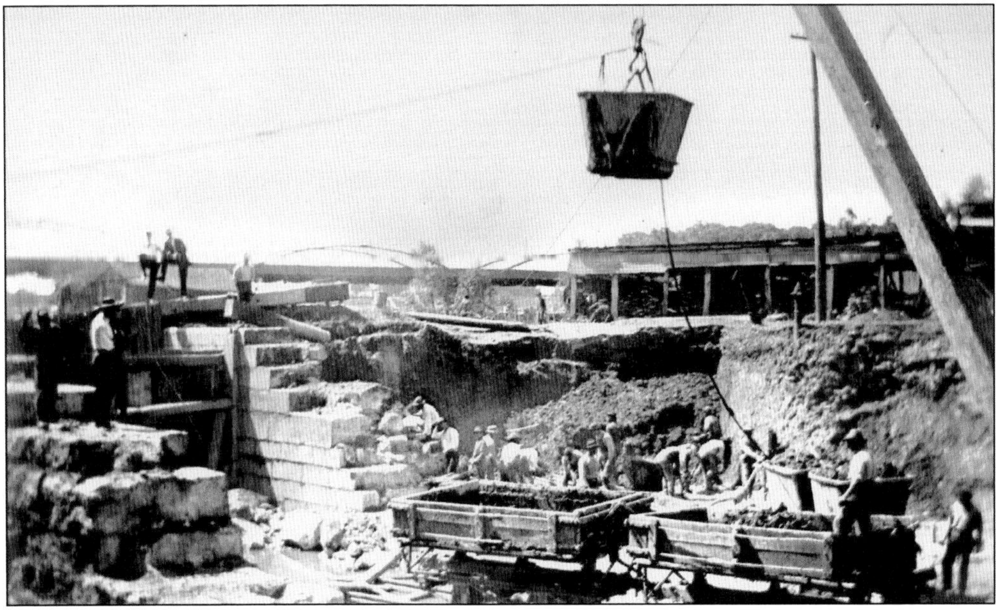

Scott Brothers is the company involved in constructing the barge canal in Phoenix c. 1909. This photograph shows the loading of debris onto narrow-gauge railroad cars. (Courtesy of Richard Huntley.)

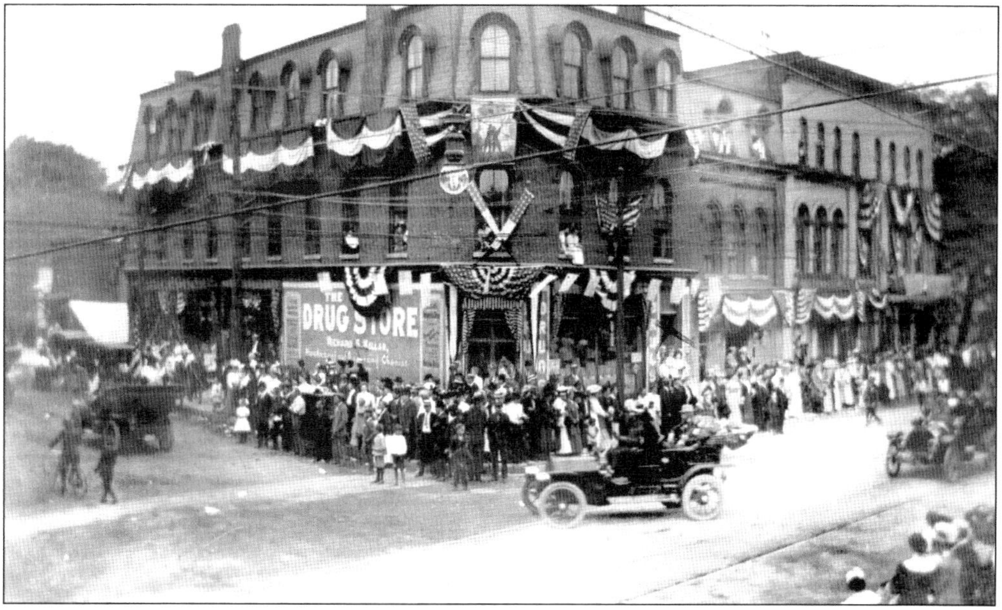

A parade moves through the business section of Phoenix. (Courtesy of Richard Huntley.)

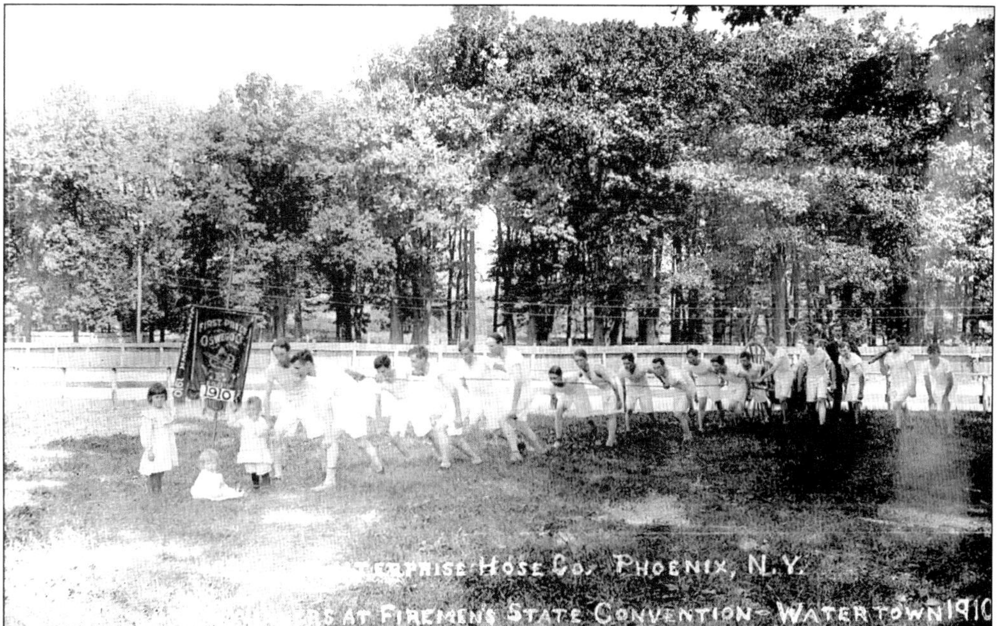

Shown is the Enterprise Hose Company in Phoenix. This was the winning team at the State Firemen's Convention in Watertown in 1910.

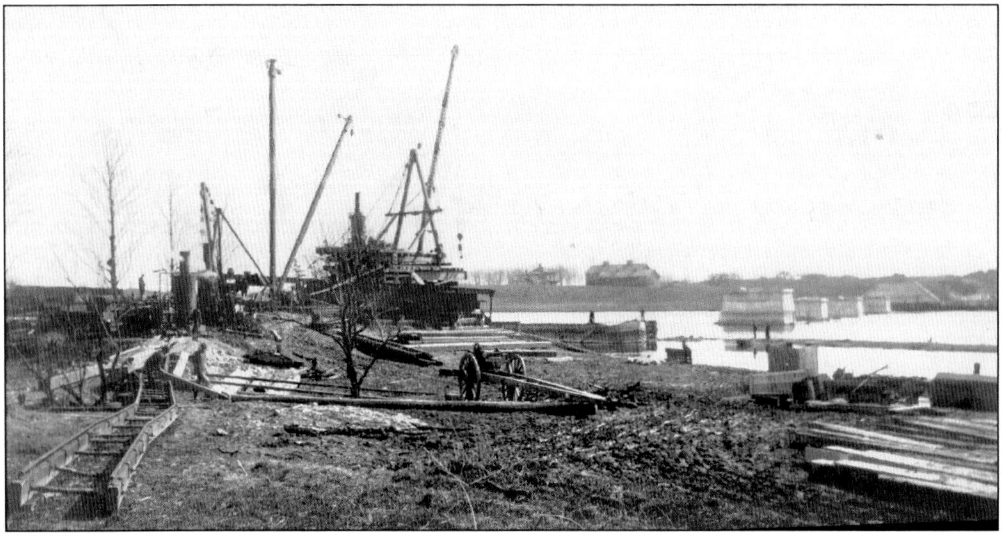

The trolley bridge of the Syracuse, Lake Shore & Northern Railroad Company is under construction in Phoenix. The bridge consisted of four decks of 94 feet each and a through-span of 357 feet. The cost of the entire line exceeded $1 million dollars. The trolley went out of business in 1931. In 1938, the steel from this bridge was dropped onto a barge and sold as scrap to Japan. (Photograph by R.S. Kellar, courtesy of Richard Huntley.)

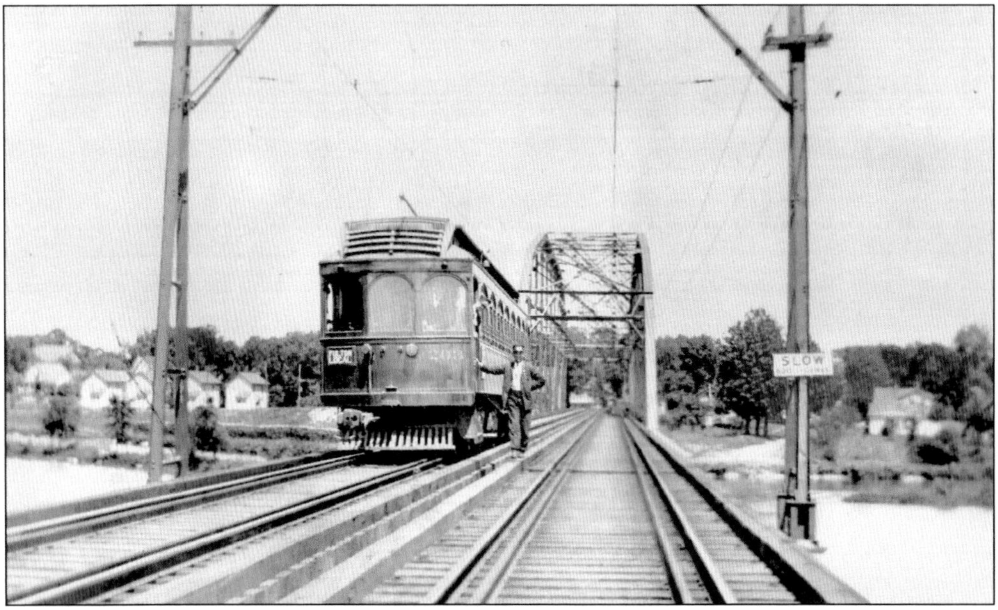

This is another view of the trolley bridge in Phoenix. The first trolley ran through Phoenix in December 1908. (Courtesy of Richard Huntley.)

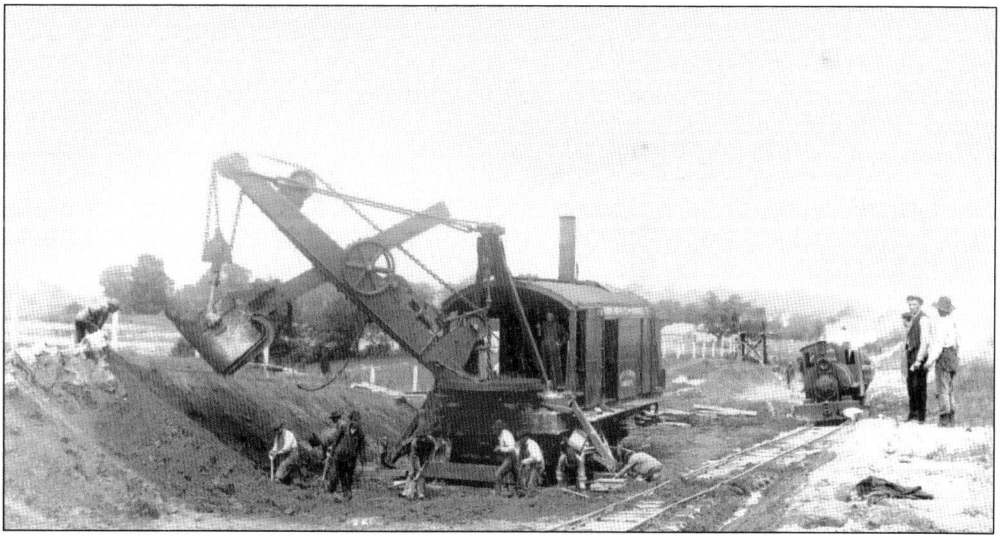

The trolley road is under construction near Phoenix. (Photographs by R.S. Kellar; above, courtesy of Lora and Doc Jones, and below, courtesy of Richard Huntley.)

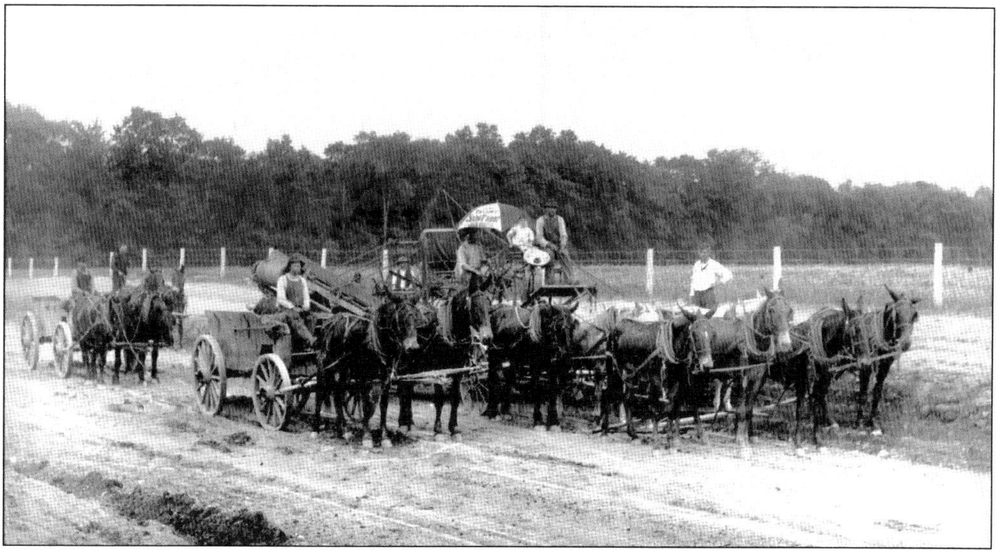

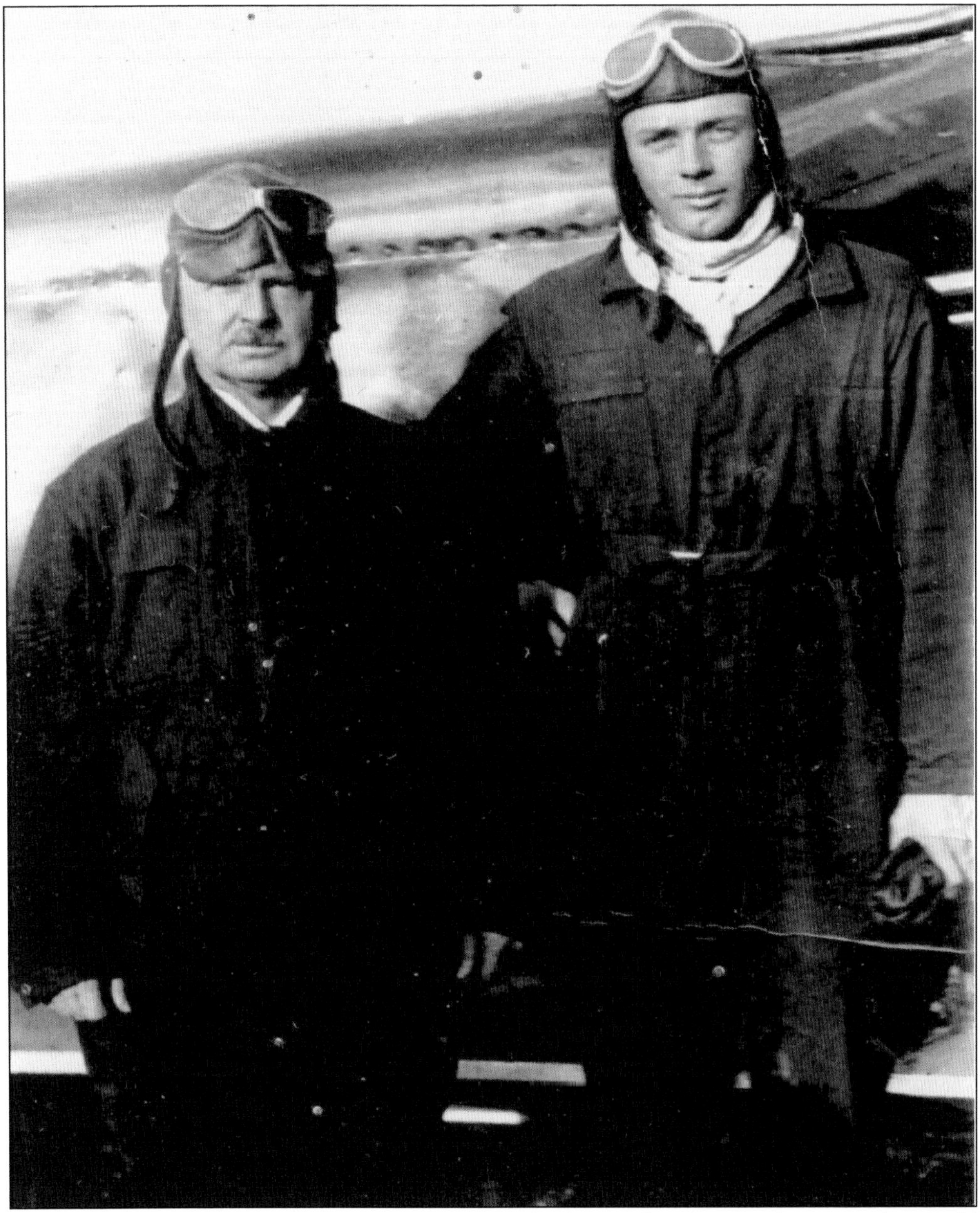

This picture of Thaddeus Sweet of Phoenix with Charles Lindbergh was taken at Boiling Field outside of Washington, D.C., when Sweet was in Congress. He was on the Ways and Means Committee and the Armed Forces Committee, and Lindbergh was trying to influence him to favor flight issues at the time. It worked. (Courtesy of Richard Huntley.)

In 1909, Thaddeus Sweet was elected to the New York State Assembly. He became speaker of the assembly in 1914. He received international notoriety in 1920 when, at the opening session, he refused to seat five members elected by the Socialist ticket from New York City. He was appointed to fill a vacancy in the U.S. House of Representatives after the death of Luther Mott in 1923. Sweet served until he was killed in an airplane crash in 1928. The U.S. Senate and House were closed on the day of his funeral, held in Phoenix. Sweet is shown at his post as speaker of the New York State Assembly. (Courtesy of Richard Huntley.)

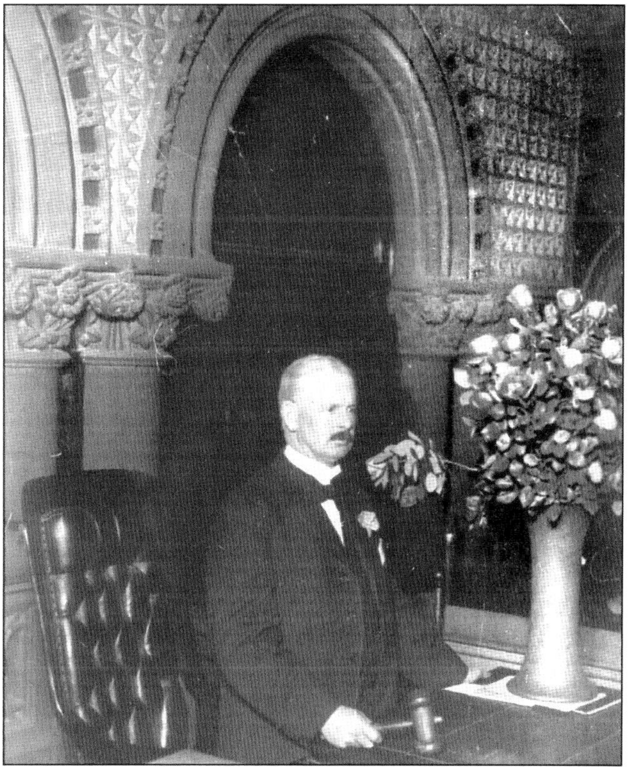

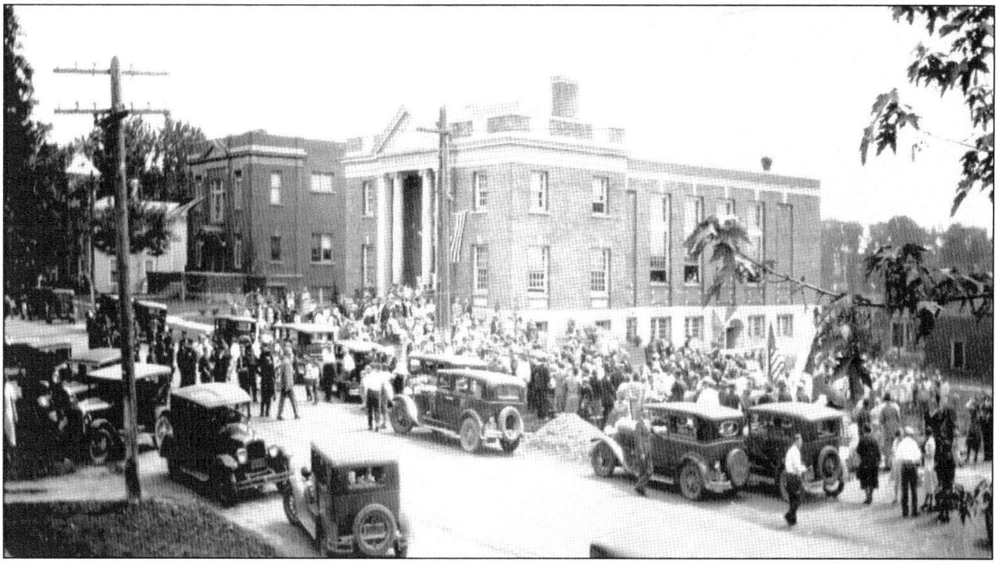

Before Thaddeus Sweet was killed in an airplane crash, he had established a fund for a community building. After his death, donations came from all over for a memorial. The memorial eventually became this community building known as the Sweet Memorial Building in Phoenix. The donations were combined with the existing fund, and plans were made to build a larger building. The building contains the village offices and an auditorium, with other areas that are available for public use. This photograph of the Sweet Memorial Building was taken during the 1933 Schroeppel centennial. (Courtesy of Lora and Doc Jones.)

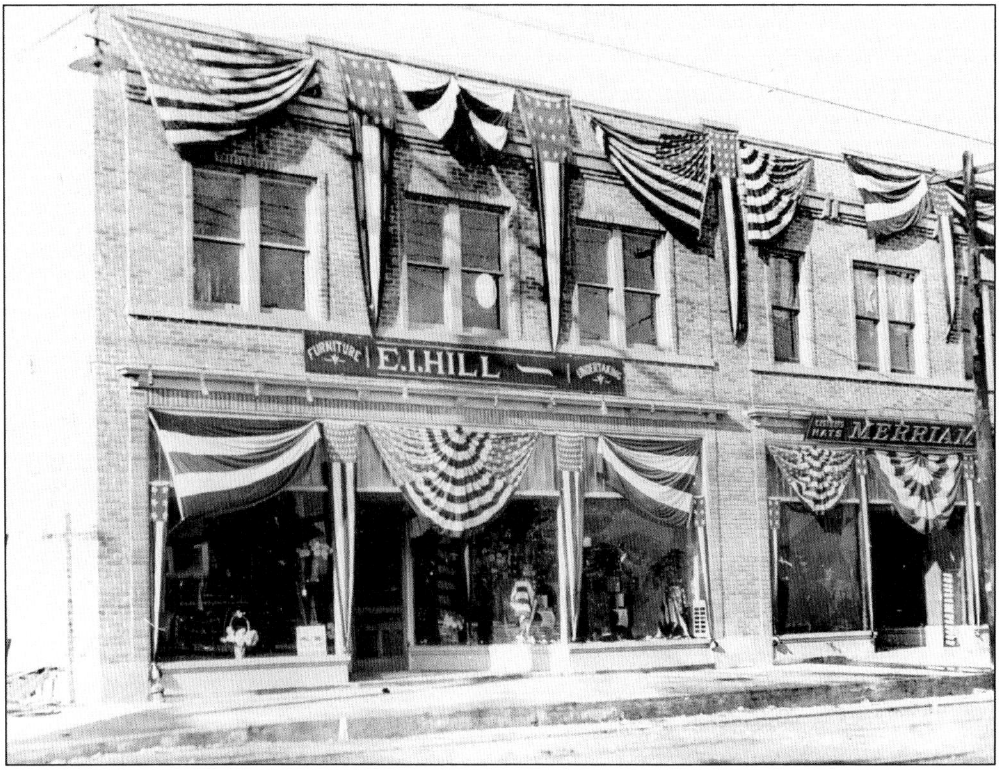

Shown are the E.I. Hill store and the Merriam store in Phoenix. (Courtesy of Richard Huntley.)

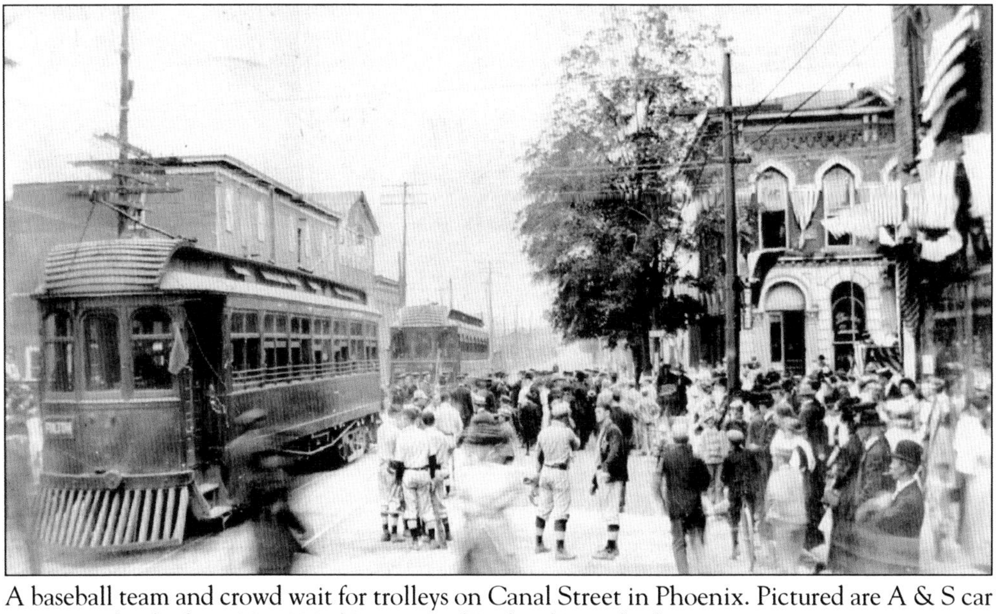

A baseball team and crowd wait for trolleys on Canal Street in Phoenix. Pictured are A & S car No. 56 and Lakeshore No. 202. (Courtesy of Richard Huntley.)

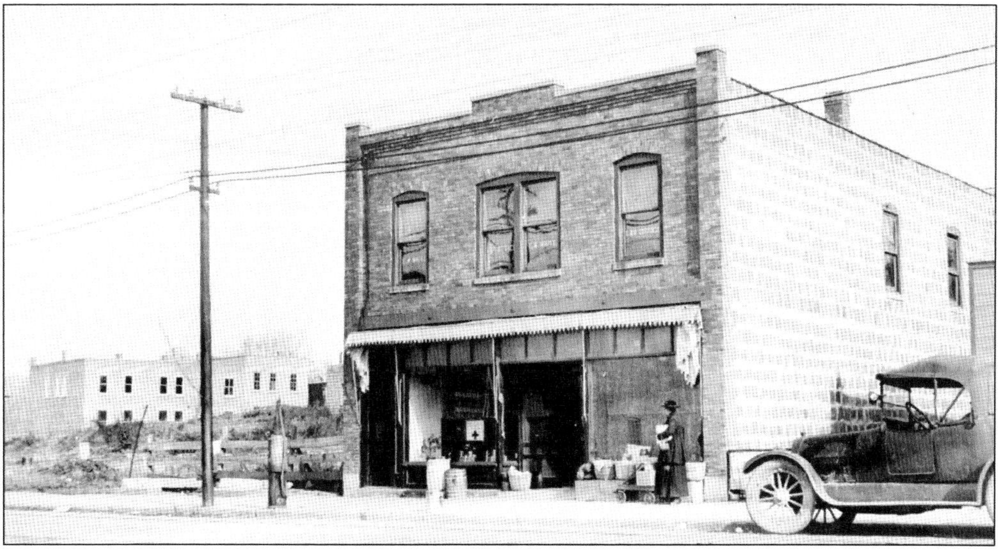

This is Potter's store in Phoenix. (Courtesy of Richard Huntley.)

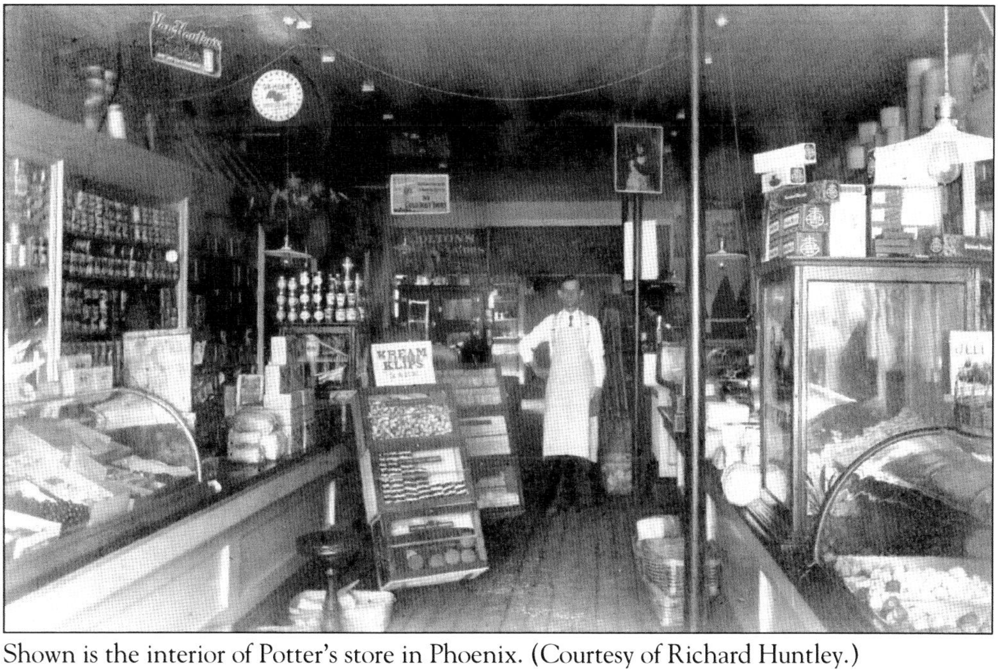

Shown is the interior of Potter's store in Phoenix. (Courtesy of Richard Huntley.)

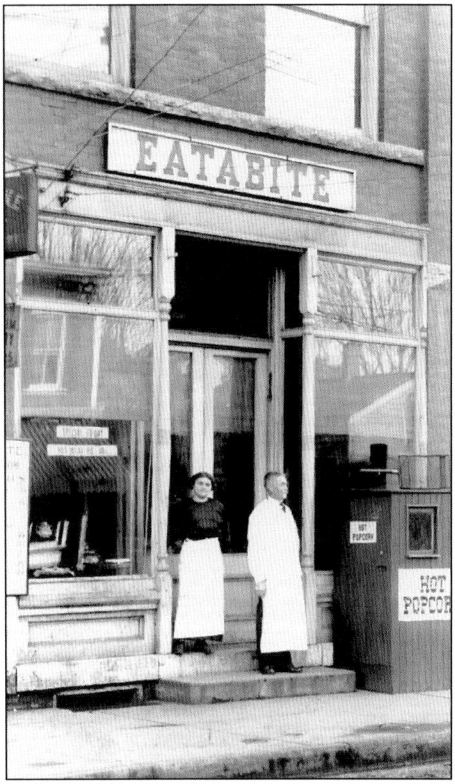

The Eatabite restaurant in Phoenix is pictured here. (Courtesy of Richard Huntley.)

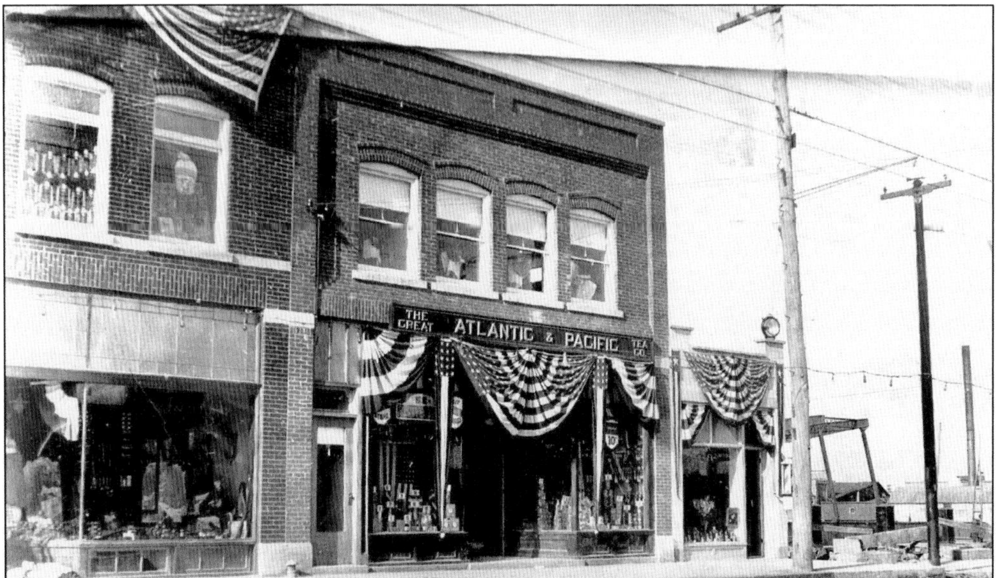

Pictured is the Atlantic & Pacific store (A & P) in Phoenix. (Photograph by R.S. Kellar, courtesy of Richard Huntley.)

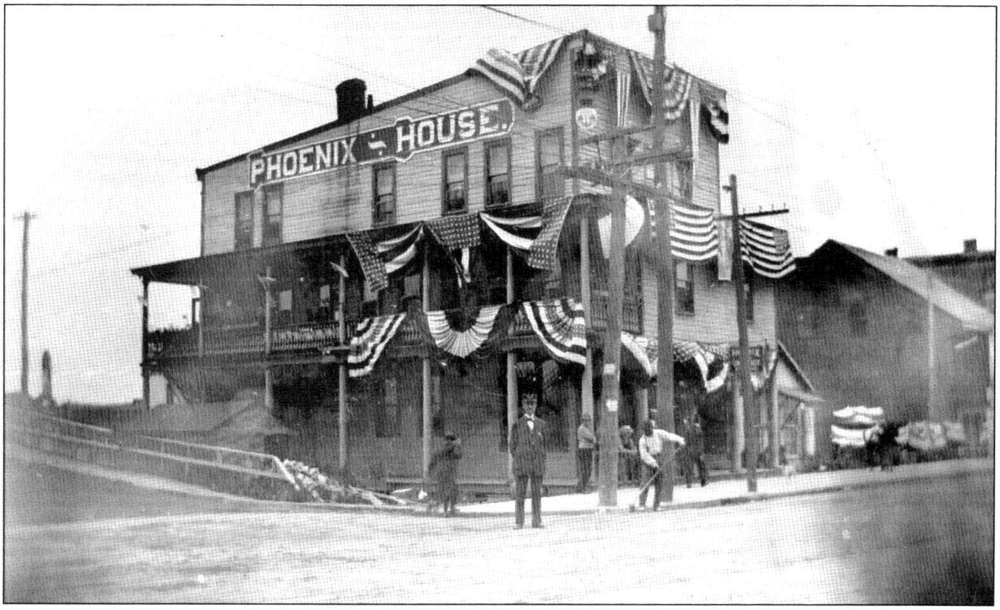

The Phoenix House is shown here. (Courtesy of Richard Huntley.)

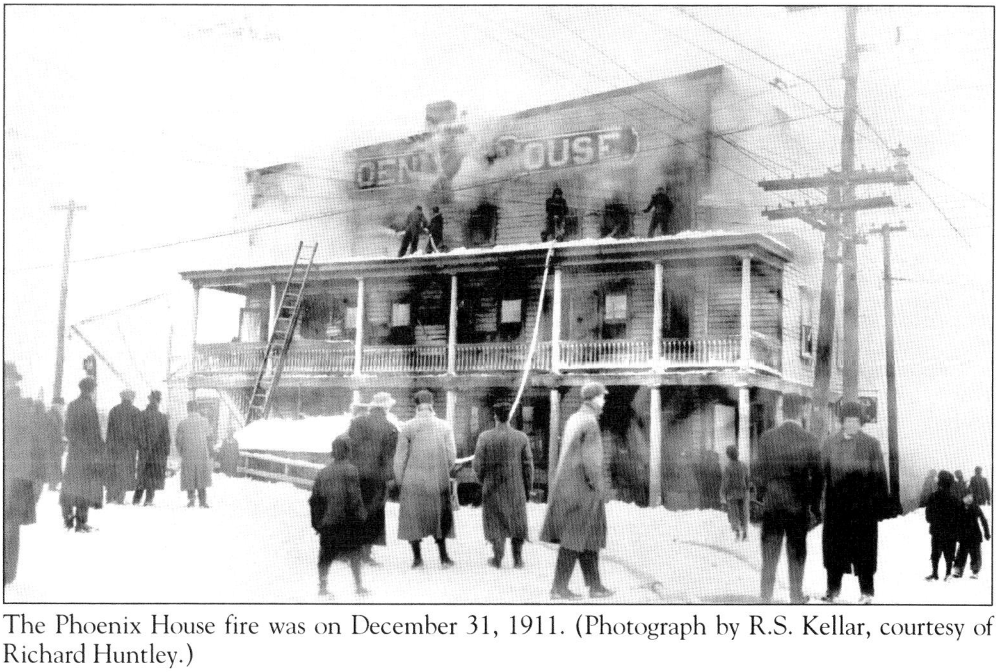
The Phoenix House fire was on December 31, 1911. (Photograph by R.S. Kellar, courtesy of Richard Huntley.)

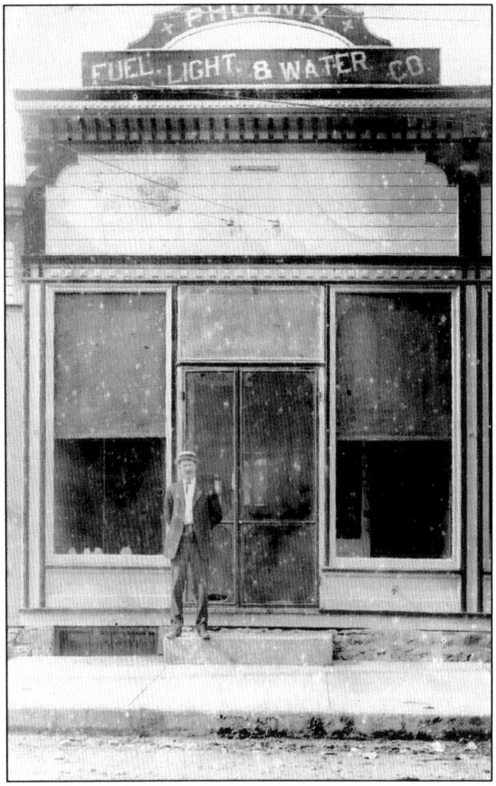

The Phoenix Fuel, Light & Water Company is pictured here. (Courtesy of Richard Huntley.)

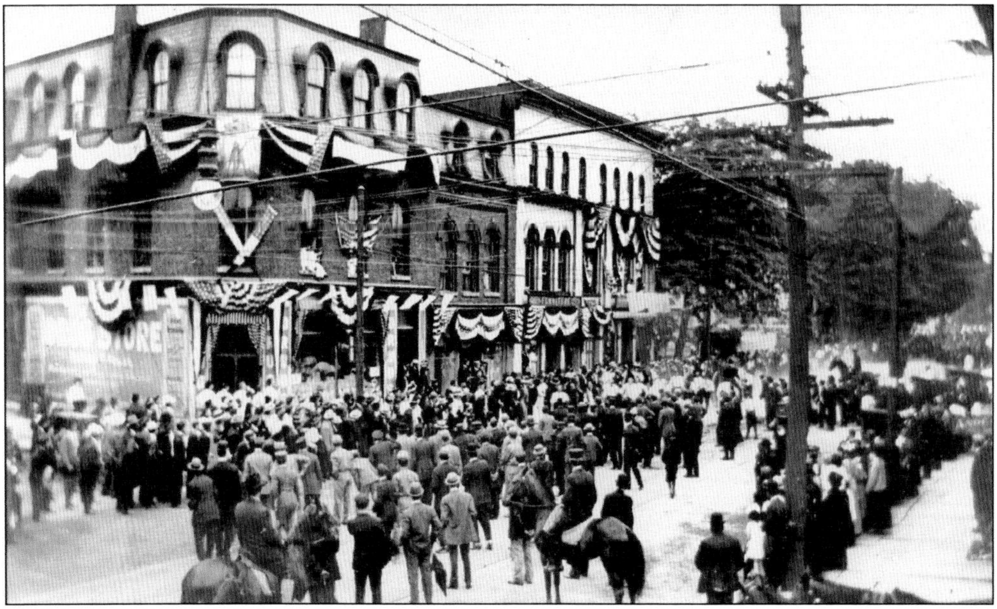

Shown is a crowd gathered on Canal Street in Phoenix for the Firemen's Convention. (Courtesy of Richard Huntley.)

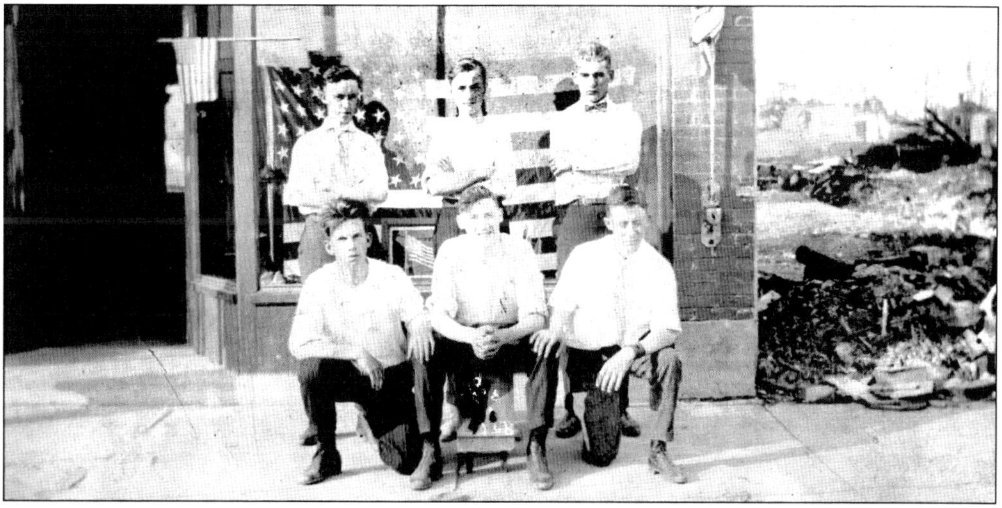

The New York State Cannon Brigade is pictured in Phoenix *c.* 1917. From left to right are the following: (front row) Royce Huntley, Myles Ragan, and Franklin Van Auken; (back row) Bert Van Auken, William Thompson, and Robert Fish. (Courtesy of Richard Huntley.)

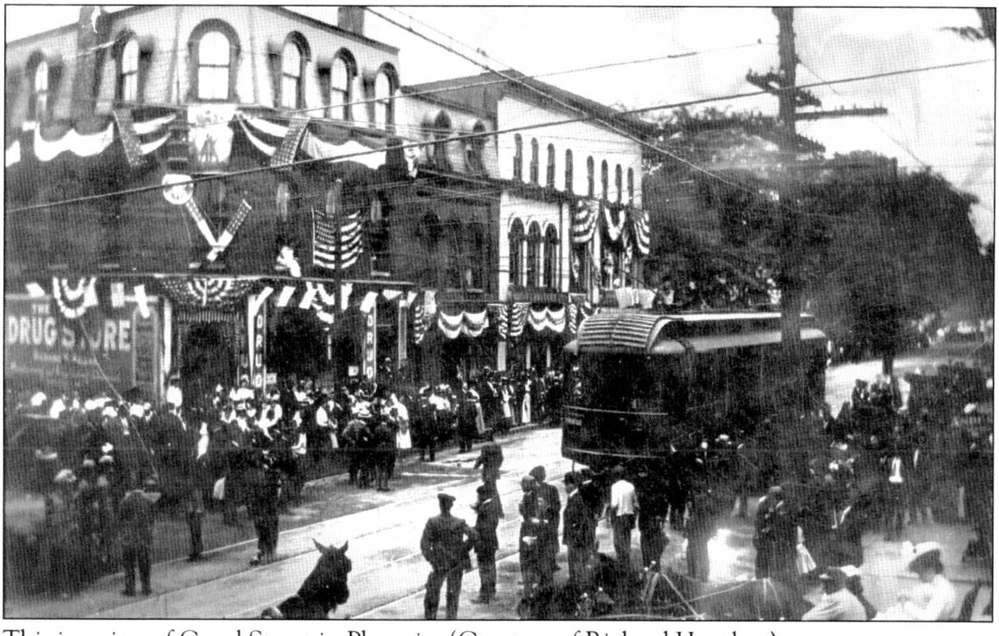

This is a view of Canal Street in Phoenix. (Courtesy of Richard Huntley.)

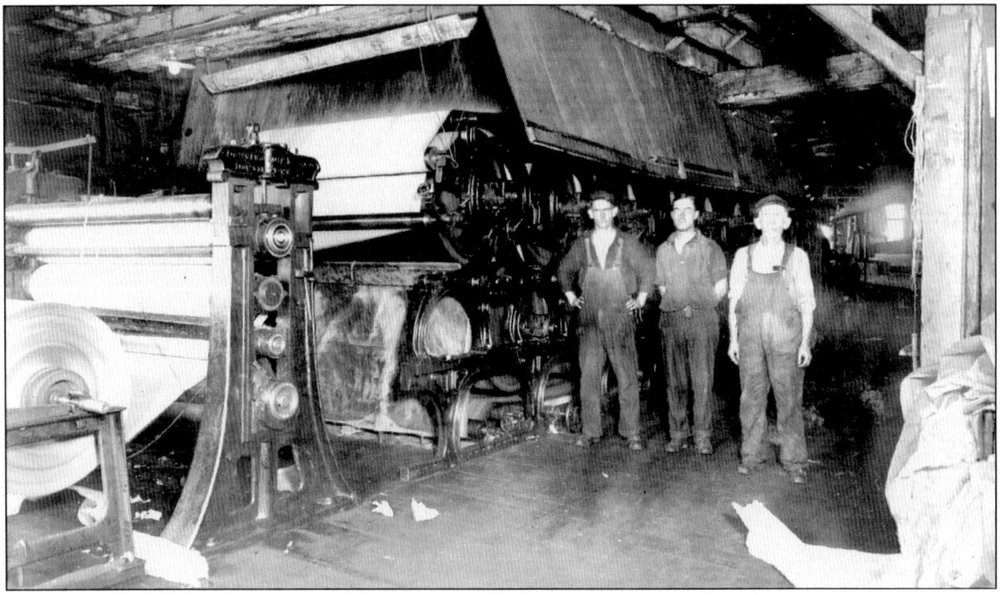

This is the interior of one of four paper mills in Phoenix that ran day and night, except on Sundays. The four mills were the Oswego River Paper Company, the Phoenix Tissue Paper Company, the Phoenix Toilet and Paper Company, and Sweet Brothers Paper Manufacturing Company. Harold Slade, another Phoenix inventor, invented the first machine to wrap toilet paper on a roll with perforated sheets. Before his invention, the work was done by hand. (Courtesy of Richard Huntley.)

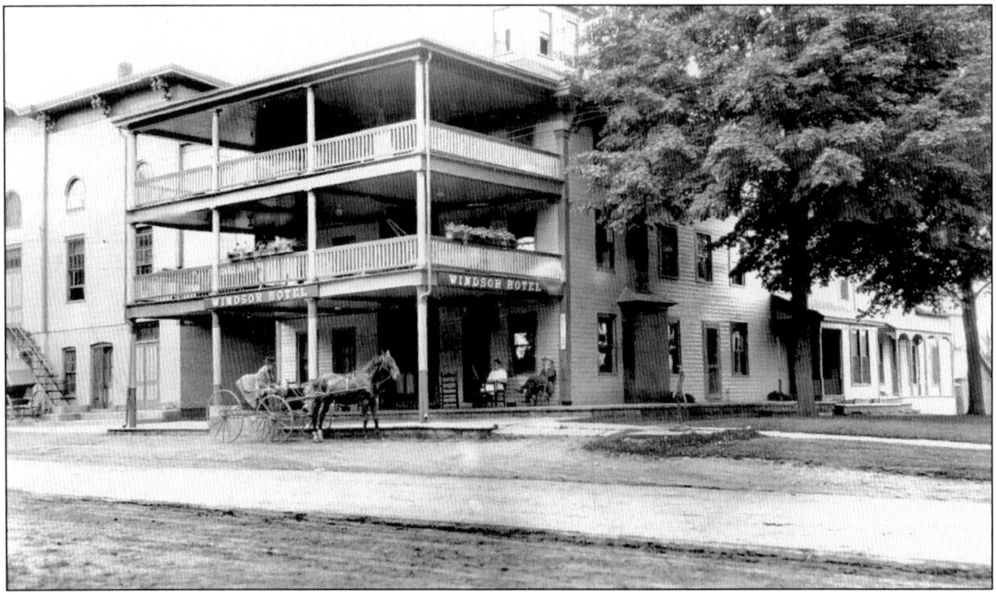

Commencement exercises for the Phoenix Academy were held in the Windsor Opera House, in Phoenix, in the late 1880s. (Photograph by R.S. Kellar, courtesy of Lora and Doc Jones.)

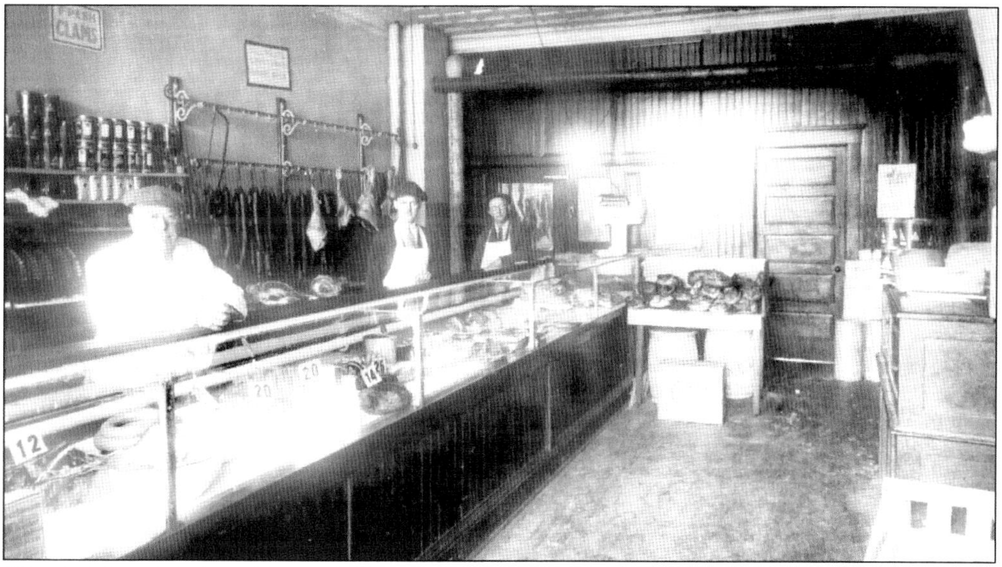

Woods Meat Market (Formerly George C. Wood & Son) was the longest continuously operating business in Phoenix (1872–1995) and the first in central New York to use mechanical refrigeration. From left to right are George Wood, Jack Spencer, and Albert Huntley. In 1872, Herbert Wood founded the business on Canal Street (now State Street). In 1883, his brother George Wood took over the management of the meat market, assisted by his son Robert Wood, who took over the market in 1935. The Wood family had its own recipes for making what was called "Wood's goods." Wood's bologna, hams, sausage, and other products were known from coast to coast. In 1957, the business was sold to Kenneth DenBleyker, who had worked at the market since he was 12 years old. Wood's Meat Market closed on November 22, 1995. It was known as the oldest customer of the Hofmann Brothers Meat Packing Company of Syracuse. (Courtesy of Joan [Wood] and Robert Coulter.)

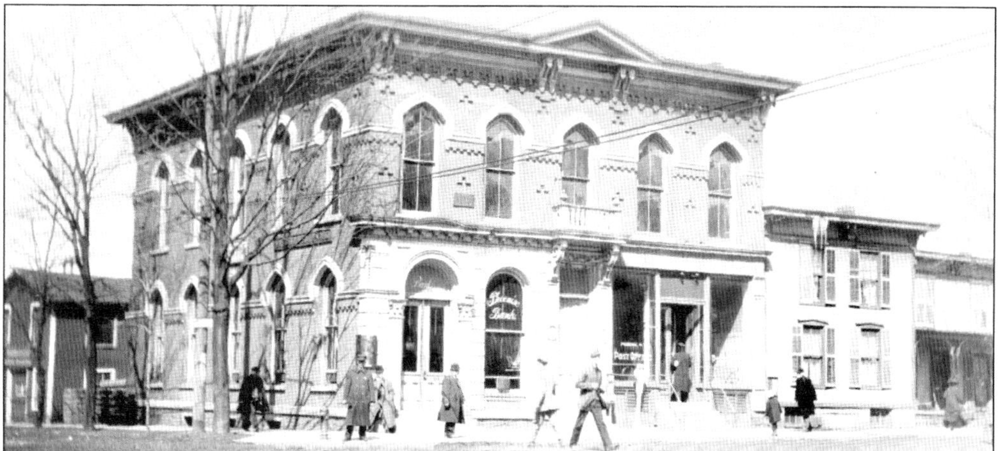

The Phoenix Bank and the post office are shown here. The bank was organized on March 1, 1869. The first banking quarters were the two front rooms of the Diefendorf & Allen store, which sold groceries and general merchandise. On January 21, 1873, the bank moved to the Betts Block. The building burned in the 1916 fire. The cornerstone for the new building was laid in 1917. Operated by different banking companies over the years, the bank closed on June 6, 2003.

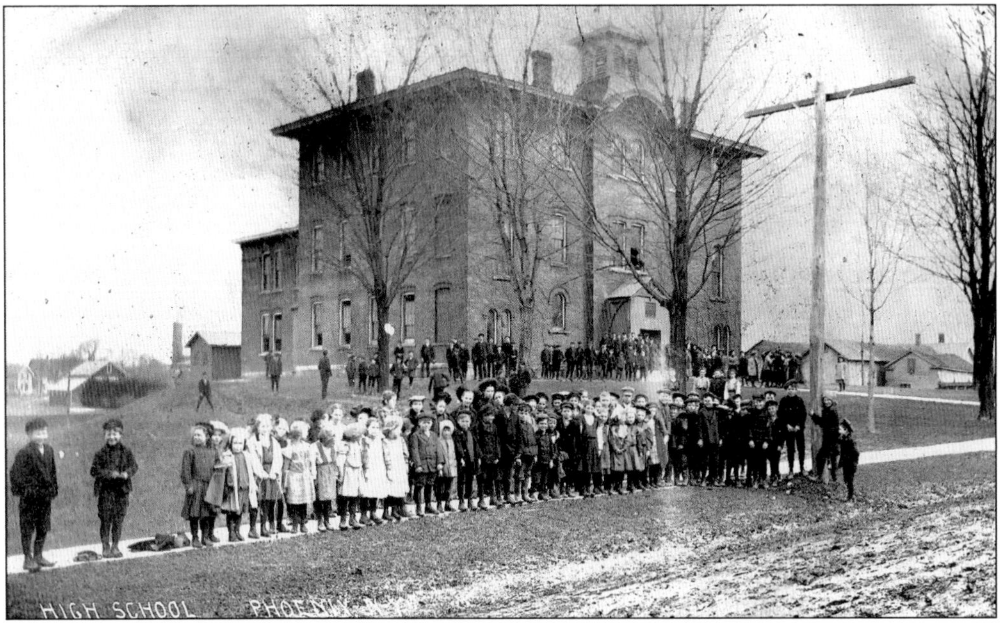

Shown is Phoenix High School on Cherry Street in Phoenix.

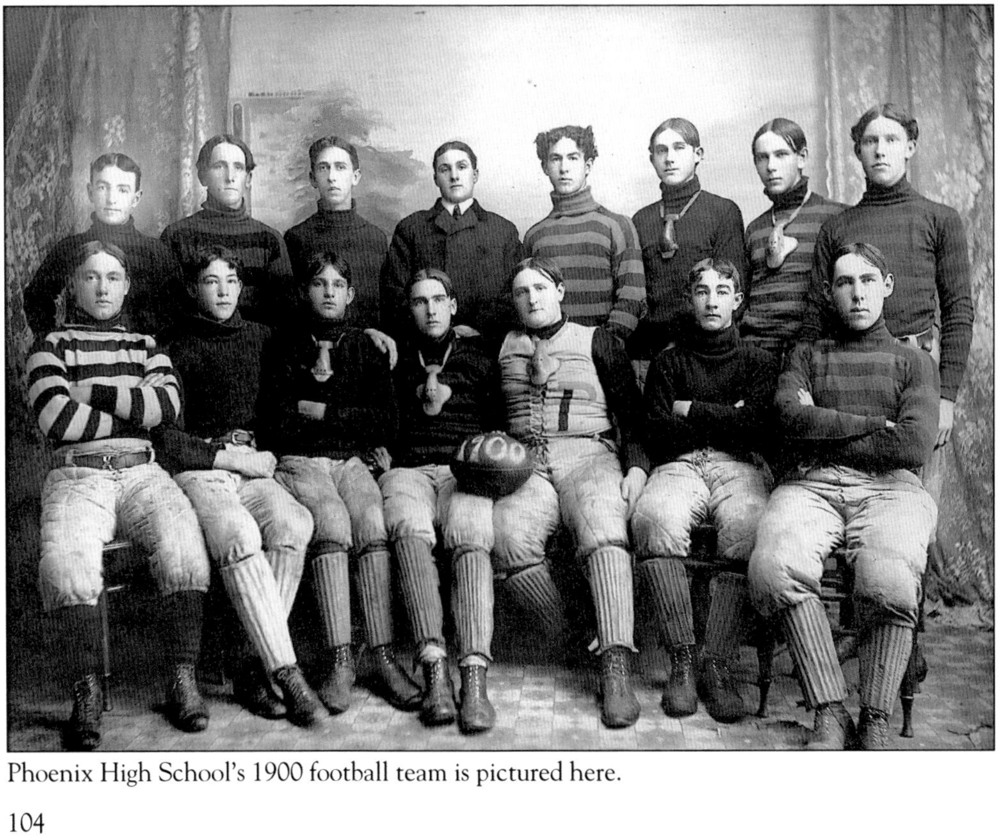

Phoenix High School's 1900 football team is pictured here.

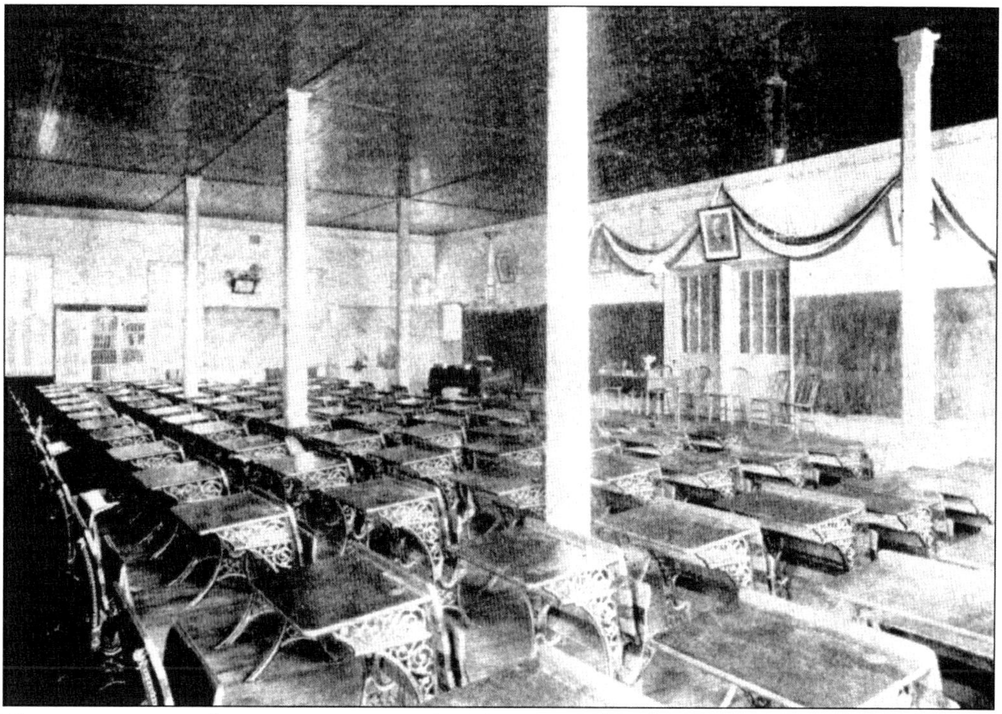

The senior primary department is pictured at Phoenix High School on Cherry Street in Phoenix in 1900. (Courtesy of Frances Chesbro.)

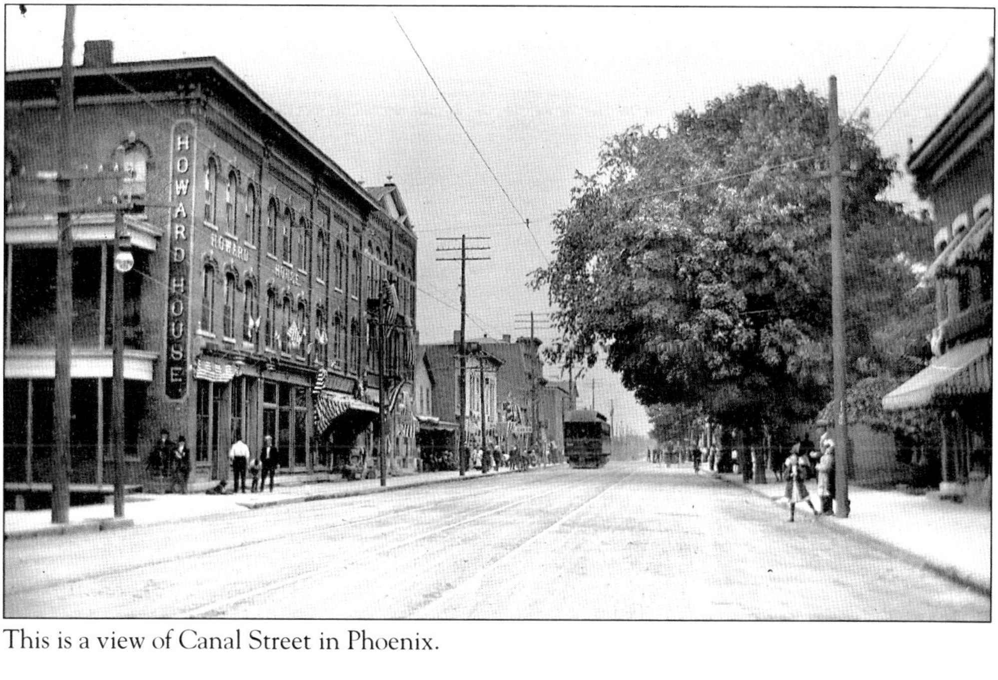

This is a view of Canal Street in Phoenix.

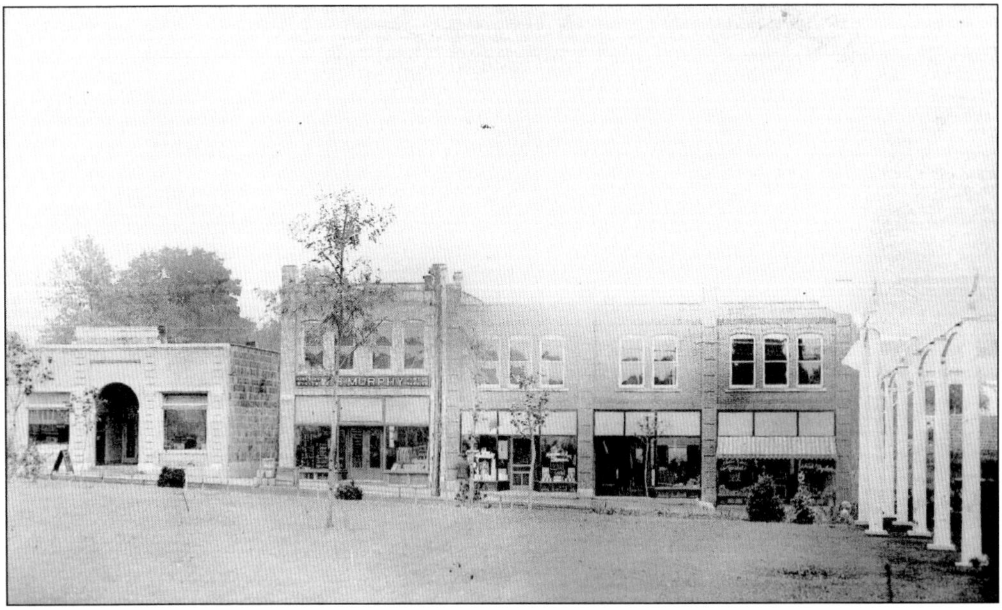

This is a view of Bridge Street in Phoenix. The columns (right) are part of a garden that was located on the north side of the street about where the Phoenix Primary Care is today.

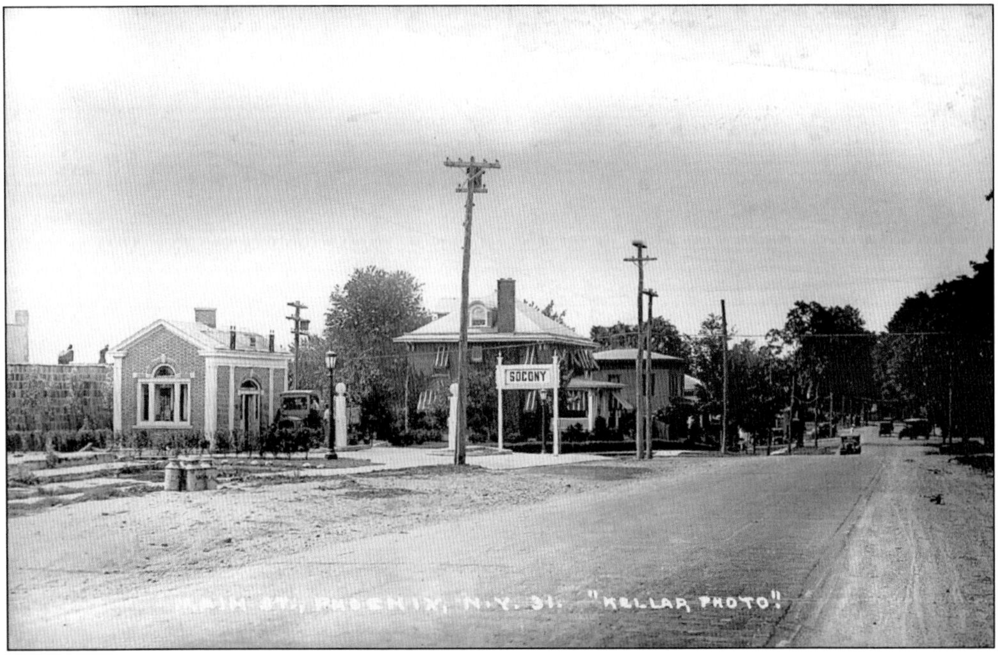

This is an early view of Main Street in Phoenix.

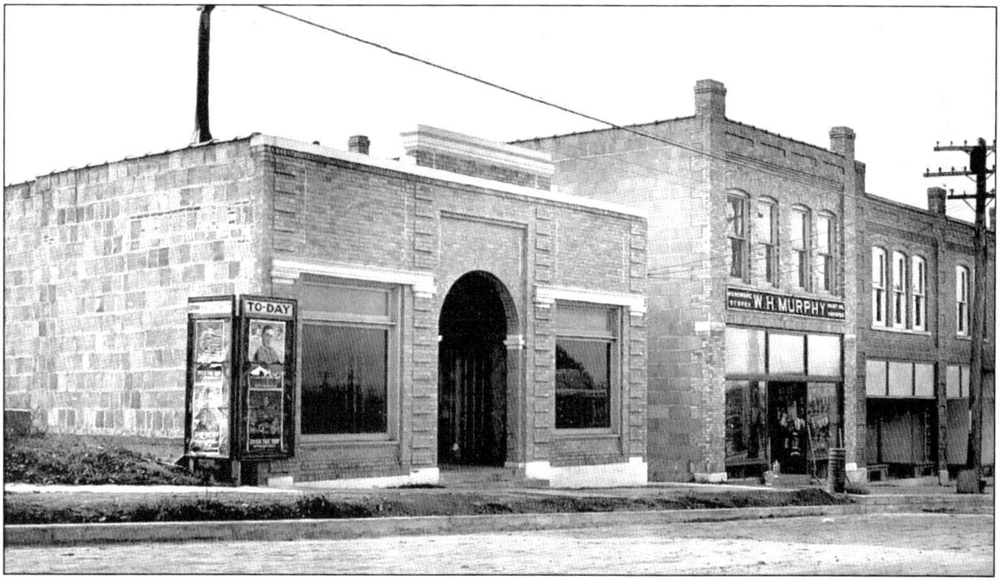

The Phoenix Theater (left) is pictured on Bridge Street, next to W.H. Murphy.

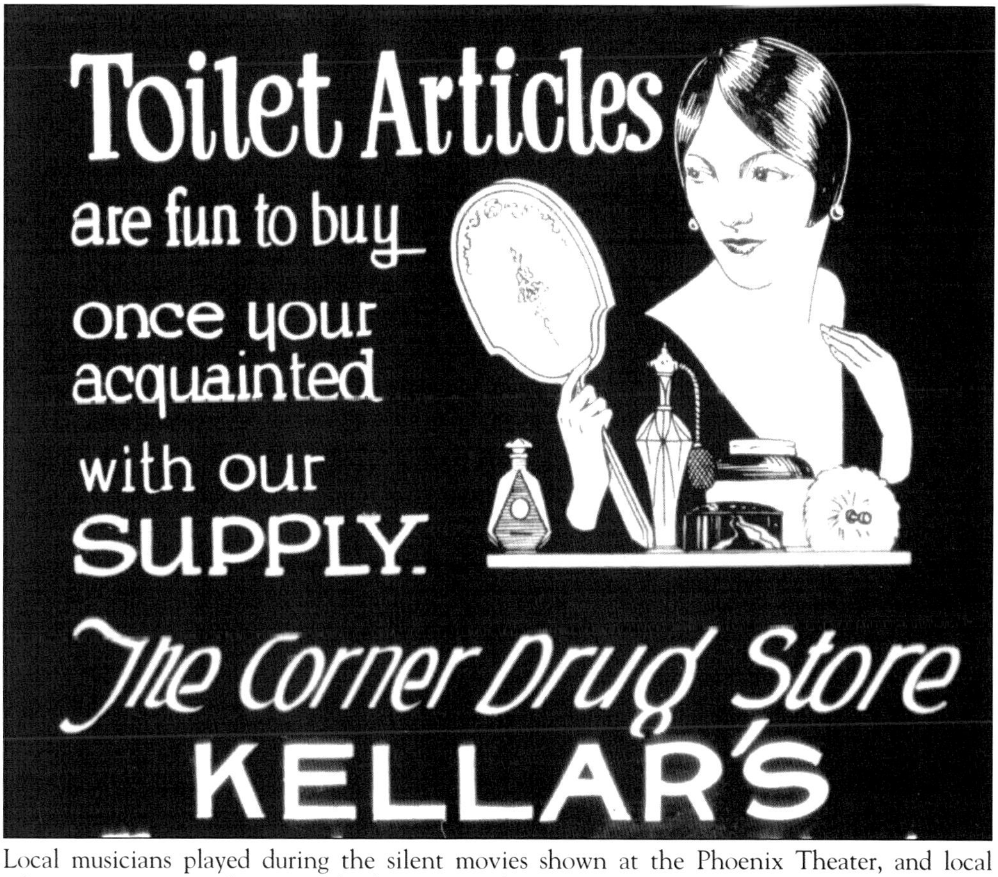

Local musicians played during the silent movies shown at the Phoenix Theater, and local advertisements were shown on the large screen by projecting slides. This print from an original Phoenix Theater slide advertises Kellar's Drug Store. (Courtesy of Richard Huntley.)

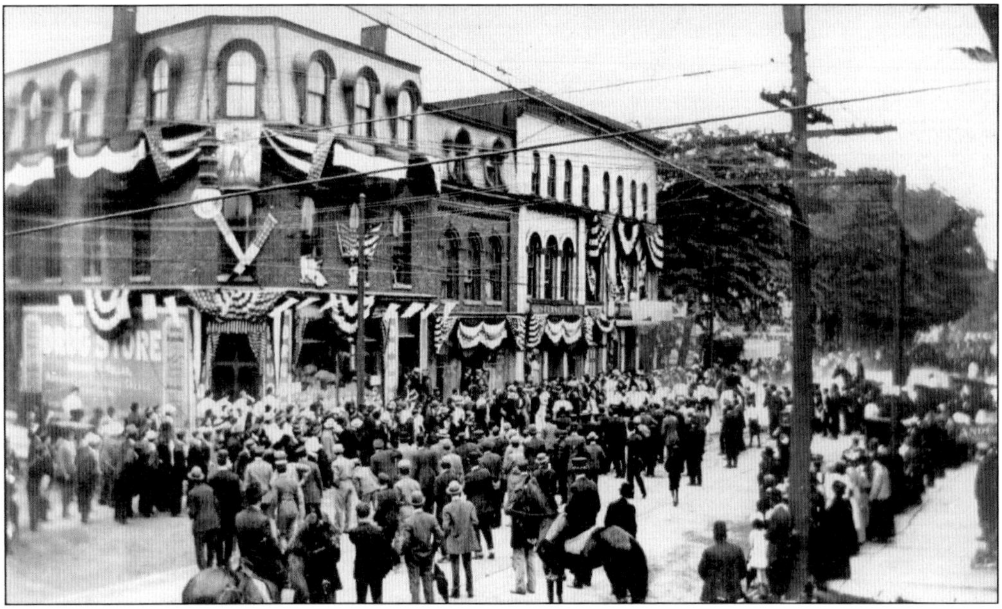

Canal Street in Phoenix is pictured during a Firemen's Convention *c.* 1908. Kellar's Drug Store is on the corner. This photograph shows the original three-story store. (Courtesy of Richard Huntley.)

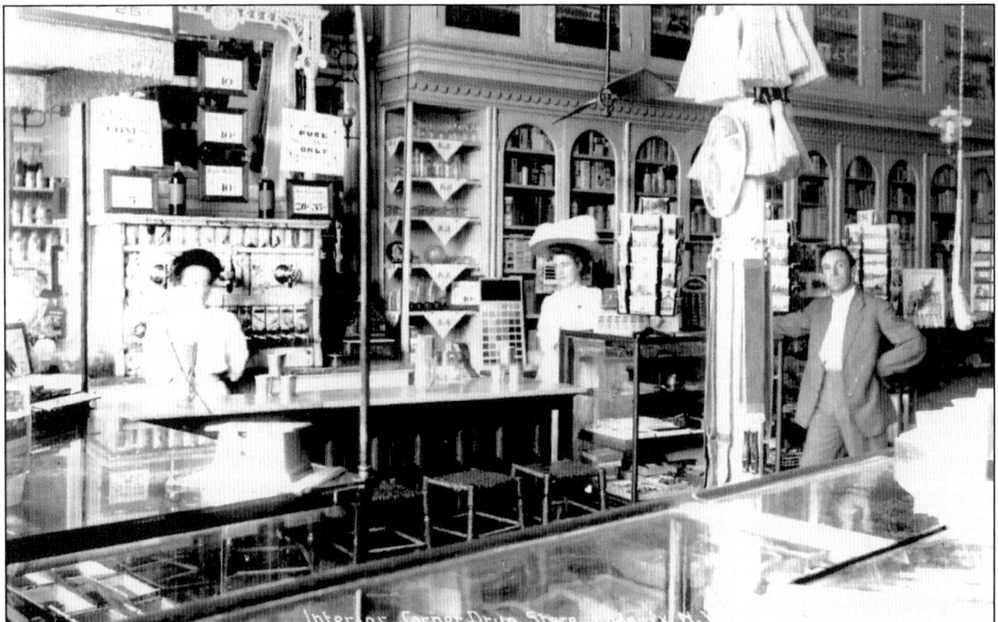

This interior photograph of Kellar's Drug Store shows the soda fountain of the early 1900s. Richard Kellar also sold photographic postcards of the local area. It is said that he took the photographs himself and that he printed the cards in the basement of the store. They are marked "Kellar Photos" and collected today as valuable pieces of local history. (Courtesy of Richard Huntley.)

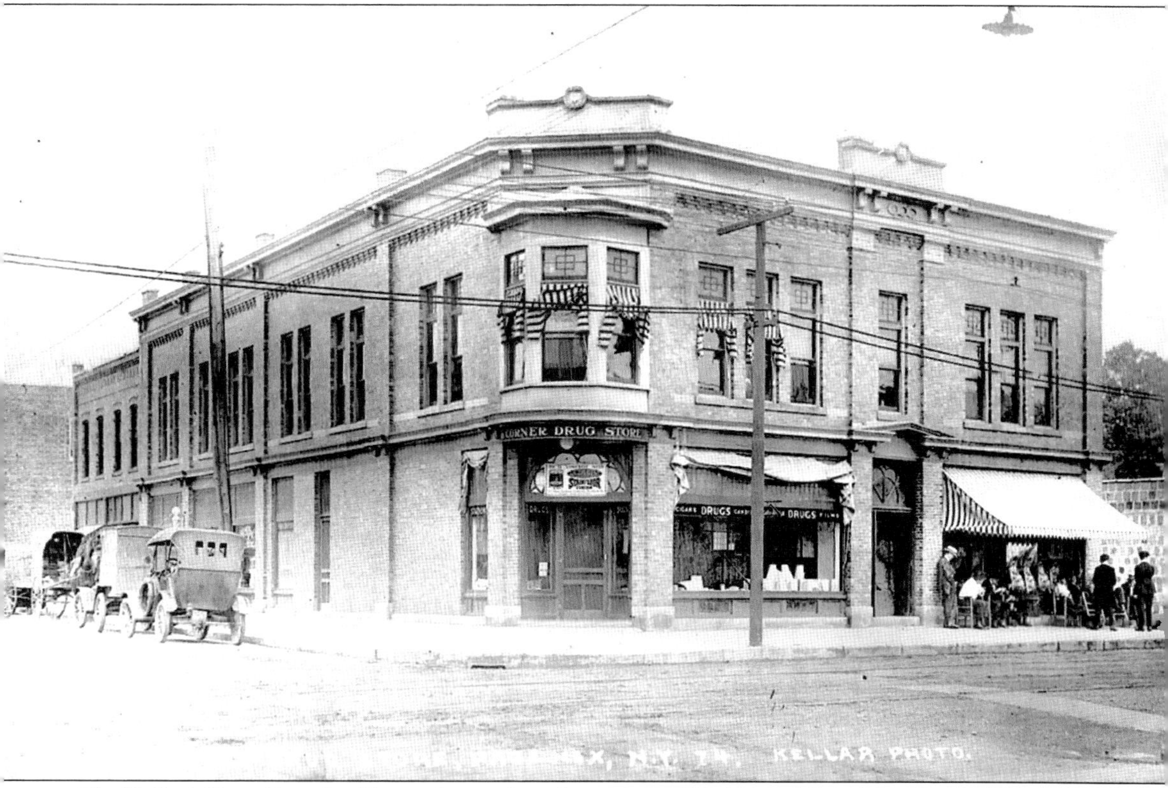

The Kellar's Drug Store building is located on the corner of Bridge and Canal Streets in Phoenix. Shown is the two-story building that replaced the three-story Kellar's that burned in the fire of 1916. It was known in later years as the Botting Drug Store and the Phoenix Pharmacy, owned by Mr. Kinney. Still standing today, it is one of the few historic buildings left in the business section of Phoenix. However, since the building is vacant and in poor condition, its fate is uncertain.

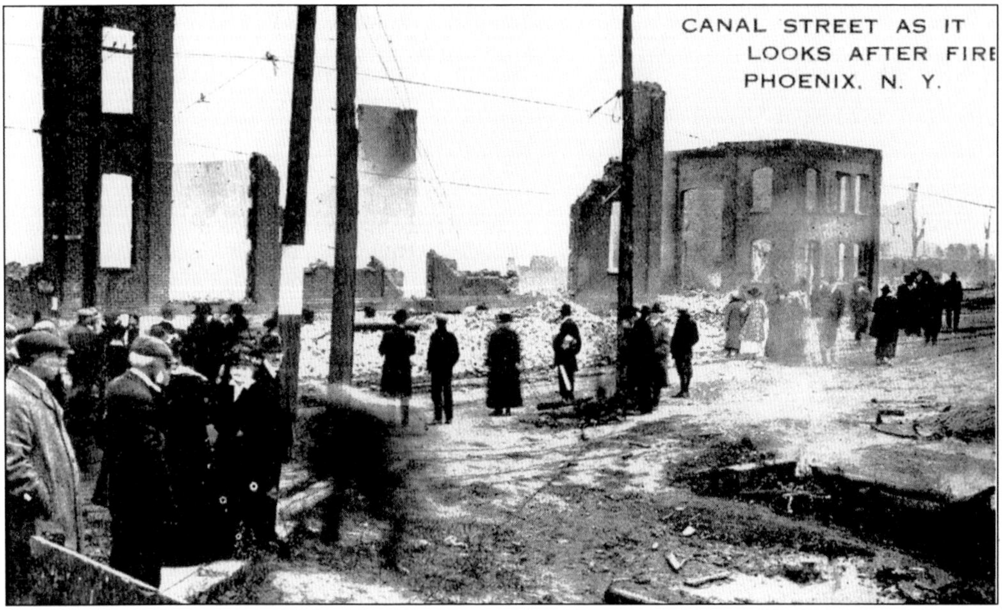

On Saturday night, September 23, 1916, most of the business section of Phoenix was destroyed by a fire that started from sparks from a generator in the Sinclair Chair Factory. It was the largest of three major fires that destroyed portions of the business and manufacturing districts, beginning with the first fire in February 1850, when the Hart & Bentley Tannery burned.

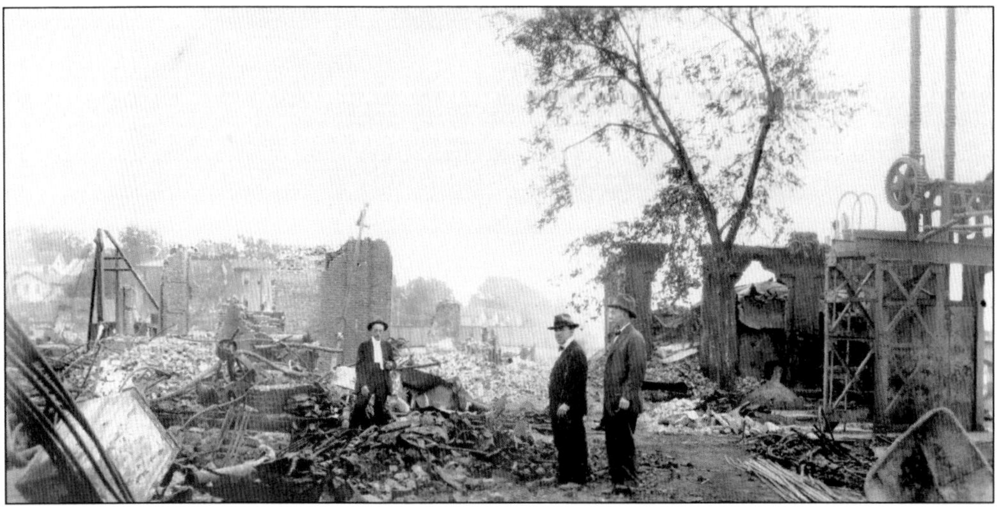

The M.C. Ryan plant is shown after the Phoenix fire.

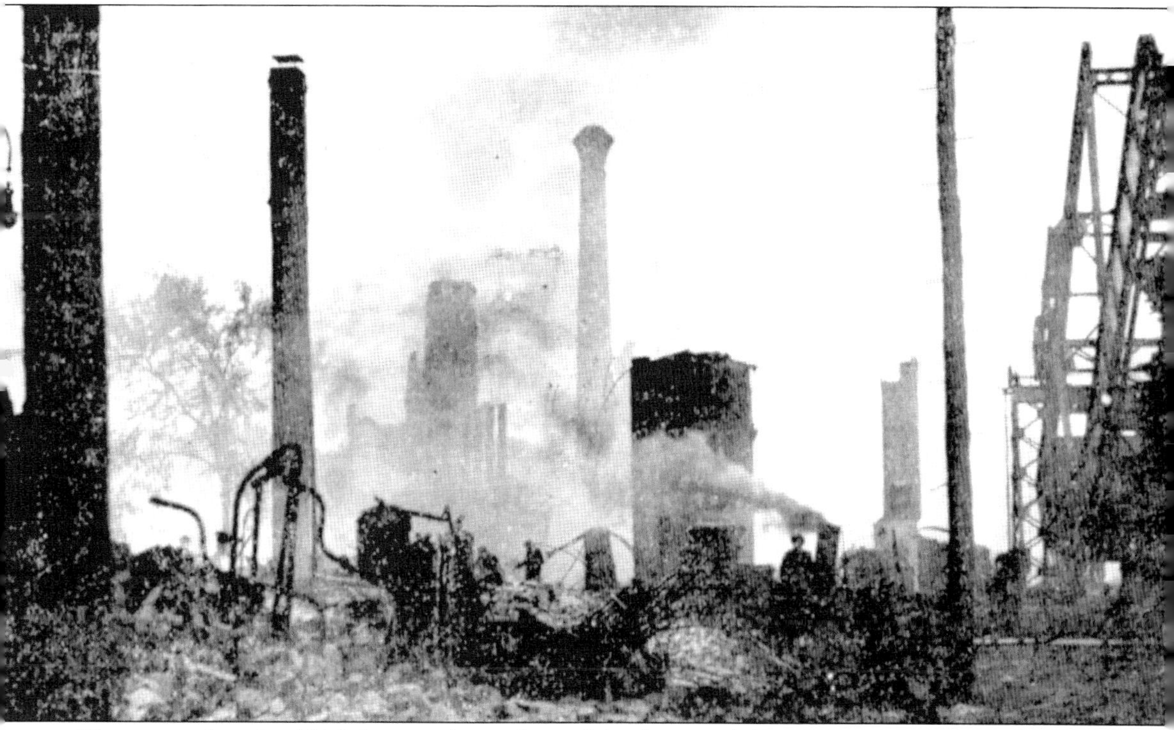

The ruins after the 1916 fire are shown here. The fire raged for 15 hours. James Goodwin, a 72-year-old inventor, was the only person to die in the fire. He reentered his room on the upper floor of the Parker Feed Mill to retrieve his patent papers for the chainless bicycle he had invented. He became trapped, and as rescuers where driven back by the heat and flames, they heard him cry out through the thick smoke, "Save yourselves boys, it's too late to get me out and I'm old and about done for. Go I tell you, go and save yourselves, I'm all in."

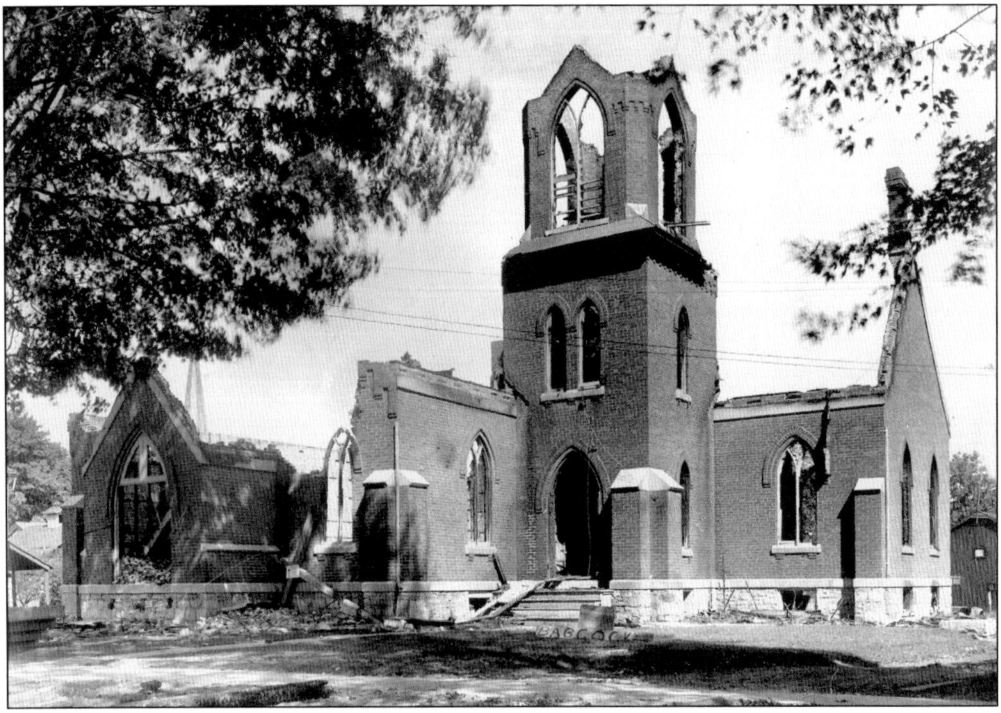

The Baptist church was in ruins after the Phoenix fire.

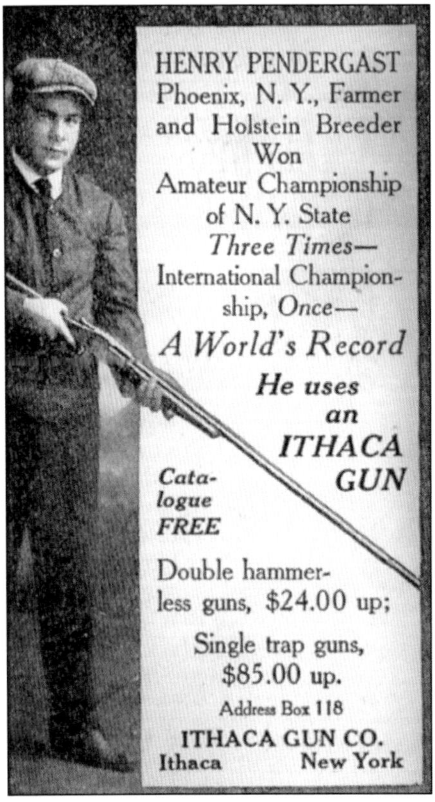

Henry Pendergast's marksmanship earned him a spot in Ithaca Gun Company advertisements. Pendergast appears in this 1917 ad.

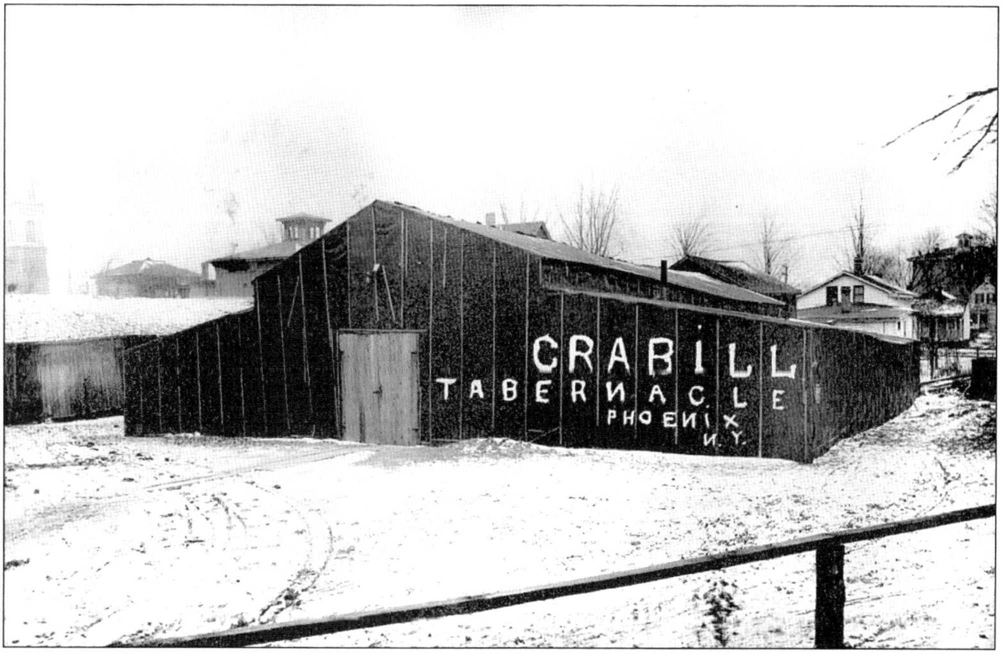

This view shows the Crabill Tabernacle in Phoenix.

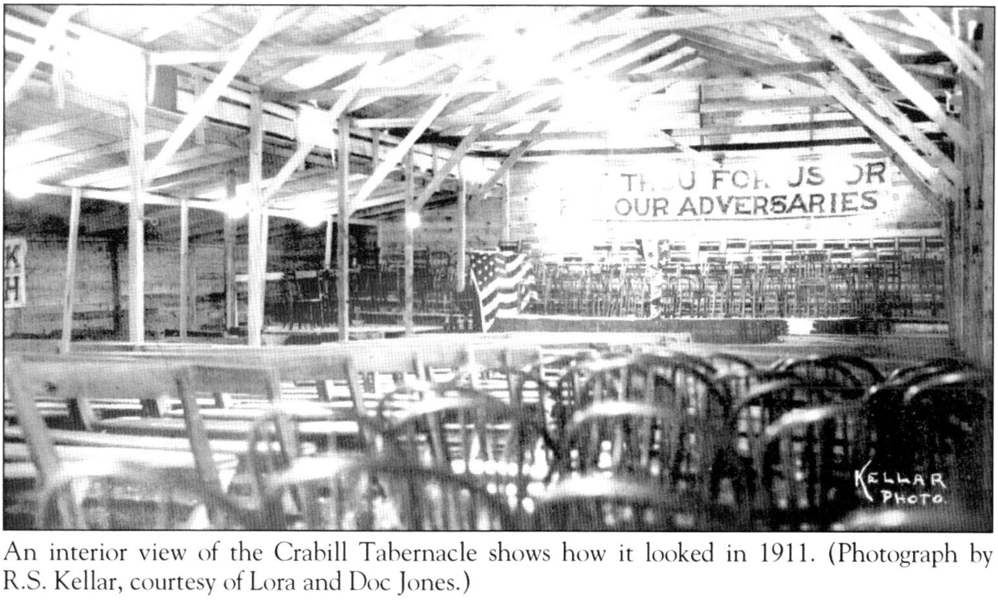

An interior view of the Crabill Tabernacle shows how it looked in 1911. (Photograph by R.S. Kellar, courtesy of Lora and Doc Jones.)

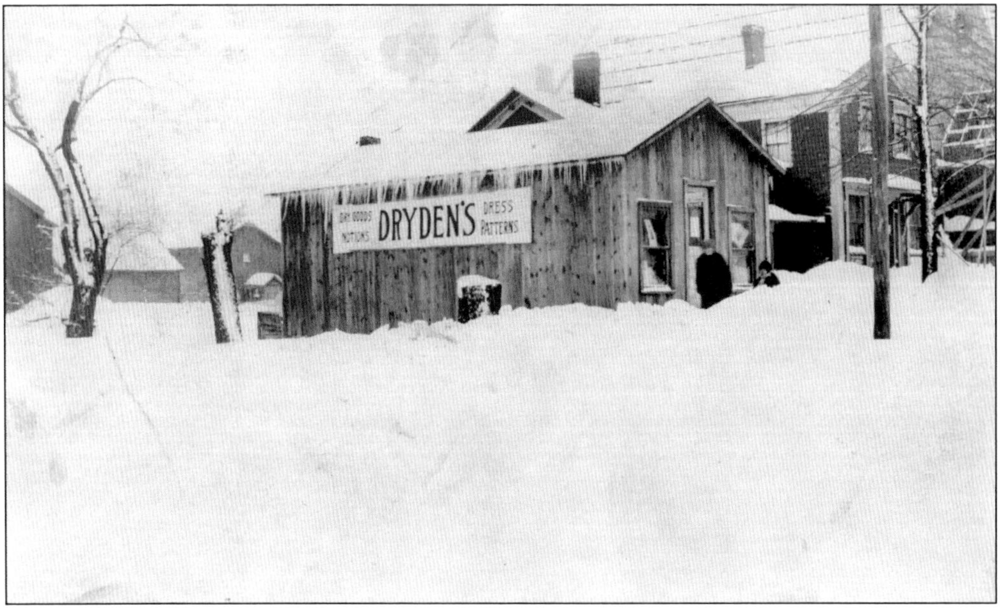

Bertha Dryden's temporary store is shown following the Phoenix fire of 1916. The store sold dry goods, notions, and dress patterns. The ruins of the Baptist church are in the background. (Courtesy of Richard Huntley.)

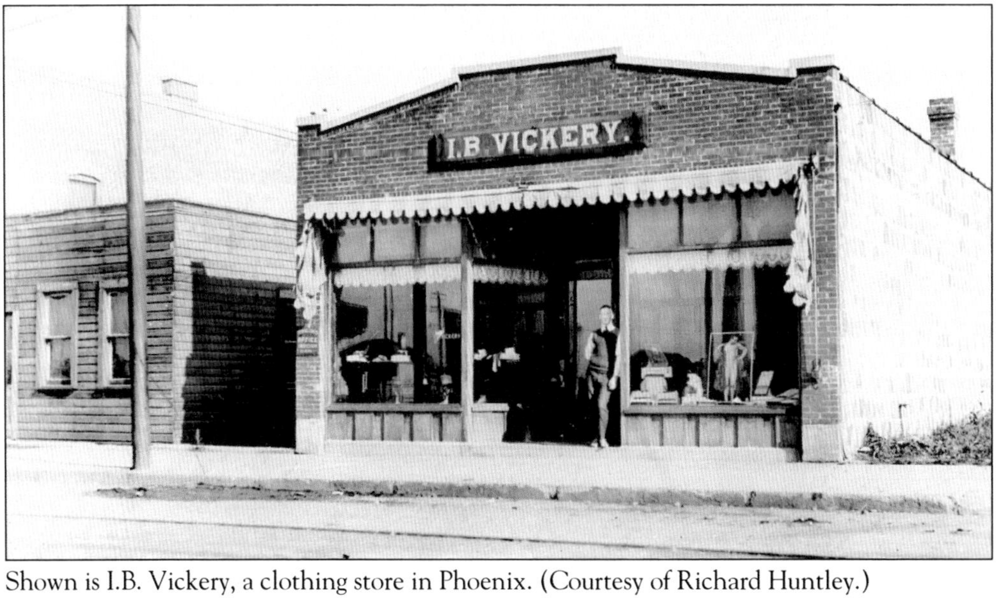

Shown is I.B. Vickery, a clothing store in Phoenix. (Courtesy of Richard Huntley.)

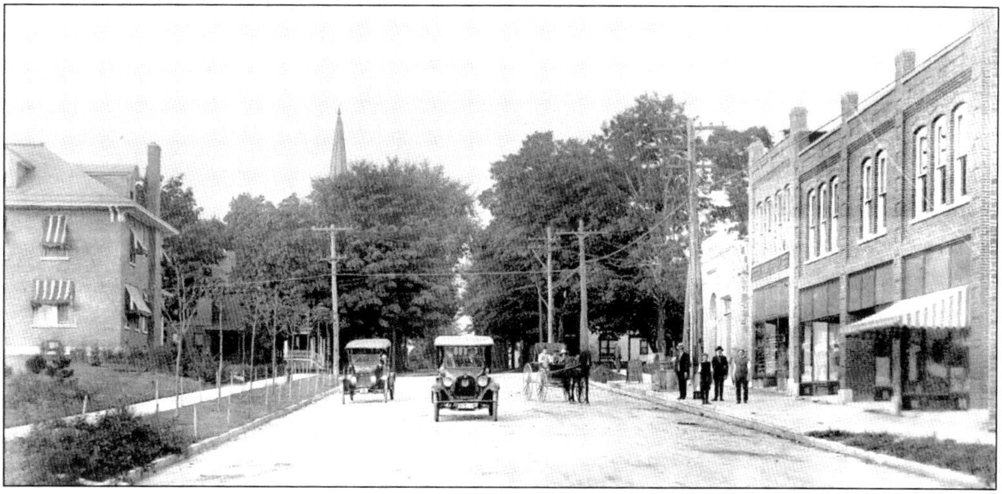

This is an early view of Bridge Street in Phoenix.

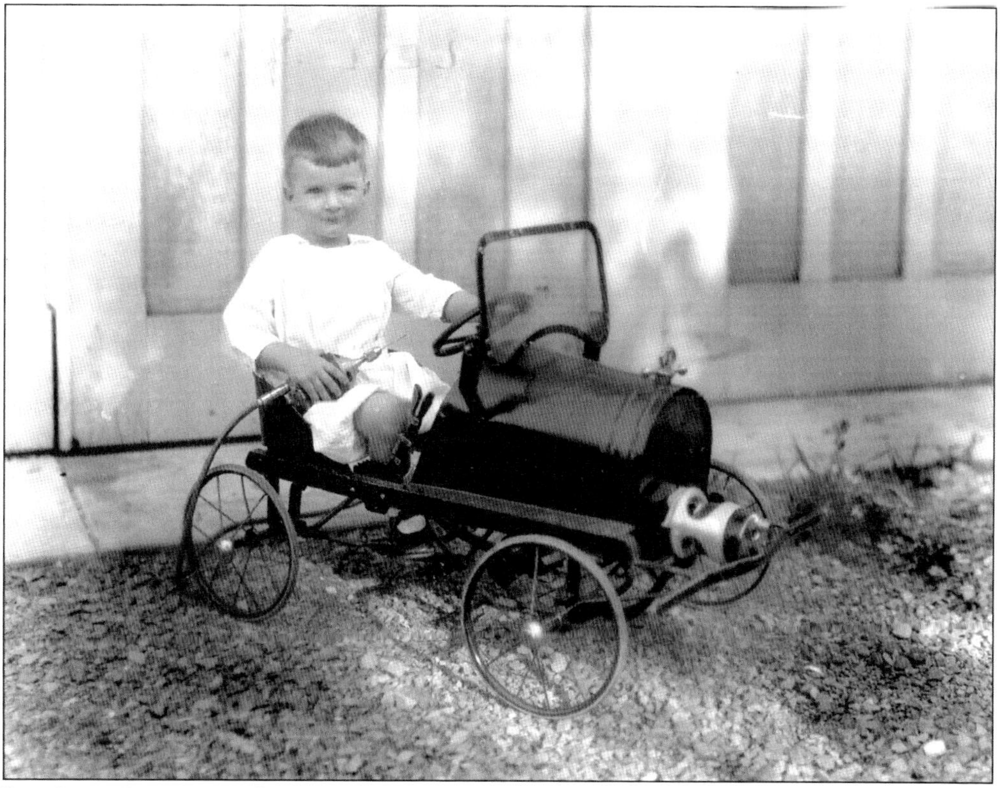

Ray Carter Jr. is pictured *c.* 1925 or 1926. The front of his car has a router motor from the R.L. Carter Company in Phoenix. His father, Ray L. Carter Sr., invented the router, the Carter Aerial Grinder, and many other tools at his tool company. All the patents and the business were eventually sold to Stanley Works, the maker of Stanley Tools, in 1929. Roy Carter Sr. was also the head of Revere Products in Phoenix for a while. (Courtesy of Richard Huntley.)

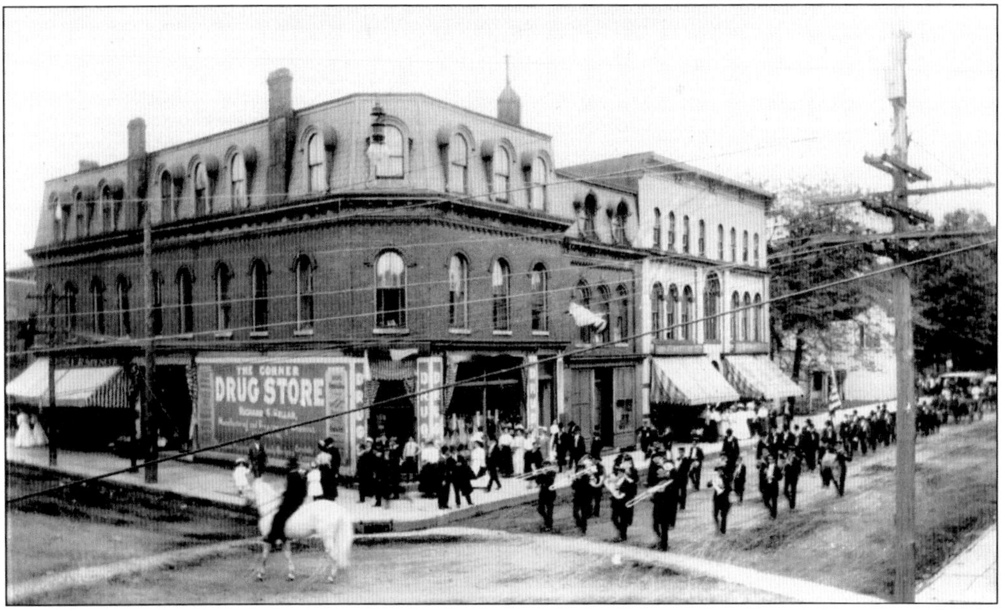

The Memorial Day parade marches on Canal Street in Phoenix. (Photograph by R.S. Kellar.)

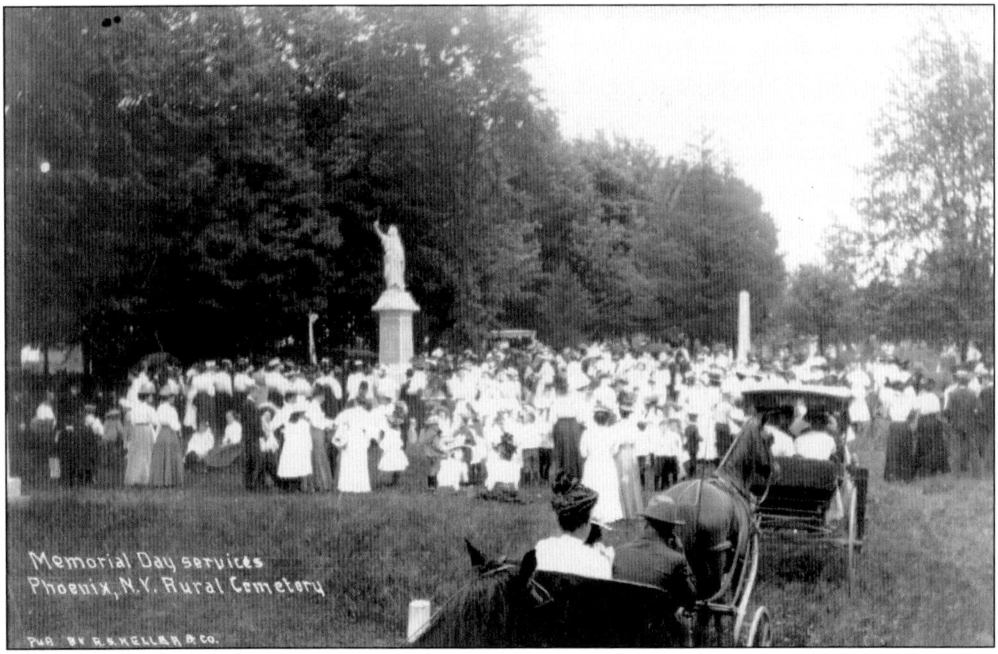

Memorial Day services take place at the Phoenix Rural Cemetery. In the early years, Memorial Day events included a picnic lunch and socializing at the cemetery following the services. Parades and services were held at both Pennellville and Phoenix throughout most of Schroeppel's history until the 1960s, when the Phoenix High School band was no longer allowed to come to Pennellville. After a couple of years of makeshift parades without the band, the Pennellville parades ended. (Photograph by R.S. Kellar, courtesy of Richard Huntley.)

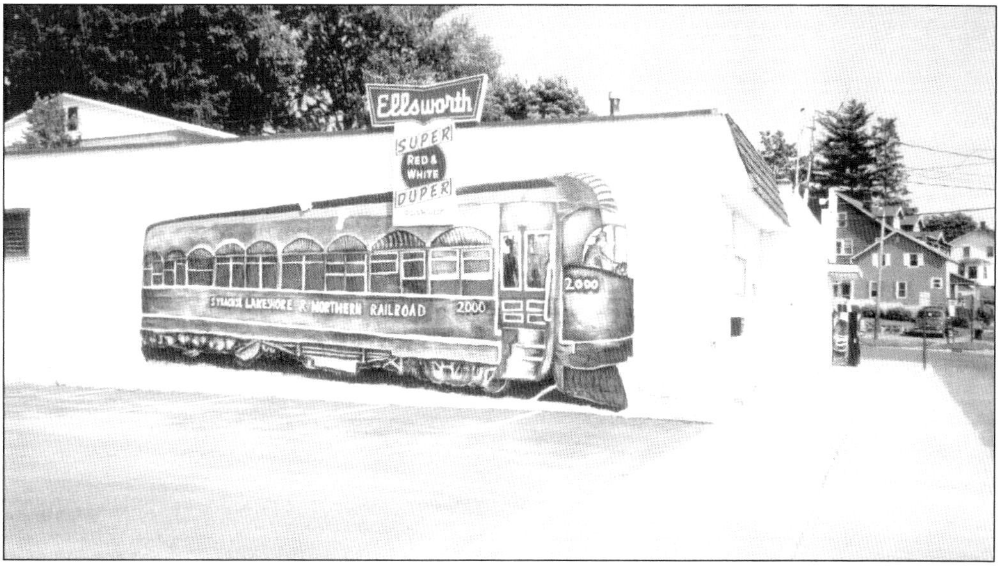

An old sign and a mural on a sidewall are all that remain of what was Ellsworth's Grocery. Today, the building is used as the Phoenix Community Nursery School. Ellsworth's Red & White was founded by Arthur R. Ellsworth in 1946. The store was later expanded into the modern building shown here. Craig Ellsworth took over the business after his father's death. His sister Jody assumed management of the 3 Rivers Super Duper. Located in the plaza just south of Phoenix for many years, it closed in 2003. Today, although there are many mini-marts that sell groceries, there is no longer a true grocery store left in Phoenix or the town of Schroeppel.

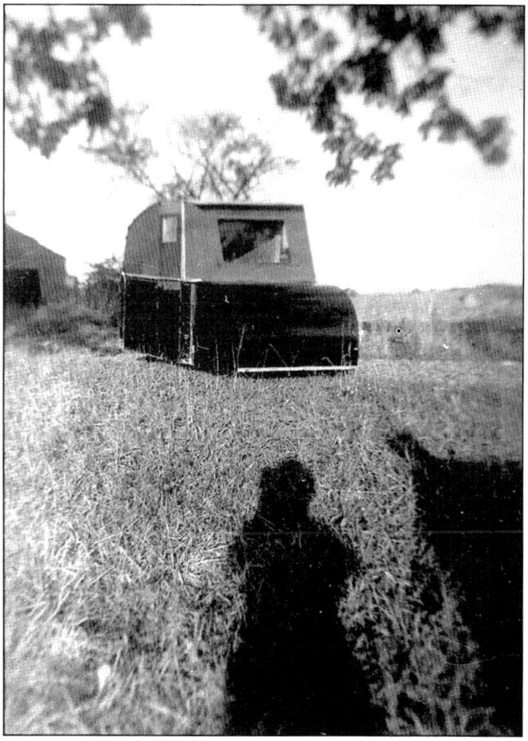

This wooden car was built by Melvin Watkins, who was born with poor sight and was legally blind by 20 years of age. Watkins and his wife, Louise, who was mentally challenged, lived during a period when there were few services to aid the disabled. The car covered their two bicycles and was their only way of transportation. They used it in all types of weather from the 1940s through the 1960s, mainly in and around Phoenix to go to the doctor or get groceries. However, they were known to have traveled as far as Cato to visit relatives. (Courtesy of Linda Sanders.)

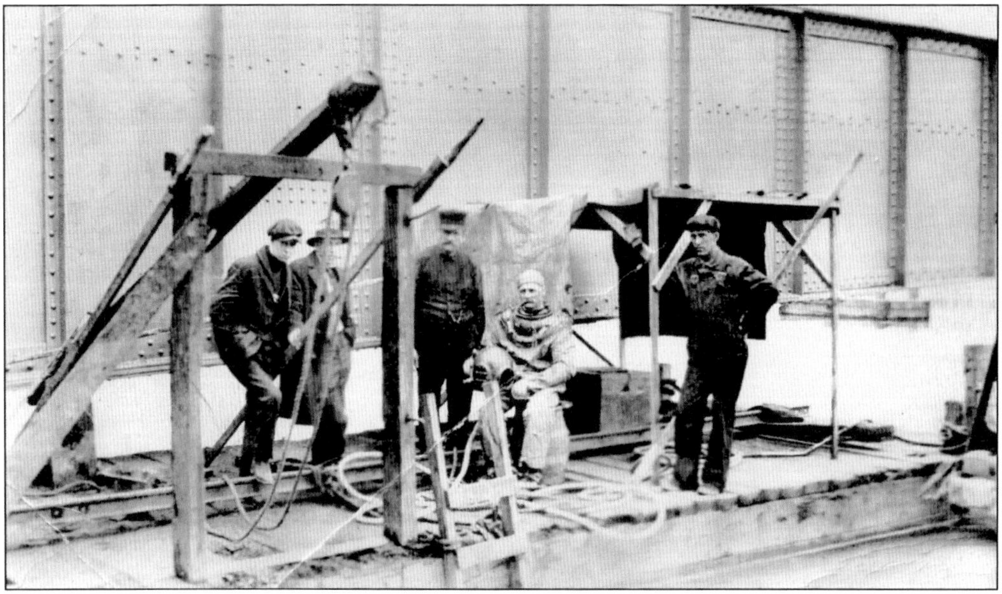

This photograph shows a diver and work crew in Phoenix. (Courtesy of Lora and Doc Jones.)

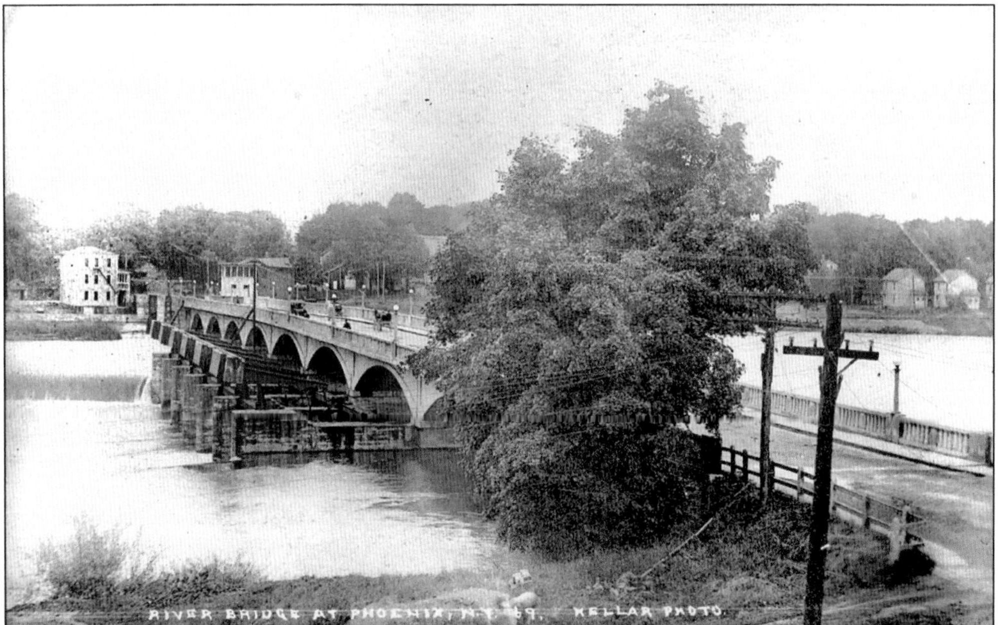

This photograph shows the old Phoenix bridge from the West Phoenix side of the river. In May 1987, the state closed the bridge to vehicle traffic because of its poor shape. Pedestrians could still walk across the bridge. By the late 1980s, a decision had already been made to build a new bridge two blocks to the north rather than to restore this bridge. That decision moved the traffic flow away from the business district. Today, Phoenix Commons and the Nice 'n Easy store located along the new traffic flow attract considerably more business than the original business district only two blocks away.

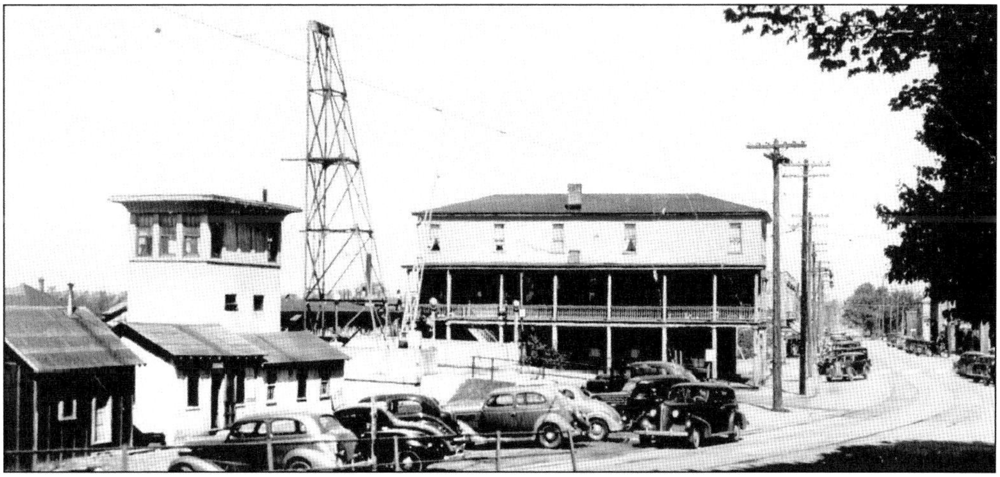

This photograph shows the on-ramp to the old drawbridge, from the Phoenix side of the river. In the early 1980s, because this was one of only two bridges of its type left in the country where each side could be operated independently, it was used for the filming of a horror movie. This area (shot from a different angle) can be seen today in the movie "Happy Birthday to Me," staring Melissa Sue Anderson, Glen Ford, Lawrence Dane, and Sharon Acker. The movie was later distributed by Columbia TriStar Home Video. (Courtesy of Richard Huntley.)

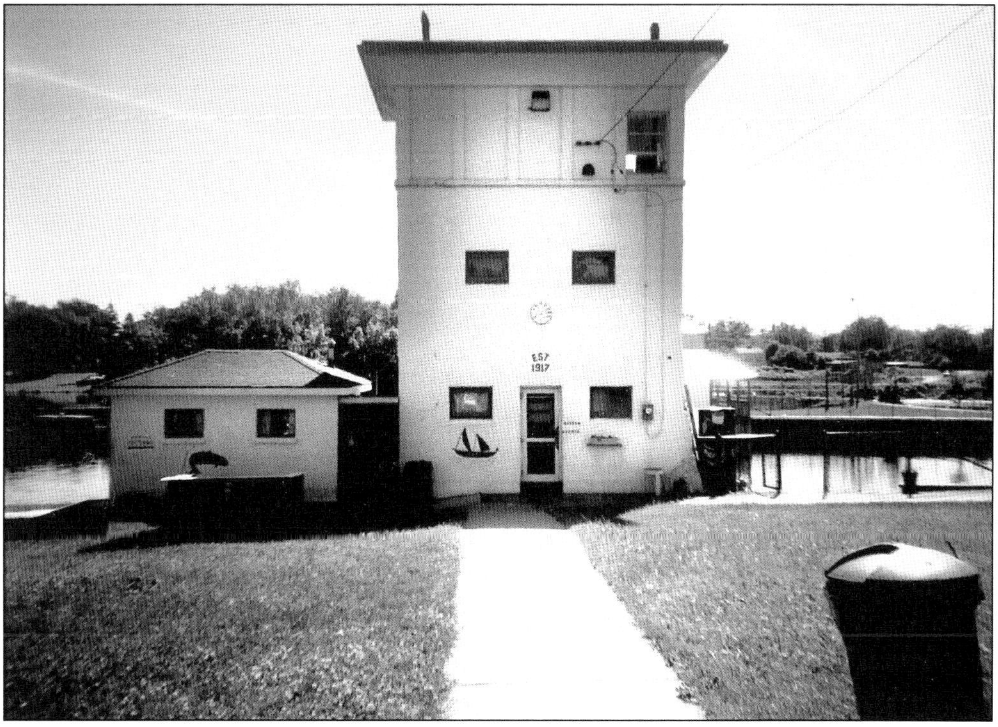

Today, the only remaining building in this area is the bridge house, which is used as a museum. The area around the bridge house is now known as Henley Park. The park and the museum are maintained by a local youth organization known as the Bridge House Brats. The Bridge House Brats also offer a wide range of services to boaters docking at the park.

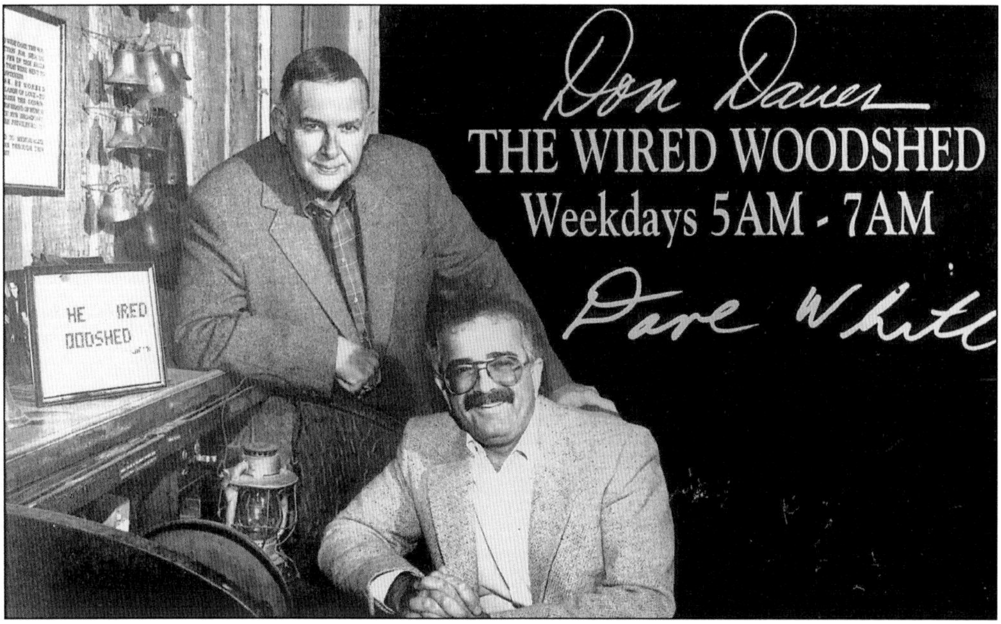

Phoenix resident Don Dauer (left) earned his place in local broadcasting history as the anchorman for WSYR's legendary *R.F.D.* morning show. Following the untimely passing of Robert "Deacon" Doubleday, it became Dauer's job to sustain the popular *Wired Woodshed* show. Dauer, who began working at WSYR in 1952, took over the program in 1971 and retired from radio in 1991. At one point when Dauer was recuperating from an illness, his show was broadcast daily via remote from his home in Phoenix. He is shown here with Dave White.

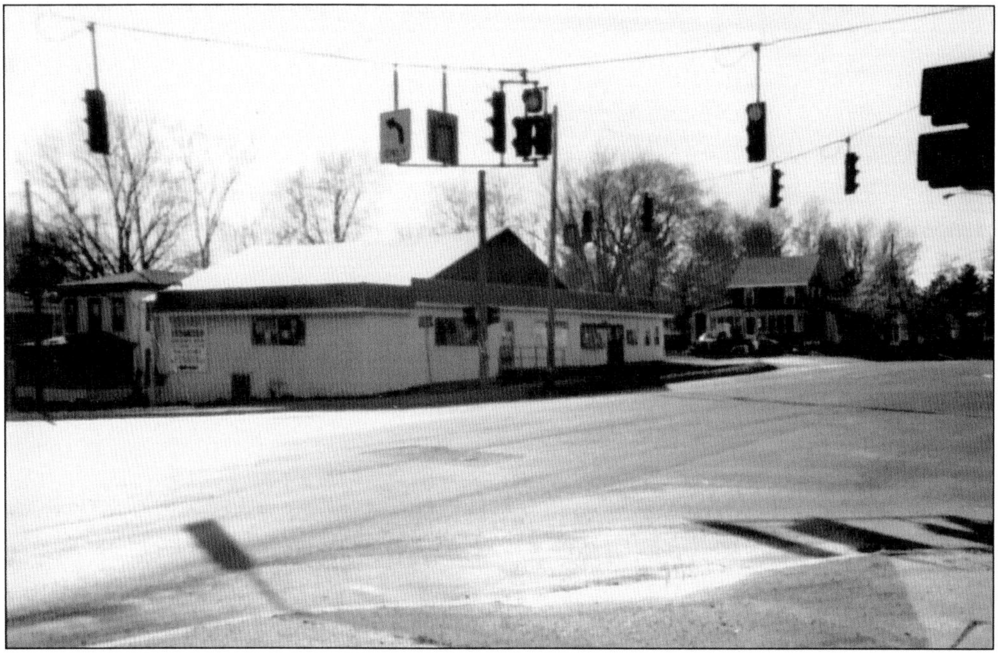

This is the corner of Main and Culvert Streets before Vecchio's Grocery and these homes were demolished for a Nice 'n Easy store.

Eight

On the Fringe

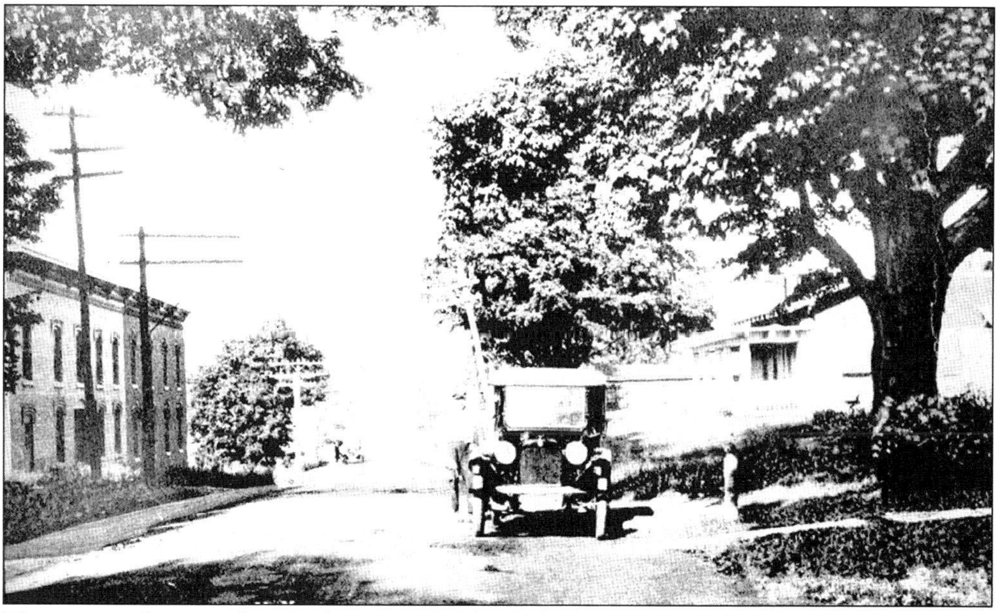

This is an early view of West Phoenix, an industrial area on the west side of the Oswego River.

To completely view the historical past of the town of Schroeppel, one must go beyond the physical boundaries of the town. Here is a look at the places and events that are on the fringe of Schroeppel.

To the west, the village of Phoenix is divided by the Oswego River. West Phoenix, its industries, the Phoenix Fair, and Lysander station all were an important part of Schroeppel's past. Yet, they are all actually in the town of Lysander and the county of Onondaga. To the south, there is the Three Rivers area within the town of Schroeppel, which is separated from the Three Rivers area in the town of Clay by the Oneida River. Although this area just across the river is within the town of Clay, it has always been associated with the village of Phoenix. Barnum's Hotel, the old baseball field, and Three Rivers Inn have all been interwoven with the history of the town of Schroeppel, even though the area is actually within the town of Clay and the county of Onondaga. The same is true to the southeast, within an area known as Oak Orchard. This area is also divided by the Oneida River, and the early history of Oak Orchard is shared by both the town of Schroeppel and the town of Clay. To the north, there is an area known as Roosevelt, which is divided by Oswego County Route 49. The Roosevelt Hotel, the Seventh-Day Adventist church, and the old one-room Roosevelt School are as much, if not more, a part of the town of Schroeppel's past, as they are of the town of Palermo, within which they reside.

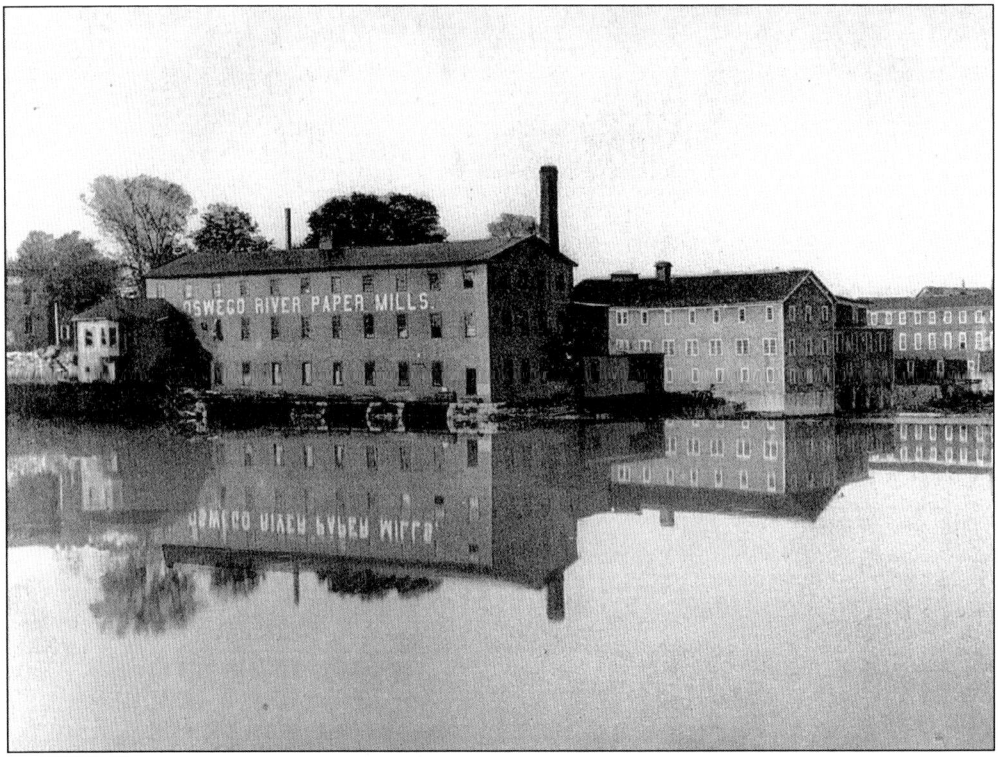

These mills were on the west side of the Oswego River, and included the Oswego River Paper Mills.

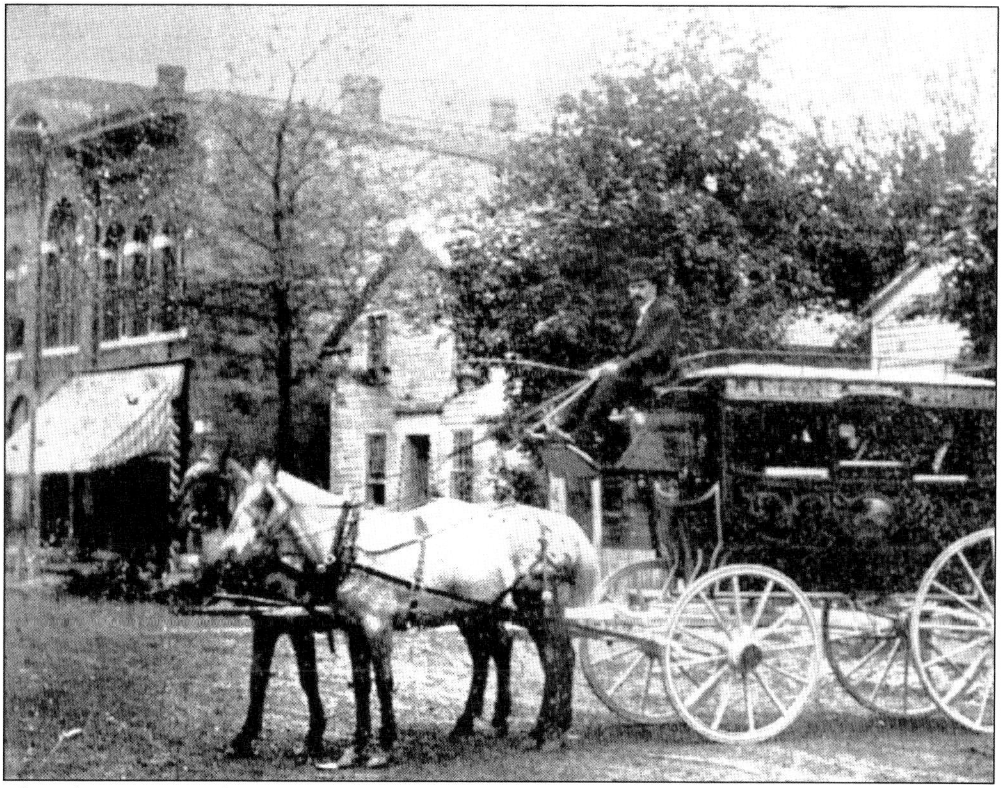

The Phoenix-Lysander stage is shown above. Below is a photograph of Lysander station, which today can be found just north of the end of Route 690, along Route 48. At one time, a stage also ran from Phoenix to Pennellville, but it is uncertain if it was operated by the Lysander Company.

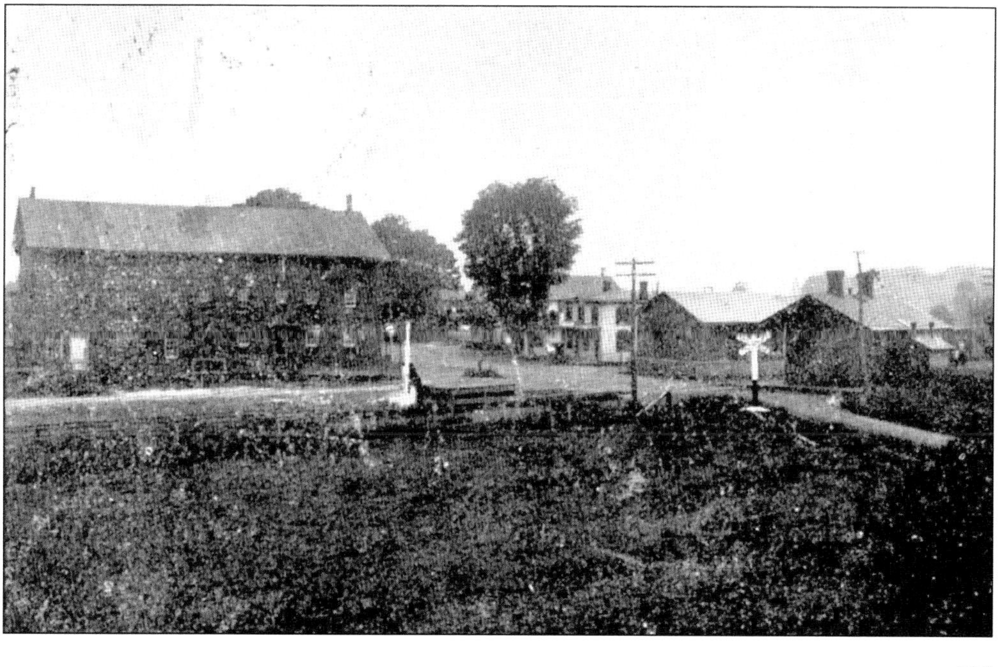

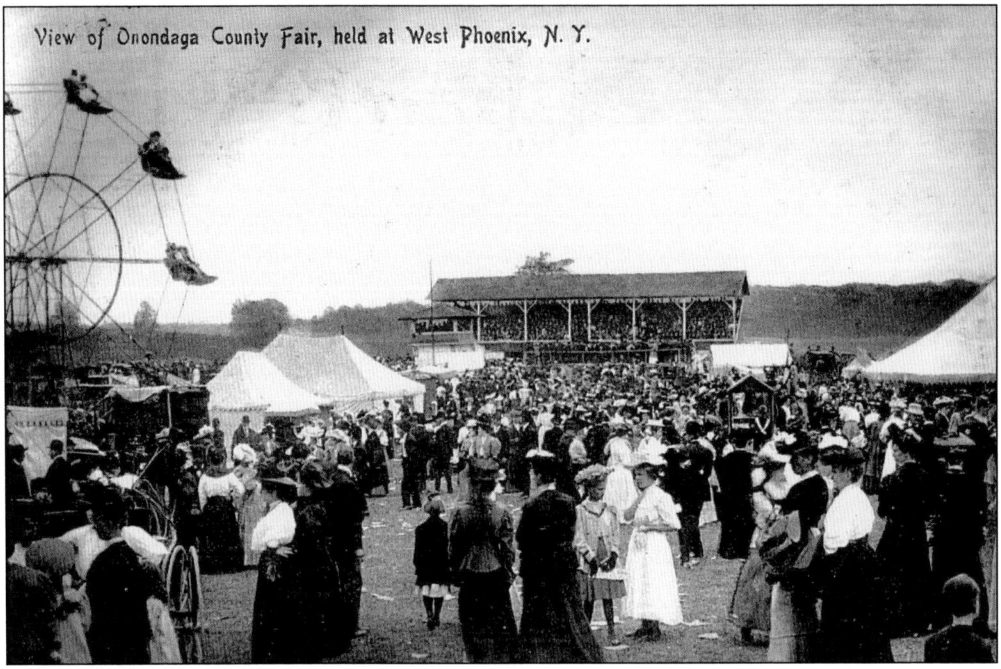

The Phoenix Fair was held across the Oswego River in West Phoenix, which is in the town of Lysander. The fair was actually the Onondaga County Fair, located at the intersection of old Lamson and West River Roads.

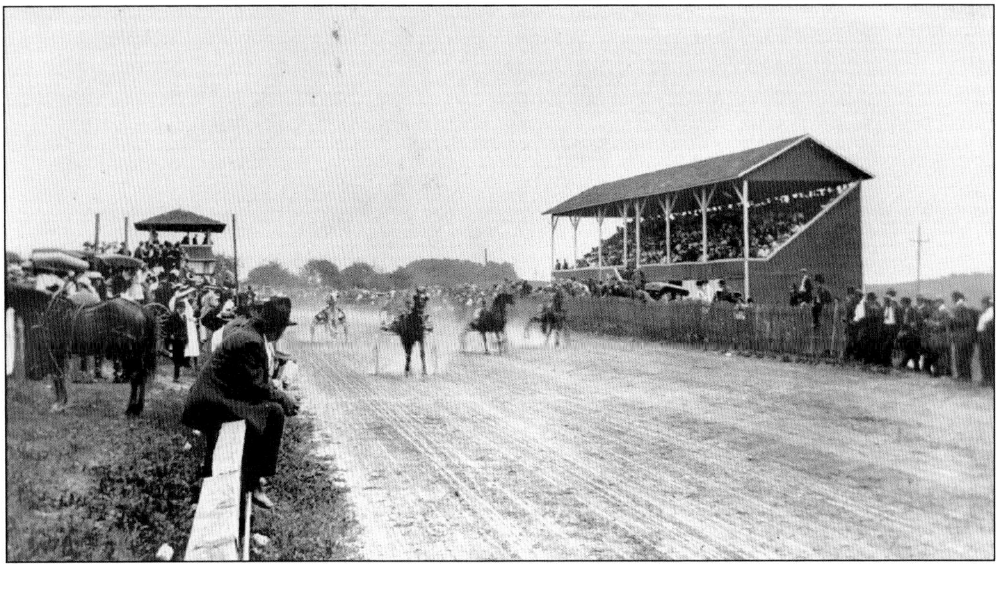

Great Bear Spring Farm's Spring House is believed to have been built in the early 1900s. Located near the Syracuse & Oswego Trolley line, it is presumed that people came here to get a drink of pure water from the spring located in the center of the building. Most of the farm is located in the town of Volney, although part of this area is located in the town of Schroeppel. (Photograph by Royce Huntley.)

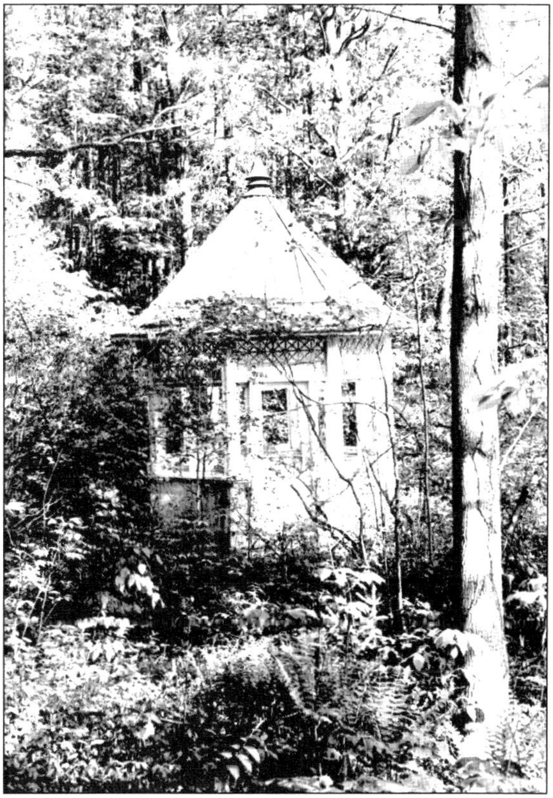

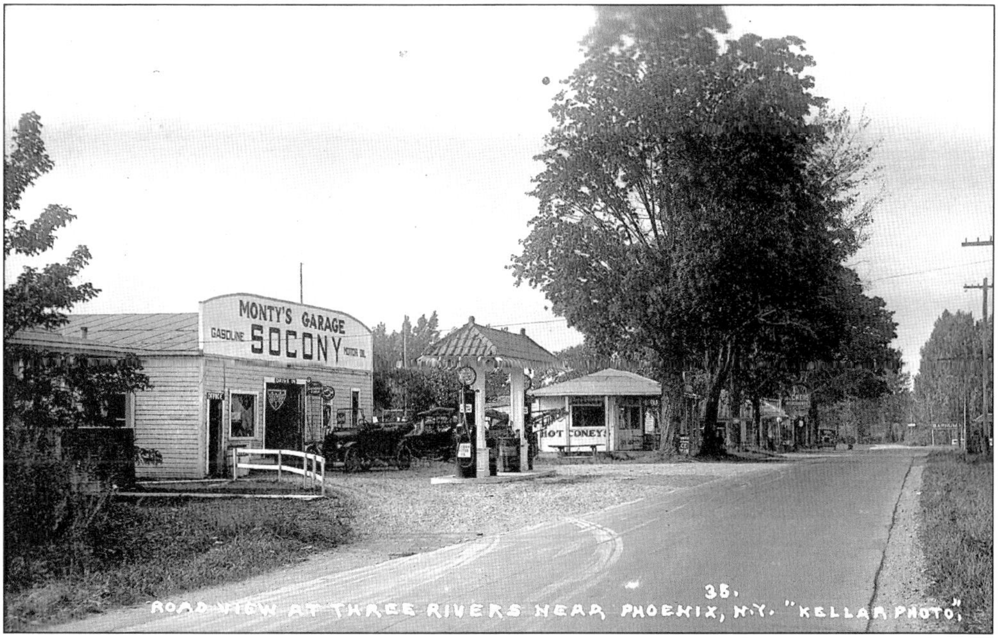

This view is at Three Rivers near Phoenix.

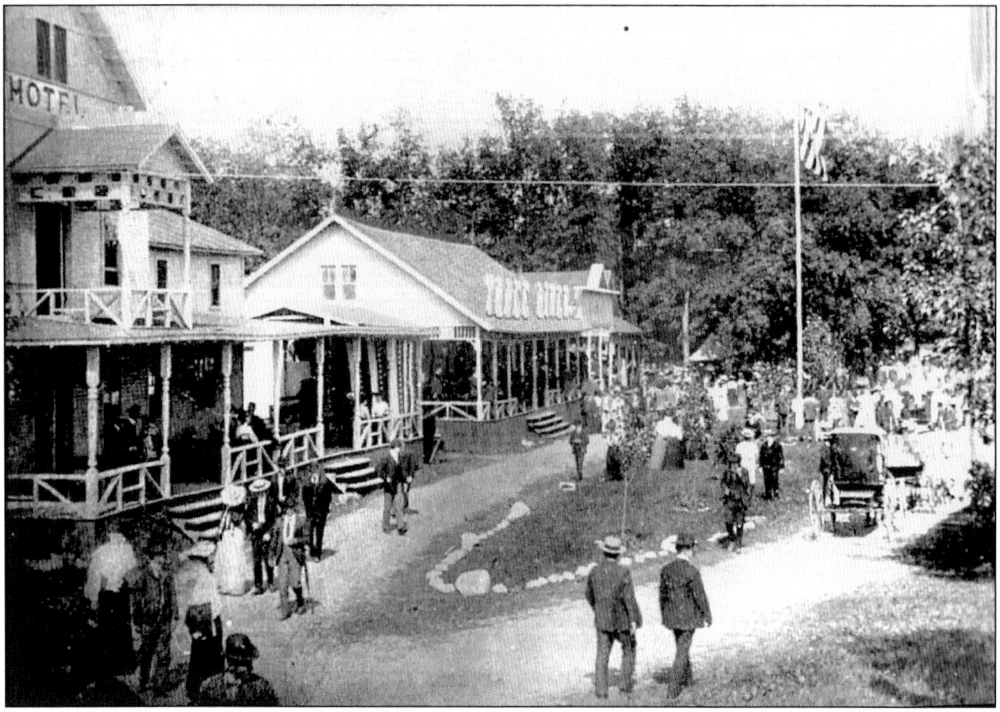

Barnum's Hotel is pictured in Three Rivers *c.* 1917.

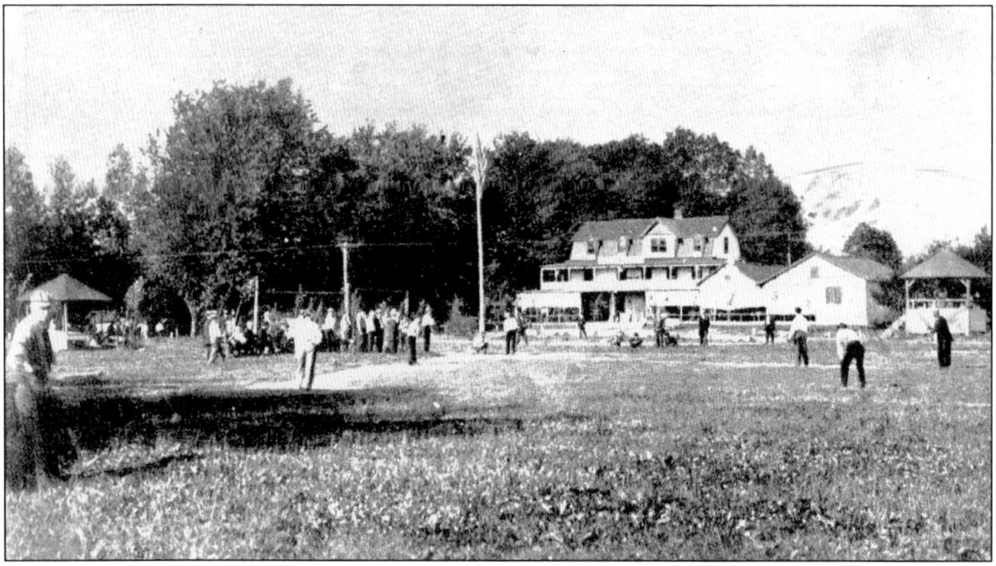

There was a baseball field behind Barnum's Hotel in Three Rivers. Both amateur and professional teams played here, including the Syracuse Stars for a short while.

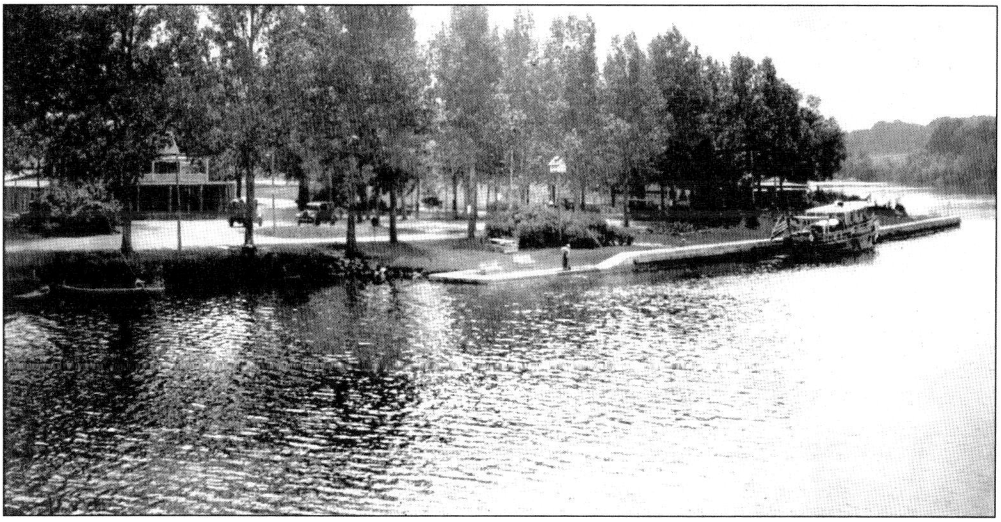

This view of the town of Clay side of Three Rivers shows the area where the Three Rivers Inn was located. Connie Francis, Jimmy Durante, and many of the top entertainers of the day performed at the inn. They often used the inn to perfect their routines before doing shows in Las Vegas, Nevada. After the inn burned in a fire that was termed "suspicious," a new Three Rivers Inn was opened in the town of Schroeppel just south of Phoenix. The new inn never regained the charm of the old one and eventually closed. (Courtesy of Richard Huntley.)

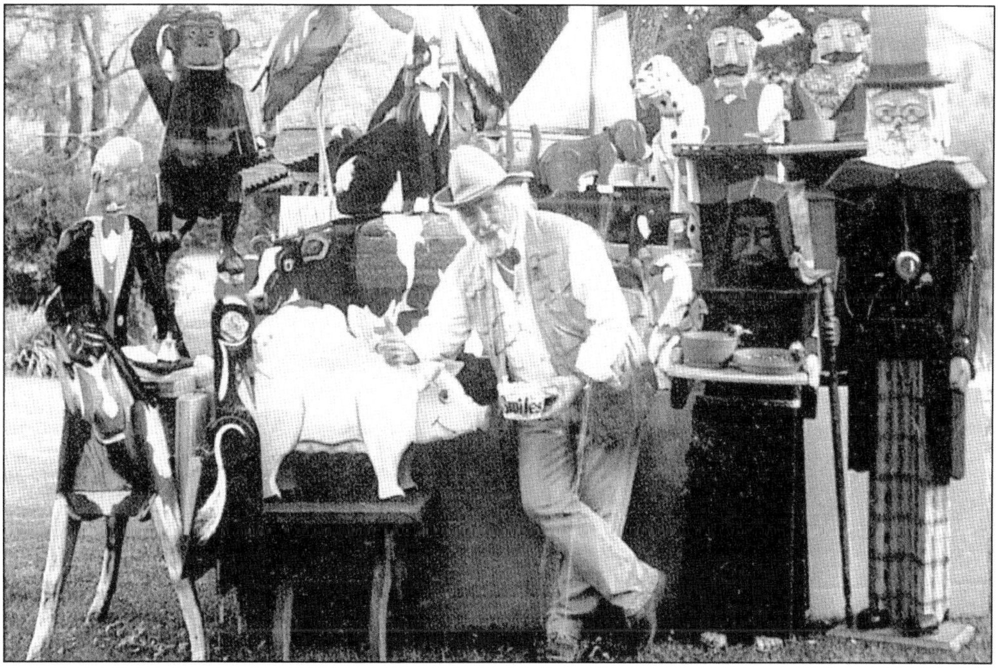

Robert DuLong is shown with some of the many wooden figures he and his artisans design and produce at Woodendipity, located on First Street in West Phoenix. Originally in the basement workshop in his home in 1984, DuLong's business is now based in one of the old Phoenix paper mills, which still has the scars from the Phoenix fire of 1916. Today, Woodendipity products are sold worldwide and are continuously featured in numerous magazines and on the Internet. (Photograph by Gerry Young.)

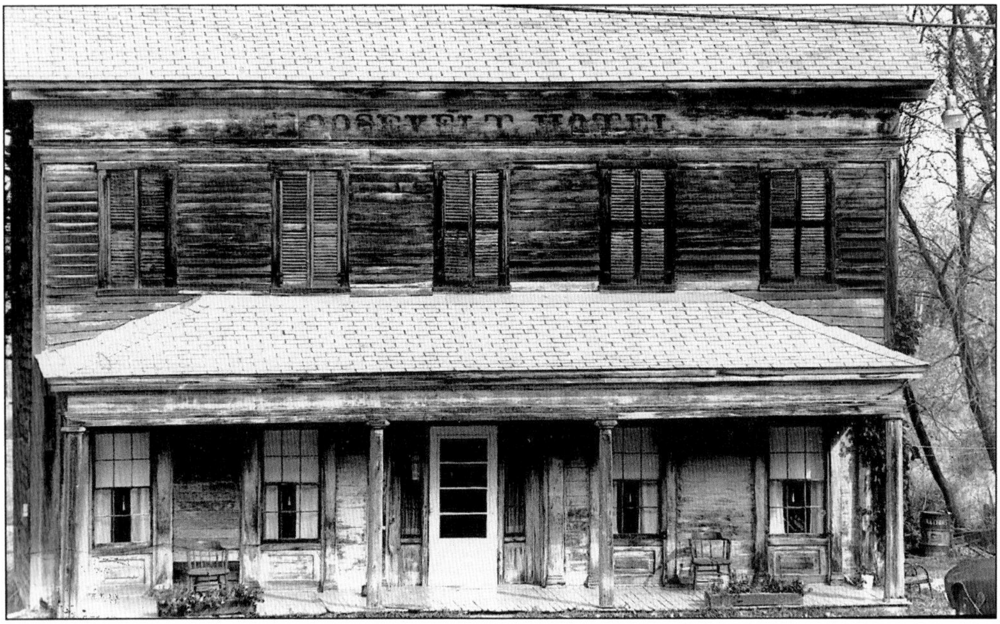

The first Roosevelt Inn was built in 1808 on the site opposite where the current hotel stands. It was torn down in 1848, and another building known as the Roosevelt Hotel was erected on the site. That building burned in 1856 and was replaced by the present building. Roosevelt, at one time, had a post office, church, blacksmith shop, stave mill, several cooper shops, and a schoolhouse. Theodore Roosevelt visited the hotel one time and had dinner there because of the association with his family history.

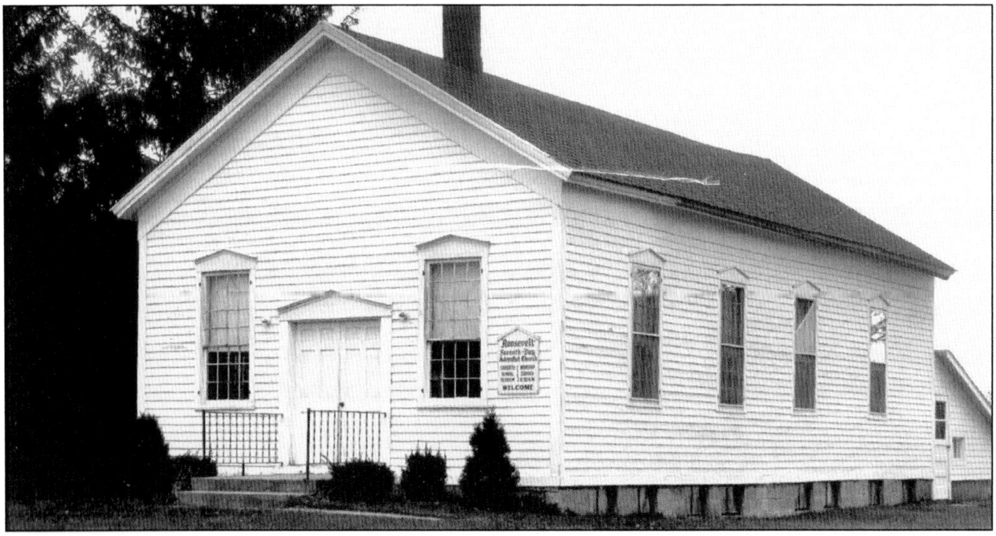

The Roosevelt Adventists Church was erected in 1858 by the Seventh-Day Adventists. The New York Conference was organized here in 1862. Hiram Edson, pioneer Adventist minister (December 30, 1806–January 8, 1882), is buried in the nearby Roosevelt Cemetery. The building fell into disuse in the early 1900s. Attempts were made to use the building as a dance hall in the 1930s, which aroused the remaining church members to restore the building. It is said that this Roosevelt Adventists Church is today the oldest church building erected, and it is still in use by the Seventh-Day Adventists.